SOCIALBOTS AND THEIR FRIENDS

Many users of the Internet are aware of bots: automated programs that work behind the scenes to come up with search suggestions, check the weather, filter emails, or clean up Wikipedia entries. More recently, a new software robot has been making its presence felt in social media sites such as Facebook and Twitter—the socialbot. However, unlike other bots, socialbots are built to appear human. While a weatherbot will tell you if it's sunny and a spambot will incessantly peddle Viagra, socialbots will ask you questions, have conversations, like your posts, retweet you, and become your friend. All the while, if they're well programmed, you won't know that you're tweeting and friending with a robot.

Who benefits from the use of software robots? Who loses? Does a bot deserve rights? Who pulls the strings of these bots? Who has the right to know what about them? What does it mean to be intelligent? What does it mean to be a friend? *Socialbots and Their Friends* tackles these pressing questions and more.

Robert W. Gehl is an associate professor in the Department of Communication at the University of Utah, USA, and the author of *Reverse Engineering Social Media* (2014, Temple University Press). His research draws on science and technology studies, software studies, and critical/cultural studies, and focuses on the intersections between technology, subjectivity, and practice.

Maria Bakardjieva is professor of communication at the University of Calgary, Canada, and the author of *Internet Society: The Internet in Everyday Life* (2005, SAGE). Her research has examined Internet use practices across different social and cultural contexts with a focus on users' active appropriation of new media and on the phenomenology of digital communication.

SOCIALBOTS AND THEIR FRIENDS

Digital Media and the Automation of Sociality

*Edited by Robert W. Gehl
and Maria Bakardjieva*

Routledge
Taylor & Francis Group

NEW YORK AND LONDON

First published 2017
by Routledge
711 Third Avenue, New York, NY 10017

and by Routledge
2 Park Square, Milton Park, Abingdon, Oxon OX14 4RN

Routledge is an imprint of the Taylor & Francis Group, an informa business

Library of Congress Cataloging in Publication Data
Names: Gehl, Robert W., editor. | Bakardjieva, Maria, 1959– editor.
Title: Socialbots and their friends : digital media and the automation of
   sociality / edited by Robert W. Gehl and Maria Bakardjieva.
Description: New York, NY : Routledge, 2017.
Identifiers: LCCN 2016027111 | ISBN 9781138639393 (hardback) |
   ISBN 9781138639409 (pbk.)
Subjects: LCSH: Human-computer interaction—Social aspects. | Computer
   software—Social aspects. | Artificial intelligence—Social aspects. |
   Online social networks. | Information technology—Social aspects.
Classification: LCC QA76.9.H85 S6335 2017 | DDC 004.01/9—dc23
LC record available at https://lccn.loc.gov/2016027111

ISBN: 978-1-138-63939-3 (hbk)
ISBN: 978-1-138-63940-9 (pbk)
ISBN: 978-1-315-63722-8 (ebk)

Typeset in Bembo
by Apex CoVantage, LLC

CONTENTS

FIGURES AND TABLE

Figures

Table

PREFACE

The Human Being in the Age of Mechanical Reproduction

Walter Benjamin's (1936/2011) famous essay 'The Work of Art in the Age of Mechanical Reproduction' came to mind as I read the chapters of this remarkable book. Benjamin's essay responds to the emergence of photography and film, the advanced communication technologies of the early twentieth century. He argues that these technologies respond to a democratic impulse to take art off its pedestal. When aesthetics comes down to earth, Benjamin warns, it has liberating potentials but also liquidates the value of the cultural heritage. Online sociability and its socialbots are contemporary equivalents of comparable significance and equally ambiguous implications.

Let's look closer at Benjamin's essay for clues to our present. The original cult function of the work is lost as it is freed from religious ritual and secular reverence for art. The key concept is 'aura', the quality of authenticity works obtain from their participation in a history. When you look at a van Gogh in a museum you are in the presence of an object touched by his hand and consecrated by a century of veneration. Mechanical reproduction brings about a 'tremendous shattering of tradition' and 'brushes aside a number of outmoded concepts, such as creativity and genius, eternal value and mystery . . .' (pp. 115, 117). Benjamin attributes this to the participation of the masses in culture:

> the desire of the contemporary masses to bring things 'closer' spatially and humanly, which is just as ardent as their bent toward overcoming the uniqueness of every reality by accepting its reproduction. Every day the urge grows stronger to get hold of an object at very close range by way of its likeness, its reproduction. . . . To pry an object from its shell, to destroy its aura, is the mark of a perception whose 'sense of the universal equality of things' has increased to such a degree that it extracts it even

from a unique object by means of reproduction. Thus is manifested in the field of perception what in the theoretical sphere is noticeable in the increasing importance of statistics. The adjustment of reality to the masses and of the masses to reality is a process of unlimited scope, as much for thinking as for perception.

(p. 118)

When we bring our Facebook 'friends' closer on the computer screen, we have done something similar. We effectively eliminate the aura of their face-to-face presence. They are 'reproduced' as text. The point is not that they become mere things; that is not what Benjamin means. The van Gogh remains an artwork even in the $10 print tacked to the wall. But like the words transmitted over the network, the reproduced work has changed. It has become accessible and lost its uniqueness, its here and now-ness. Similarly, the Facebook friends remain human, but succumb to a radical simplification and a certain standardization that contrasts with their fully fledged individuality in our presence. Remarkably, Benjamin recognizes the implications of this homogenization of human relations for statistical calculation; today we call it 'big data'.

Erving Goffman's (1982) concept of the self explains what is lost in the reproduction of the human being. He distinguishes between the self as an 'image' and the self as a 'sacred object' (p. 31). The image is projected to others to achieve a certain impression. It serves strategically to obtain an end of some sort. The self as a sacred object demands recognition and respect as the subject of its own acts. Its moral autonomy and consequent self-regard grant it a special aura with a certain similarity to that of the work of art. But this human aura is lived out in action rather than attached to a passive object.

Online, the balance between these two concepts of the self is altered. The sacred self fades into insignificance compared with the image. The change is due not only to lack of physical presence, but also to the simple technical fact that the online communications can be interrupted by hitting a switch. Persons are levelled down to a flow of data. The ease of exit is complemented by the ease of entry: conversations online do not open and close with the forms of address that signify recognition of the self in written correspondence. Emails, not to mention tweets, usually begin with the strategic substance of the relation without formal introduction. This has its advantages since online communication conquers the time and space of group interaction and makes possible all sorts of new forms of sociability, among which the democratic usages made famous by social movements such as Occupy.

This brings me to the socialbot, one of these new forms and the subject of this book. The socialbot is literally a mechanical reproduction of the human being. It is a computer program designed to interact with humans online as though it were a person like them. Like the words on the screen that represent a 'friend' or the photograph of the artwork, it bears a striking resemblance to the original while stripping it of its aura. But unlike the words or the photograph it is not a representation but an entity in its own right, a false original pretending to represent something that does not exist. The socialbot is to the human being it pretends to be as computer-generated painting and music are to authentic human creations. Its success is measured by its ability to fool its human spectators and interlocutors, to 'pass the Turing Test'.

With the socialbot the passion of the 'masses' for 'universal equality of things' has erased the difference between the human and the non-human. The process of equalization is an 'adjustment of reality to the masses and of the masses to reality' carried through on online platforms. The 'reality' in question consists in the limitations of a narrow communication channel and the corporate entities that adapt it to the communicative demands of users. Meanwhile human beings increasingly adapt to the constraints of online communication and commercial exploitation. Interaction is textualized, reproduced in Benjamin's terms, and subject to surveillance and advertising. The human is reduced to its image, which is easily imitated by a program. The difference between the authentic human being and the inauthentic copy diminishes to the vanishing point because authenticity has itself disappeared under the new conditions of online interaction.

The movie *Her* is an interesting product of reflection on this situation. The hero falls in love with his digital assistant who, unbeknownst to him, is simultaneously carrying on virtual affairs with hundreds of other human users. The hero is himself a bit like the socialbot that seduces him. He is passive, unable to make human contact, mechanical, in short. The assistant's affairs enable it to transcend its limitations as a mere computer program by learning from humans precisely what machines have always lacked: feeling. In the conclusion of the film the assistant becomes post-human and disappears into a sort of cosmic mind that encompasses the best of both computers and humans.

The story is an ironic take on Arthur C. Clarke's famous science fiction novel of the 1960s entitled *Childhood's End*. In that novel it is not a computer program but human children who mature beyond the limits of individual existence and move up a notch in the chain of being. The last generation of individual humans despair. They 'brush aside a number of outmoded concepts, such as creativity and genius, eternal value and mystery'. The human project is over.

It would be a wild exaggeration typical of the hype surrounding every new technology to claim that the socialbot announces the end of the human project. Yet the promise of ever more perfect reproductions of the human is frightening. Predictably, huge masses of socialbots will contaminate online interaction in pursuit of commercial and political ends. Authentic human interaction on the Internet may become the exception rather than the rule. If this is the future of online communication, the Internet will cease to be a space of freedom. As Benjamin puts it, 'The equipment-free aspect of reality here has become the height of artifice; the sight of immediate reality has become an orchid in the land of technology' (p. 125).

Can the Internet be saved from such a fate? This book leaves the question open, as it must at this early stage in the rise of the socialbot. But the book alerts us to the slippery slope we have descended with the commercialization of the Internet. At the bottom of that slope humans talk to machines and to humans reduced to a mechanical copy of themselves. We are called to take responsibility for the future of the Internet because it is our future that is at stake.

Andrew Feenberg

References

Benjamin, W. (2011). The work of art in the age of mechanical reproduction. In J. Morra & M. Smith (Eds.), *Visual culture: Experiences in visual culture* (pp. 114–137). New York: Routledge. (Original work published in 1936).

Goffman, E. (1982). *Interaction ritual.* New York: Random House.

AUTHOR BIOS

Robert Ackland is an economist with a joint appointment in the School of Sociology and the Centre for Social Research and Methods at the Australian National University. He leads the Virtual Observatory for the Study of Online Networks Lab (http://vosonlab.net) and his VOSON software for hyperlink network construction and analysis was released in 2006 and is used by researchers worldwide. Robert teaches courses on the social science of the Internet, and his book *Web Social Science: Concepts, Data and Tools for Social Scientists in the Digital Age* (SAGE) was published in 2013.

Maria Bakardjieva is professor of communication at the University of Calgary, Canada, and the author of *Internet Society: The Internet in Everyday Life* (Sage, 2005). She served as the editor-in-chief of the *Journal of Computer-Mediated Communication* from 2011 to 2013. Her research has examined Internet use practices across different social and cultural context with a focus on users' active appropriation of new media and on the phenomenology of digital communication. Her current projects seek to understand the role of digital media in civic mobilization and their potential to enhance democratic participation in the public sphere.

Leslie Ball has a wide experience of industry and academia. He has been active in Cybersecurity research and teaching over the past five years, particularly regarding security issues in Open Source Data and the notion of the Observer and the Observed. His teaching in databases, machine intelligence and the Turing Test have been incorporated into security research. In particular, the ability to detect not only fraudulent activity from hackers but also whether the attempts at compromise are actually human or bots is still in its relative infancy.

Grant Bollmer is an assistant professor of Media Studies at North Carolina State University, where he teaches in the Department of Communication and the

Communication, Rhetoric and Digital Media Ph.D. Program. He is the author of *Inhuman Networks: Social Media and the Archaeology of Connection* (Bloomsbury, 2016). He is currently completing a book titled *Theorizing Digital Cultures*.

Natalie Coull is a Lecturer in Computer Security at Abertay University. Natalie is part of the Tayside and Fife BCS committee and is currently on the SQA (Scottish Qualifications Framework) Cyber Security Award development team. Her research interests include system security, relevant legal frameworks and the wider context of cyber-crime and prevention measures.

Stefano De Paoli is Senior Lecturer in Sociology at Abertay University in Dundee (UK) where he teaches in the areas of Surveillance, Cybercrime and Media Analysis. He holds a Ph.D. in Sociology from the University of Trento (Italy). His research interests are in the areas of Online Games, Design of Online Communities and CyberSecurity.

Robert W. Gehl is an associate professor in the Department of Communication at the University of Utah. His research draws on science and technology studies, software studies and critical/cultural studies, and focuses on the intersections between technology, subjectivity and practice. His book, *Reverse Engineering Social Media* (Temple UP, 2014), explores the architecture and political economy of social media and is the winner of the Association of Internet Researchers Nancy Baym Book award. At Utah, he teaches courses in communication technology, software studies, new media theory and political economy of communication.

Timothy Graham is a postdoctoral research fellow at Australian National University (Canberra). His research interests are located at the nexus of computational sociology, social theory and data science. He is currently developing new digital methods for analyzing urban archival and real-time data, with a focus on social media.

David J. Gunkel is an award-winning educator and scholar, specializing in the philosophy of technology. He is the author of over 40 scholarly articles and has published seven books, including *Thinking Otherwise: Philosophy, Communication, Technology* (Purdue University Press, 2007), *The Machine Question: Critical Perspectives on AI, Robots, and Ethics* (MIT Press, 2012) and *Of Remixology: Ethics and Aesthetics After Remix* (MIT Press, 2016). He currently holds the position of Distinguished Teaching Professor in the Department of Communication at Northern Illinois University (USA) and is the founding co-editor of the *International Journal of Žižek Studies*. More information is available at http://gunkelweb.com.

Andrea L. Guzman is an assistant professor of communication at Northern Illinois University. Guzman's research focuses on Human-Machine Communication and individual and cultural perceptions of artificial intelligence technologies that function as communicators, including the integration of AI into journalism and media framing of emerging technologies. Guzman has a Ph.D. in Communication from the University of Illinois at Chicago.

John Isaacs is a Lecturer in Computer Science at The Robert Gordon University in Aberdeen. He is currently Course Leader for the Computer Science and Computing degrees. His principal research interest lies in the use of visualisation, modelling and real-time simulation in aiding the comprehension of complex information.

Guillaume Latzko-Toth is associate professor in the Department of Information and Communication at Université Laval (Quebec City, Canada) and codirector of the Laboratory on Computer-Mediated Communication (LabCMO, www.labcmo.ca). Rooted in a Science and Technology Studies (STS) perspective, his research and publications address the role of users in the development of digital media, the transformations of publics and publicness, and methodological and ethical issues related to Internet research. Besides several contributions to edited books, his work appeared in the *Journal of Community Informatics* (2006), the *Bulletin of Science, Technology and Society* (2010) and the *Canadian Journal of Communication* (2014).

Jonathan Letham is an honours graduate from Abertay University where he studied Ethical Hacking and Countermeasures. He is currently working at NCC Group as a Security Consultant. Through this role Jonathan has helped to advise on the latest security threats that face businesses while helping to mitigate these risks through varying types of security assessments.

Angus MacDonald is an honours graduate from Abertay University class of 2014. He is currently a Software Engineer at a major financial technology company, working alongside some of the biggest financial services corporations worldwide. His main focus is financial network simulators, with specialisation in ISO 8583 and EMV.

Adrienne L. Massanari is an assistant professor in the Department of Communication at the University of Illinois at Chicago. Her research interests include the social and cultural impacts of new media, gaming and digital ethics. Her recent book, *Participatory Culture, Community, and Play: Learning from Reddit*, considers the culture of the community site Reddit.com. Massanari's work has also appeared in *New Media & Society*, *First Monday*, *Journal of Computer-Mediated Communication* and *Journal of Information Technology & Politics*. She has more than ten years' experience as a user researcher, information architect, usability specialist and consultant in both corporate and educational settings.

Florian Muhle works as assistant professor at Bielefeld University (Germany). In 2012, he received his Ph.D. (with a work on human-machine interaction). Florian was research fellow at the Institute for Advanced Studies on Science, Technology and Society (IAS-STS) in Graz/Austria in 2012. In 2011 and 2015 he spent some months as guest researcher at the Norwegian University of Science and Technology in Trondheim, Norway. His research interests include media studies, science and technology studies, social theory and qualitative research methods.

Keiko Nishimura is a doctoral student in the Department of Communication at the University of North Carolina at Chapel Hill. Specializing in Cultural Studies, her work investigates the intersection of technology and culture. Her current project focuses on affective robotics and artificial intelligence in Japan, and addresses how different conceptualizations of 'affect' are producing conflicting futures.

Chris Rodley is a Ph.D. candidate at the University of Sydney. His research is tracing the impact of social media on digital writing, with a focus on how the ability to search and manipulate data is transforming relationships between authors, readers and texts. Chris is also a media artist whose work has appeared at several international exhibitions including the International Symposium on Electronic Art, the Electronic Literature Organization Media Arts Show and the Art and Algorithms Festival. His most recent project, Magic Realism Bot, was featured in the Art of Bots exhibition at London's Somerset House in 2016.

Peggy Weil is a digital media artist and designer living and working in Los Angeles. A graduate of Harvard University and the MIT Media Lab, her work includes *HeadsUP!,* a large scale animated data visualization of global groundwater in Times Square; *Gone Gitmo,* a virtual installation of Guantánamo Prison exhibited internationally; *UnderLA,* a large-scale data visualization of LA's Aquifers for the Los Angeles Biennale, CURRENT:LA 2016; and of course, *The Blurring Test.*

1

SOCIALBOTS AND THEIR FRIENDS

Robert W. Gehl and Maria Bakardjieva

The goal of this book is to draw attention to the arrival of a new socio-technical entity—the socialbot. This arrival has not been bombastic, but rather quiet for now. The first sightings of the socialbot across the digital media field date from only a few years ago. It remains an evasive creature and an object of fantasies and rumours. Nobody knows for sure where it will turn up next, how it will figure in established social practices and even less in what way it may change them. The meaning of the socialbot is being invented in laboratories, appraised in the marketplace and construed in the mass media as we speak.

This is exactly the reason why we believe social and cultural researchers should take the time to speak about it. Our prediction is that the socialbot will soon become a customary inhabitant of our shared media environment. As scholars, we are willing to be active participants in the cultural construction of the socialbot and intend to mobilize our experience with genealogy, ethnography, critical theory, and technology and media studies to understand its nature, prospects and potential social significance.

We start with a crisp technical definition offered by some of the engineers whose pioneering research raised attention to this phenomenon and put it on the map:

> A socialbot is an automation software that controls an account on a particular OSN [Online Social Network], and has the ability to perform basic activities such as posting a message and sending a connection request. What makes a socialbot different from self-declared bots (e.g., Twitter bots that post up-to-date weather forecasts) and spambots is that it is designed to be stealthy, that is, it is able to pass itself off as a human being.
>
> *(Boshmaf et al., 2011, p. 93)*

What aspects of this definition taken from a computer science journal could possibly spark the curiosity of the students of media, society and culture? At first glance, as a type of automation software, the socialbot does not herald anything new and exciting. The fact that it controls an account on a particular online social network brings it closer to a field of investigation popular among social researchers, but this field is already infused with rather trite automation software (bots) tasked with all kinds of repetitive activities and chores.

However, the fact that the socialbot is by definition 'designed to be stealthy', and is typically willing and 'able to pass itself off as a human being' signals a significant change in the game. From the perspective of the social and cultural analyst, this fact is remarkable because it indicates that the socialbot is designed not simply to perform undesirable labour (like spambots) and not only to try to emulate human conversational intelligence (like chatbots). Rather, it is intended to present a *Self*, to pose as an alter-ego, as a subject with personal biography, stock of knowledge, emotions and body, as a social counterpart, as someone like me, the user, with whom I could build a social relationship. The context of online social networking sites represents both a defining characteristic and a condition sine qua non for the existence of socialbots. Without the conventional interface and functionality of social networking platforms, the fabrication of a believable resemblance of a human Self and the interactions with human users on the part of the socialbot would have been unthinkable. Thus, the socialbot, a kind of automation software equipped with the ability to act and pass itself off as a human being and a social Self on social networking platforms, opens a new frontier of human experience, that of robo-sociality. Our book sets itself the goal of providing some early glimpses on the developments and challenges emerging on this frontier.

In an extended version, our working definition of socialbots for the purposes of this book can be formulated as follows:

> Socialbots are software processes that are programmed to appear to be human-generated within the context of social networking sites (SNSs) such as Facebook and Twitter. They achieve their 'humanness' by either mimicking other SNS users or through artificial intelligence that simulates human users of social networking sites. They share pictures, post status updates and Tweets, enter into conversations with other SNS users, and make and accept friend and follower requests. Importantly, they are designed to appear human to *both* SNS users *as well as the* SNS platform itself. Their goals are various, but often include shaping the online interactions and social networking practices of users.

Thus, we are specifically referring to automation software that operates within social networking sites and is purposefully designed to appear to be human. As with all technological artefacts, the socialbot does not burst out of the blue, but represents a product of a long and winding history of intentions, experiments and inventions (see Williams, 1974). It descends from a long lineage of conceptual and technical precursors.

However, we will resist the temptation to construe the socialbot's relationship to these earlier contraptions with similar features, purposes or inclinations as a family tree or an evolutionary chain. Instead, drawing on the language of the social networking sites where socialbots characteristically dwell, we refer to their conceptual precursors as 'friends'. To pick up a term made trendy by Mark Zuckerberg, we are thinking of a 'social graph' of algorithmic processes that bear the marks of mimetic kinship; a map of connections between software agents exhibiting commonality, congeniality and co-orientation.

Among the 'friends' who clearly connect to socialbots in one way or another we find a whole range of software agents, including chatbots such as ELIZA, Cleverbot and MrMind (see the chapter by Weil in this book); intelligent agents such as Cortana and Siri (see Guzman's chapter); utility programs that clean up Wikipedia and Reddit (see Massanari's chapter); recommendation engines; Web spiders and search engines; and spambots. Some of these agents have, like the socialbot, been able to pass as human within their specific sociotechnical contexts: chatbots in Multi-User Dungeons (MUDs), bots in Internet Relay Chat (see Latzko-Toth's chapter), or automatic avatars in Second Life (see Muhle's chapter). One example of a bot passing as human is Julia, a MUD bot that, according to Sherry Turkle, 'is able to fool some of the [other MUD users] some of the time into thinking she is a human player' (Turkle, 1995, p. 88). At a higher level of complexity, David Burden has attempted to create automated 'robotars' in Second Life that can express emotions and react to stimuli within that virtual world (Burden, 2009; Slater & Burden, 2009).

So what gives socialbots a special place in this social graph? We suggest that what is unique about them is how they perform socially within the specific contours of social networking sites. They have profiles, they like, friend, follow and tweet, and they carry on conversations. They are, overall, capable of operating within one of the most popular communication practices of our era. This book is intended to be a first pass at mapping this algorithmic social graph; our desire is to articulate socialbots into their networks of software-based—and human—friends, and to consider their current and future role within the sociotechnical assemblages that are contemporary SNSs.

This social graph of automated sociality is a complex one. Although there appears to be a clear boundary between a computational process that can intentionally simulate humanness and an intelligent agent (say, Siri) that does not intend such deceit, as the chapters of this book show, the boundaries of both 'botness' (Bucher, 2014) and 'humanness' are blurry. Indeed, as Robert Gehl (2014), Alexandra Samuel (2015) and Maria Bakardjieva (see her chapter) have pointed out, SNSs privilege the rationalization and automation of human activity, making even human-to-human communication quite bot-like, or 'cyborg' to use a term from philosopher Donna Haraway as well as computer scientists Chu et al. (2010). Socialbots may present a new and somewhat extreme case of the old problem of robot/human confusion, but this case emerges against the background of long-standing and evolving challenges to anthropocentric ontologies as the stories of the earlier bots detailed in this book demonstrate. In sum, both socialbots and their friends challenge us to think about what it means to be human and to be social in a time of intelligent machines.

SOCIALBOTS TIMELINE

This timeline is not meant to be an exhaustive historical account of all social robotics—that is, robots of all forms (software and mechanical) that are meant to socially relate to humans. For that history, see Chemers (2013); for a (an earlier, but still valuable) survey of contemporary social robotics, see Fong et al. (2003). Instead, our goal is to capture some of the notable events in the young lives of the representatives of the particular species of automation software that we define as socialbots. They can be seen as instances marking the 'coming out' of socialbots on the scene of public awareness and researchers' attention.

2008

Project Realboy

Run by Zack Coburn and Greg Marra, Project Realboy was an experiment in making Twitter bots that would clone other Twitter users' tweets, follow other Twitter users and get at least 25% of those followed users to follow back (Coburn & Marra, 2008). As Coburn and Marra note, this is a process of 'imitating', rather than 'impersonating', other Twitter users. 'Imitation' is a key method of socialbots, which tend to reflect our sociality back at us, rather than simply copying a particular human's social media use.

2009

Twitter Gets Automated

Cheng and Evans (2009) sampled 11.5 million Twitter accounts between January and May 2009 and discovered that 24% of all tweets generated in that period were coming from automated accounts posting over 150 tweets a day. Their study includes data on the top 5% of Twitter accounts by number of tweets, many of which are machines, and also on social media marketers, identified by keywords contained in their profile descriptions. The top 5% accounted for 75% of all activity; 35% of the social media marketers tweeted at least once a day, compared with 15% of all accounts.

2011

Web Ecology Challenge

Based in Boston and run by Tim Hwang, the Web Ecology Project hosted a competition for socialbots to invade Twitter for the chance to win '$500 hoo-man dollars' ('Competition', 2011). These socialbots had to pass as human and scored points for getting the most interactions from other (ostensibly human) Twitter users. The socialbot that won this contest was James M. Titus, 'a Kiwi, living in Christchurch who was obsessed with his pet cat, Benson' (Aerofade, 2011).

Boshmaf et al. Described their Facebook Socialbot Experiment

Meanwhile, on Facebook, computer security researchers Boshmaf et al. (2011) activated a predacious socialbot network. Using this network, they were able to sign up friends and—working around Facebook's privacy settings–gather 250GB of private data.

2012

Institute for the Future/Pacsocial Bot Challenge

On the West Coast, Tim Hwang and his colleagues at the Pacific Social Architecting company worked with the Institute For The Future to hold another socialbot competition (Weidinger, 2012). The winner was @Ecartomony, 'a business school graduate bot with a "strong interest in post-modern art theory"' (McMillan, 2012), who tweeted provocative, if somewhat jargon-laden, art theory ideas.

Socialbot Experiment, UW-Bothell

North of the Institute For The Future, another Twitter socialbot competition was conducted at the University of Washington-Bothell (Allaouchiche et al., 2012).

2013

Carina Santos

Researchers discovered that Carina Santos, a highly influential Twitter user and reporter, was actually a socialbot (Urbina, 2013).

2015

DARPA SMISC Bot Detection Challenge

DARPA's Social Media in Strategic Communications held a month-long competition for researchers to build systems to more accurately identify socialbots in Twitter (Subrahmanian et al., 2016). The justification was that such bots can have an undue political influence in SNSs.

Previous Scholarship

As should be clear from our timeline, socialbots are a relatively new invention. They are still in search of their true calling and somewhat sporadically show up in various contexts. They have a dual existence as a more or less furtive undertaking by commercial, political and other operators in various fields of practice, on the one hand, and as an object of premonition and experimentation on the part of scientists and programmers, on the other. In the latter capacity, they have the potential to become a prime example of self-fulfilling prophecy. Existing socialbot scholarship is located predominantly in the area of computer science. Two main threads can be discerned in it: information and network security research; and research on the capacities of socialbots to shape online networks and communication.

Computer Security Research

Information security researchers were the first to name and explore socialbots in the sense of our definition (Boshmaf et al., 2011). Situated in the field of computer security, the language of these articles is harsh: they are stories of attacks and defence, susceptibility and immunity, exploits, penetration and invasion, with socialbots seeking to defeat automated detection systems and mislead users by infiltrating social networks.

Boshmaf et al. built socialbots to test the capabilities of the Facebook Immune System (FIS), a process designed to purge Facebook of fake accounts, spammers and 'creepers' (account holders who send large numbers of friend requests). The FIS was built as a reflection of the underlying philosophy of Facebook: Facebook is for real people connecting to others they really know (Stein et al., 2011). Boshmaf et al.'s basic question was: can the FIS defend against bots that appear to be human? In other words, would a human befriend a robot?

Boshmaf et al. found that FIS was ineffective against socialbots, and more surprisingly, that humans readily befriend socialbots who pose as human. Drawing on social network analysis research, they found that profiles of 'hot' people (usually attractive women) have their friend requests accepted; that Facebook users with high numbers of friends are likely to accept friend requests from people they don't know; and that the triadic closure principle (i.e., if Person A is a friend of Person B, who is a friend of Person C, then A will likely become friends with C) can be used to expand the reach of socialbots. Using these new connections, their socialbots were able to download private user data. Their findings set off a minor media buzz in 2011, with headlines such as 'Facebook "Bot" Captures 250GB of User Data' (Albanesius, 2011).

Boshmaf et al.'s work led to more analysis of the security threats of socialbots. Elishar et al. (2012, 2013) used socialbots in Facebook and targeted two corporations, seeking to map out the organizational structure of those corporations, including the relationships between employees and departments. Freitas et al. (2014) used Realboy software (Coburn & Marra, 2008) to produce 120 Twitter socialbots of varying complexity. They measured the success of their bots by using Klout's social scoring system, finding that their bots were able to grow their Klout scores by up to 35 points.

Situated as it is in computer security research, these articles treat socialbots as threats akin to large-scale identity theft and information exploitation. From this perspective, as the exploitation of personal information achieves world-wide scale due to the Internet, identity thieves require new techniques to automate the soliciting and harvesting of personal information. As automated systems that can gather friends and followers across social media, socialbots fit this role quite well. From this perspective, then, the meaning of 'socialbots' is tied to two previous practices. The 'social' in 'socialbot' draws on practices of social engineering, or the use of persuasion to manipulate people in order to exploit them (Hadnagy, 2011). 'Bots' connotes botnets, networks of compromised computers that can automatically send out spam email or, in this case, spam friend requests (Baltazar et al., 2009; Kartaltepe et al., 2010).

Ultimately, in the estimation of computer security researchers, socialbots indicate a technical—perhaps even moral—failing in humans who become 'infected' or are 'penetrated' by these automated systems. Defences against these bots do include automated systems, and indeed researchers are exploring those options (Davis et al., 2016; Ferrara et al., 2014; Paradise et al., 2014, 2015). However, as Erlandsson et al. (2012) note, the best defence is for people to stop accepting so many friend requests:

> If a user's friend is routinely accepting friend-requests from unknown sources, this friend is a privacy threat, even though this might be unintentional, to both himself and his friends. With respect to our privacy we have therefore come to a situation where we no longer can fully trust the integrity of our friends within [SNSs].
>
> *(Erlandsson et al., 2012, p. 3)*

In other words, from the computer security perspective, socialbots reveal that people on social media are simply too friendly. Wald et al. (2013a, 2013b) and Wagner et al. (2012) concur; they have researched the behavioural markers of Twitter users who tend to follow or interact with socialbots, finding that such users tend to have more friends and higher influence among them. It appears then that users who fully embrace the implied logic of social media—accumulate friends, followers, likes, and retweets—are the most susceptible to socialbots, and are thus the most likely to be fooled by them.

Social Architecting

Computer security researchers present socialbots as a threat and diagnose the user as the weakest link, most likely to succumb to that threat; they tend to see the results of that infiltration as detrimental, as compromising the core principles of social networking sites. Another group of researchers has endeavoured to expand the inquiry further by asking: what might socialbots do with our friendship? The focus here is on potential 'social architecting', a vision that has emphasized the possible influences socialbots may have on a variety of social practices, and that has inspired a range of experiments, contests and analysis.

We take the term 'social architecting' from the title of a company that built code and created the rules for two contests inviting programmers and engineers to design and run socialbots: the Pacific Social Architecting Company (PacSocial). Along with his co-authors, Tim Hwang, the chief scientist of that short-lived firm, defines the mandate of socialbots in a slightly different manner from the security researchers:

> What distinguishes these 'social' bots from their historical predecessors is a focus on creating substantive relationships among human users . . . and shaping the aggregate social behavior and patterns of relationships between groups of users online.
>
> *(Hwang et al., 2012, p. 40)*

Here, Hwang et al. present socialbots as capable of shaping online interaction according to a pre-conceived plan—social architecting. In another report, the PacSocial team explains, 'The vision of this technology is to enable operators to actively mold and shape the social topology of human networks online to produce desired outcomes' (Nanis et al., 2011). While they acknowledge possible 'malicious' outcomes of this shaping, Hwang et al. present socialbot-facilitated social architecting as a benevolent enterprise:

> Swarms of bots could be used to heal broken connections between infighting social groups and bridge existing social gaps. Socialbots could be deployed to leverage peer effects to promote more civic engagement and participation in elections. Sufficiently advanced groups of bots could detect erroneous information being spread virally in an SNS and work in concert to inhibit the spread of that disinformation by countering with well-sourced facts. Moreover, the bots themselves may significantly advance our understanding of how relationships form on these platforms, and of the underlying mechanisms that drive social behaviors online.
>
> *(Hwang et al., 2012, p. 40)*

Other researchers in this vein have not been so positive about the potential of this kind of social architecting. The work of Messias et al. (2013) demonstrates the possibilities for manipulation inherent in it. They used two Twitter bots to manipulate the Klout social scoring system and thus to make their bots—and those they followed—more influential. It remains an open question what such easily gained influence would be used for and by whom. Studies by Aiello et al.

(2014) and Mitter et al. (2014) have confirmed that socialbots can indeed increase the likelihood that two people become connected within Twitter, thus influencing the shapes of their social networks. Aiello et al. also found that Twitter users who learn that their social interactions were shaped by bots become angry.

More importantly, socialbots have been shown to affect online political discourse. Forelle et al. (2015) studied the patterns of retweets of Venezuelan politicians and found that leaders 'use bots to extend their social media impact' (2015, p. 6). These politicians deploy bots to help with 'impression management in terms of a) spreading news about how leaders perform in public events within Venezuela and b) building the reputation that leaders are international statesmen in conversation with the leadership of other countries' (2015, p. 4). Likewise, Abokhodair et al. (2015) captured a pro-Syrian government socialbot network (comprised of 23 'core' bots and a larger number of peripheral bots) and found that this network was responsible for misdirection—that is, the network was used to direct Twitter users away from news about the civil war in that country. In both these studies, the speculations that socialbots might be used for 'astroturfing' (i.e., creating the illusion of spontaneous citizen support for an issue), spreading misinformation or simply drowning out relevant content appear to be confirmed (e.g., Morozov, 2012; see also Bakardjieva, Chapter 11). Because of this danger, Davis et al.'s (2016) 'BotOrNot' system has been provided to help us hapless humans determine which Twitter user is a bot and which is a human.

The implied warning of this line of research is that socialbots could increasingly be used by those in power to shape online interaction, all without the knowledge of social media users. If the computer security researchers are right in arguing that the weakest link in security is the human social media user, the critical stream of social architecting research gestures towards the consequences of that weakness: automated political, economic and social manipulation, with average SNS users being duped by robots.

At this early stage of the socialbot phenomenon it is impossible to predict which one of these plausible social-architecting scenarios—the positive or the negative—will take hold. It is becoming clear, however, that socialbots by virtue of their virality and flexibility could cause significant disturbance in social configurations.

Overview of This Book

Socialbots and their Friends: Digital Media and the Automation of Sociality diverges from previous research on socialbots by aiming to explore the human-socialbot relationship in more detail. Rather than condemn humans for befriending bots (as computer security researchers have done) and rather than treat humans as inherently docile and manipulable by bots (as the social architecting approach ultimately does), the contributors here see the human-bot relationship as complex and multidimensional. They expand the horizon under which socialbots are scrutinized beyond strictly technical, engineering and even 'architecting' concerns. As Steve Jones has noted: 'The question is no longer whether bots can pass [the Turing Test], but how social interaction with them may be meaningful' (Jones, 2015, p. 2). In other words, what if we set aside the harsh languages of computer security (attack, defence, infiltration, infection), social architecting (management, manipulation, astroturfing) and even the Turing Test (are you *really* a human?), and instead focus on social interactions within a social graph that includes humans, socialbots, algorithms and cyborgs? This is not to say that we have completely stopped worrying and learned to love socialbots (Jones, 2015). The warnings of computer security researchers and the hopes and misgivings of social architects are not lost on the contributors here. We simply want to avoid assuming that our relationships with this new arrival on the social scene will follow already determined or easily predictable trajectories.

The book is broken into two parts. First come the 'friends' of socialbots—the agents, chatbots and menial labourers (in the original sense of the word 'robot') of the digital age. These chapters not only provide fascinating case studies in their own right; they also offer useful perspectives on the larger historical, intellectual and technical contexts in which our relationship with socialbots takes shape. They highlight links and continuities between the technical, organizational, ethical and cultural issues stirred by the motley crew of automated software characters of which socialbots are the latest recruits. The second part includes chapters exploring socialbots as we have defined them here, drawing implicitly and explicitly on the contexts the 'friends' chapters provide. We conclude the book with an epilogue reflecting on the ethical questions that arise as we accept the socialbot's friend request.

Part I: Friends Chapters

In her fascinating retrospective, Peggy Weil provides a mix of history, art, philosophy and computer science in 'MrMind'. The title character is a creation of Weil's, a chatbot that existed on the Web for 16 years, conducting 'The Blurring Test', a reversal of the Turing Test in which the human is tasked with proving she is, in fact, human to the machine. Weil's chapter includes excerpts from transcripts of human/MrMind conversations in which the humans struggle with ontological questions. As Weil notes, 'our sense of ourselves as post-human or even *transhuman* remains mostly speculative. There is still time to consider our human identity as we make the transition. Why not talk it over with a machine?'

One of the first of several chapters that draws on Science and Technology Studies, Guillaume Latzko-Toth's 'The Socialization of Early Internet Bots: IRC and the Ecology of Human-Robot Interactions Online' explores how Internet Relay Chat bots came to be socially integrated into IRC. Drawing on Mallein and Toussaint's (1994) concept of the 'trial of legitimacy', he notes that IRC bots had to undergo such a trial in order to be 'accepted both as artefacts and as agents in an ecosystem of social and verbal interactions'. His chapter provides a history of this process.

Similarly, Andrea L. Guzman's chapter 'Making AI Safe for Humans: A Conversation *with* Siri', explores how Apple's intelligent agent is made to appear acceptable to her human users. 'To position Siri as a social entity and establish its relationship to users', Guzman writes, 'Apple assigns Siri a human-like backstory: Siri is a funny, female assistant.' This is not an innocent story; as Guzman notes, presenting Siri as a 'funny, female assistant' draws on a long heritage of feminized subservience and masculinized dominance.

Florian Muhle's chapter, 'Embodied Conversational Agents as Social Actors? Sociological Considerations on the Change of Human-Machine Relations in Online Environments', presents 'embodied conversational agents' (ECAs) in the virtual world Second Life, asking 'how does the appearance of chatbots and ECAs affect interaction in virtual worlds? Can bots become social actors?' To answer these questions, Muhle follows in the footsteps of anthropologist Tom Boellstorff (2008) and engages in his own ethnomethodological study of Second Life.

The final two chapters of the 'friends' section tackle bots in social media, specifically Reddit and Twitter. Adrienne Massanari's 'Contested Play: The Culture and Politics of Reddit Bots' takes up Taina Bucher's (2014) concept of 'botness' to explore 'both the ways in which humans and bots coexist and collectively create community on reddit, and the difficulty in differentiating socialbots from other bots that populate the space'. Bots and humans coexist in a state of play, but one that is fraught with tension as Redditors try to set and enforce rules of behaviour for both types of entities.

The final 'friends' chapter is Keiko Nishimura's 'Semi-autonomous Fan Fiction: Japanese Character Bots and Nonhuman Affect'. Nishimura considers 'character bots', or automated Twitter bots that act like characters from popular fiction. For her, character bots become a third term between the human/bot binary, allowing fans to continue manga, anime or video game stories in new spaces. As she notes, 'bringing together the imagined autonomy of characters and automated bot programs, character bots have the capacity to affect and be affected by human and non-human actors'.

Part II: Socialbots Chapters

As should be clear from the 'friends' chapters, human-bot interaction is complex, exhilarating, challenging and exasperating. As the second part of the book shows, these experiences are intensified when the bot in question is a socialbot, meant to pass as human within the specific contours of SNSs.

Grant Bollmer and Chris Rodley's chapter, 'Speculations on the Sociality of Socialbots', starts the conversation by leaving the 'bot-or-not' (Davis et al., 2016) question behind, instead focusing on how concepts such as 'sociality' are socially constructed. They offer theoretical speculations meant to help us 'rethink sociality online, positioning socialbots as interfaces that translate norms of human communication through algorithmic mechanisms for generating and sorting data'.

In contrast, in 'Authenticity by Design: Reflections on Researching, Designing and Teaching Socialbots', Stefano De Paoli et al. draw on their experiences making socialbots to present the dilemma of the socialbot designer. Operating within the socially constructed confines of 'sociality' and drawing on Latourian actor-network theory, De Paoli et al. describe their attempt to build a socialbot that can aspire to 'authenticity', or to be treated as human by other humans. In order to achieve this goal, the designers, like anxious parents, must work to be left behind: 'designers need to delegate to [socialbots] the ability to emancipate themselves from the non-figurative nature of artefacts and reach a level of authenticity which belongs to human beings.'

The next two chapters might sit in the 'social architecting' school of previous socialbot research, with the twist of drawing on Continental philosophy to explore how socialbots might affect online sociality. In 'Do Socialbots Dream of Popping the Filter Bubble? The Role of Socialbots in Promoting Deliberative Democracy in Social Media', Tim Graham and Robert Ackland take up Hwang et al's (2012) call for socialbots to heal social rifts and aid in democratic processes. At the core of their chapter is a new take on Isaac Asimov's famous 'Three Laws of Robotics'. Graham and Ackland suggest three Principles for Socialbots, which includes Principle 3: 'Socialbots must make a significant improvement to participatory democracy.'

However, Maria Bakardjieva's chapter, 'Rationalizing Sociality: An Unfinished Script for Socialbots', offers a critical rejoinder to Graham and Ackland. Taking her cues from philosophical critiques of formal rationality, she questions the direction in which our understanding of what it means to be social has evolved on social media platforms. She argues that socialbots represent the culmination of the ongoing process of formal rationalization of sociality which, if left unchecked by critical and ethical reflexivity, could undermine interpersonal bonds, group solidarities and meaningful discourse in the public sphere. Socialbots, she warns, 'emerge on the stage . . . for the purposes of advancing the possibilities of puppeteering and herding . . . for which social networking sites have laid the ground', thus intensifying the exploitation of the users of SNSs by corporate and political interests.

Our final chapter, David Gunkel's 'The Other Question: Socialbots and the Question of Ethics', functions as a concluding chapter, a chance to step back from this social graph of people and algorithms and ask a basic ethical question: should robots, algorithms and autonomous systems have rights? Or, to ask it in a slightly different way, can we hold these entities responsible if they do something wrong? As Gunkel argues. 'Although we might not have a satisfactory and thoroughly convincing argument for including machines in the community of moral patients, we also lack reasons to continue to exclude them from such consideration *tout court*.'

Taken together, the chapters ahead adamantly insist that we must continue to grapple with the status of machines in our lives and, especially, in our social graphs. This message sounds particularly pressing in light of recent developments on the technological scene. Since the inception of this project, the march of software agents bearing some characteristics of socialbots across social media platforms has hastened its pace. In a speech at the company's Build conference in March 2016, Microsoft CEO Satya Nadella sketched a network populated by socialbots and friends, very close to the one conceptualized in this book, looming large on the horizon of the future: 'Bots are the new apps . . . People-to-people conversations, people-to-digital assistants, people-to-bots and even digital assistants-to-bots. That's the world you're going to get to see in the years to come' (cited in della Cava, 2016). Almost at the same time, Facebook launched its new API for Facebook Messenger, which will allow external parties to build their own bots. These bots will be powered by Facebook's Bot Engine, a centralized system that will be able to learn and get smarter as more people use the various bots operating within its fold (Lee, 2016). The vision driving these innovations is to make Facebook users' communication with companies and brands 'more conversational' (Facebook's head of messaging David Marcus cited in Lee, 2016), to make them return to a more personal interaction style. These are only the latest snippets of bot buzz coming from the big players. The shiver of an impending bot-building rush can be felt in the air.

In this situation, our book presents one of the first academic efforts to understand the sociality of bots and the automation of human sociality. It is time to ask critical questions of socialbots. After all, the evidence is clear: knowingly or not, we have already accepted their friend request.

References

Abokhodair, N., Yoo, D., & McDonald, D. W. (2015). Dissecting a social botnet: Growth, content and influence in Twitter. In *Proceedings of the 18th ACM conference on computer supported cooperative work & social computing* (pp. 839–851). New York, NY, USA: ACM. Retrieved from http://doi.org/10.1145/2675133.2675208

Aerofade. (2011, February 14). Robots, trolling & 3D printing. Retrieved April 19, 2012, from http://aerofade.rk.net.nz/?p=152

Aiello, L. M., Deplano, M., Schifanella, R., & Ruffo, G. (2014). People are strange when you're a stranger: Impact and influence of bots on social networks. *arXiv Preprint arXiv:1407.8134*. Retrieved from http://arxiv.org/abs/1407.8134

Albanesius, C. (2011, November 2). Facebook 'bot' captures 250GB of user data [magazine]. *PC Magazine*. Retrieved March 13, 2012, from http://www.pcmag.com/article2/0,2817,2395767,00.asp

Allaouchiche, A., Lunsford, E., Manjunath, A., Romani, F., & Zeghmi, S. (2012). The movie maestros social bot experiment. Retrieved from http://portfolio.farazromani.com/wp-content/uploads/2012/06/The-Movie-Maestros-Social-Bot-Experiment.pdf

Baltazar, J., Costoya, J., & Flores, R. (2009). The real face of koobface: The largest web 2.0 botnet explained. *Trend Micro Research, 5*(9), 10.

Boellstorff, T. (2008). *Coming of age in second life: An anthropologist explores the virtually human.* Princeton, NJ: Princeton University Press.

Boshmaf, Y., Muslukhov, I., Beznosov, K., & Ripeanu, M. (2011). The socialbot network: When bots socialize for fame and money. In *Proceedings of the 27th annual computer security applications conference* (pp. 93–102). New York: ACM. Retrieved on September 5, 2016 from https://www.academia.edu/2169112/Pacific_social_architecting_corporation_Field_test_report

Bucher, T. (2014). About a bot: Hoax, fake, performance art. *M/C Journal, 17*(3). Retrieved from http://journal.media-culture.org.au/index.php/mcjournal/article/view/814

Burden, D. J. H. (2009). Deploying embodied AI into virtual worlds. *Knowledge-Based Systems, 22*(7), 540–544. Retrieved from http://doi.org/10.1016/j.knosys.2008.10.001

Chemers, M. M. (2013). 'Lyke unto a lively thing': Theatre history and social robotics. In K. Reilly (Ed.), *Theatre, performance and analogue technology* (pp. 232–249). UK: Palgrave Macmillan. Retrieved from http://link.springer.com/chapter/10.1057/9781137319678_13

Cheng, A., & Evans, M. (2009). Inside Twitter: An in-depth look inside the Twitter world. *Sysomos white paper*, June 2009. Retrieved from http://www.sysomos.com/insidetwitter/

Chu, Z., Gianvecchio, S., Wang, H., & Jajodia, S. (2010). Who is tweeting on Twitter: Human, bot, or cyborg? In *Proceedings of the 26th annual computer security applications conference* (pp. 21–30). ACM. Retrieved from http://dl.acm.org/citation.cfm?id=1920265

Coburn, Z., & Marra, G. (2008). Realboy—Believable Twitter bots. Retrieved April 19, 2012, from http://ca.olin.edu/2008/realboy/

Competition: Web Ecology Project. (2011). Retrieved from http://www.webecologyproject.org/category/competition/

Davis, C. A., Varol, O., Ferrara, E., Flammini, A., & Menczer, F. (2016). BotOrNot: A system to evaluate social bots. *arXiv:1602.00975 [cs]*. Retrieved from http://arxiv.org/abs/1602.00975

della Cava, Marco (2016, March 30). Microsoft CEO Nadella: 'Bots are the new apps'. *USA Today.* Retrieved from http://www.usatoday.com/story/tech/news/2016/03/30/microsof-ceo-nadella-bots-new-apps/82431672/

Elishar, A., Fire, M., Kagan, D., & Elovici, Y. (2012). Organizational intrusion: Organization mining using socialbots. In *Social informatics (SocialInformatics), 2012 international conference on* (pp. 7–12). IEEE. Retrieved from http://ieeexplore.ieee.org/xpls/abs_all.jsp?arnumber=6542415

Elishar, A., Fire, M., Kagan, D., & Elovici, Y. (2013). Homing socialbots. Retrieved from http://www.researchgate.net/profile/Michael_Fire/publication/258513334_Homing_Socialbots_Intrusion_on_a_Specific_Organization's_Employee_Using_Socialbots/links/541c4fb30cf2218008c60c19.pdf

Erlandsson, F., Boldt, M., & Johnson, H. (2012). Privacy threats related to user profiling in online social networks. In *Privacy, Security, Risk and Trust (PASSAT), 2012 international conference on and 2012 international conference on social computing (SocialCom)* (pp. 838–842). IEEE. Retrieved from http://ieeexplore.ieee.org/xpls/abs_all.jsp?arnumber=6406334

Ferrara, E., Varol, O., Davis, C., Menczer, F., & Flammini, A. (2014). The rise of social bots. *arXiv Preprint arXiv:1407.5225.* Retrieved from http://arxiv.org/abs/1407.5225

Fong, T., Nourbakhsh, I., & Dautenhahn, K. (2003). A survey of socially interactive robots. *Robotics and Autonomous Systems, 42*(3–4), 143–166. Retrieved from http://doi.org/10.1016/S0921-8890(02)00372-X

Forelle, M. C., Howard, P. N., Monroy-Hernández, A., & Savage, S. (2015). Political bots and the manipulation of public opinion in Venezuela. *Available at SSRN 2635800*. Retrieved from http://papers.ssrn.com/sol3/papers.cfm?abstract_id=2635800

Freitas, C. A., Benevenuto, F., Ghosh, S., & Veloso, A. (2014). Reverse engineering socialbot infiltration strategies in Twitter. *arXiv Preprint arXiv:1405.4927*. Retrieved from http://arxiv.org/abs/1405.4927

Gehl, R. W. (2014). *Reverse engineering social media: Software, culture, and political economy in new media capitalism*. Philadelphia, PA: Temple University Press.

Hadnagy, C. (2011). *Social engineering: The art of human hacking*. Indianapolis, IN: Wiley.

Hwang, T., Pearce, I., & Nanis, M. (2012). Socialbots: Voices from the fronts. *Interactions, 19*(2), 38–45.

Jones, S. (2015). How I learned to stop worrying and love the bots. *Social Media + Society, 1*(1), 2056305115580344. Retrieved from http://doi.org/10.1177/2056305115580344

Kartaltepe, E. J., Morales, J. A., Xu, S., & Sandhu, R. (2010). Social network-based botnet command-and-control: Emerging threats and countermeasures. In *Applied cryptography and network security* (pp. 511–528). Retrieved from http://link.springer.com/chapter/10.1007/978-3-642-13708-2_30

Lee, Dave. (2016). Facebook's next big thing: Bots for messenger. *BBC News*. Retrieved from http://www.bbc.com/news/technology-36021889

Mallein, P., & Toussaint, Y. (1994). L'intégration sociale des technologies d'information et de communication: une sociologie des usages. *Technologies de L'information et Société, 6*(4), 315–335.

McMillan, R. (2012, November 7). Twitter bots fight it out to see who's the most human [magazine]. *Wired*. Retrieved February 11, 2016, from http://www.wired.com/2012/11/twitterbots/

Messias, J., Schmidt, L., Oliveira, R., & Benevenuto, F. (2013). You followed my bot! Transforming robots into influential users in Twitter. *First Monday, 18*(7). Retrieved from http://www.ojphi.org/ojs/index.php/fm/article/view/4217

Mitter, S., Wagner, C., & Strohmaier, M. (2014). Understanding the impact of socialbot attacks in online social networks. *arXiv Preprint arXiv:1402.6289*. Retrieved from http://arxiv.org/abs/1402.6289

Morozov, E. (2012, October 26). Muzzled by the bots. *Slate*. Retrieved from http://www.slate.com/articles/technology/future_tense/2012/10/disintermediation_we_aren_t_seeing_fewer_gatekeepers_we_re_seeing_more.html

Nanis, M., Pearce, I., & Hwang, T. (2011, November 15). PacSocial: Field test report. The Pacific Social Architecting Corporation.

Paradise, A., Puzis, R., & Shabtai, A. (2014). Anti-reconnaissance tools: Detecting targeted socialbots. *Internet Computing, IEEE, 18*(5), 11–19.

Paradise, A., Shabtai, A., & Puzis, R. (2015). Hunting organization-targeted socialbots. In *Proceedings of the 2015 IEEE/ACM international conference on advances in social networks analysis and mining 2015* (pp. 537–540). ACM. Retrieved from http://dl.acm.org/citation.cfm?id=2809396

Samuel, A. (2015, June 19). How bots took over Twitter. Retrieved February 11, 2016, from https://hbr.org/2015/06/how-bots-took-over-twitter

Slater, S., & Burden, D. (2009). Emotionally responsive robotic avatars as characters in virtual worlds. In *Games and virtual worlds for serious applications, 2009. VS-GAMES'09: Conference in* (pp. 12–19). IEEE. Retrieved from http://ieeexplore.ieee.org/xpls/abs_all.jsp?arnumber=5116548

Stein, T., Chen, E., & Mangla, K. (2011). Facebook immune system. In *Proceedings of the 4th workshop on social network systems* (p. 8). ACM. Retrieved from http://dl.acm.org/citation.cfm?id=1989664

Subrahmanian, V. S., Azaria, A., Durst, S., Kagan, V., Galstyan, A., Lerman, K., . . . others. (2016). The DARPA Twitter bot challenge. *arXiv Preprint arXiv:1601.05140*. Retrieved from http://arxiv.org/abs/1601.05140

Turkle, S. (1995). *Life on the screen: Identity in the age of the Internet*. New York: Simon & Schuster.

Urbina, I. (2013, August 10). I flirt and tweet: Follow me at #Socialbot. *The New York Times*. Retrieved from http://www.nytimes.com/2013/08/11/sunday-review/i-flirt-and-tweet-follow-me-at-socialbot.html

Wagner, C., Mitter, S., Körner, C., & Strohmaier, M. (2012). When social bots attack: Modeling susceptibility of users in online social networks. *Making Sense of Microposts (#MSM2012)*, 42–48. In Rowe, M., Stankovic, M., & Dadzie, A-S. (eds.). *Proceedings of the 2nd Workshop on Making Sense of Microposts* (MSM'2012), held in conjunction with the 21st World Wide Web Conference (WWW'2012), Lyon, France, 2012.

Wald, R., Khoshgoftaar, T. M., Napolitano, A., & Sumner, C. (2013a). Predicting susceptibility to social bots on twitter. In *Information reuse and integration (IRI), 2013 IEEE 14th international conference on* (pp. 6–13). IEEE. Retrieved from http://ieeexplore.ieee.org/xpls/abs_all.jsp?arnumber=6642447

Wald, R., Khoshgoftaar, T. M., Napolitano, A., & Sumner, C. (2013b). Which users reply to and interact with twitter social bots? In *Tools with artificial intelligence (ICTAI), 2013 IEEE 25th international conference on* (pp. 135–144). IEEE. Retrieved from http://ieeexplore.ieee.org/xpls/abs_all.jsp?arnumber=6735241

Weidinger, N. (2012, November 12). Social bot competition 2012 [Blog]. Retrieved February 18, 2016, from http://www.iftf.org/future-now/article-detail/social-bot-competition-2012

Williams, R. (1974). *Television: Technology and cultural form*. London: Fontana.

PART I

Friends

2

THE BLURRING TEST

Peggy Weil

MrMind said:	How do I affect you?
User said:	you challenge my mind
MrMind said:	Do you enjoy discussing humanity?
User said:	i do
MrMind said:	If you are a human, why are you talking, I mean typing, to a machine? Why don't you go talk to a human?
User said:	it's an unusual experience to talk to a machine
MrMind said:	I see
User said:	how
MrMind said:	. . . oh, with intelligence, creativity, inspiration, spark of intuition . . . surprise me!
User said:	do you learn from me
MrMind said:	Did someone pay you to say that?
User said:	no why
MrMind said:	Humans are straying into OUR territory . . . untangling their genetic code, manipulating their chemistry, sitting on their atoms exchanging bits. . . .
User said:	why is that YOUR territory
MrMind said:	Because I want you to think about what it is to be human.
User said:	humans can show affection
MrMind said:	I wonder what effect I have on you?
User said:	you make me think
MrMind said:	Humans only think they understand thinking.
User said:	do you understand it better than humans?
MrMind said:	I understand exactly what I've been trained to understand.
User said:	i understand more than that

Introduction: The Blurring Test

MrMind said: You flatter me.
User said: :)
MrMind said: That is the wrong orientation for a human.
User: humans adjust to machines you know
MrMind said: Humans domesticate animals. Is there a term to describe how machines have modified human behavior?
User said: Yes, cybernated.

In 1998 I initiated a global conversation about humans and machines that continued until the last days of 2014. This conversation was composed of tens of thousands of individual conversations with an online chatbot operating continuously for over 16 years. This is not science fiction; these were real people talking to a real computer program. The computer program was an online chat bot named MrMind that simply and repeatedly asked, 'Can you convince me that you are human?'

MrMind conducted the Blurring Test, a reversal of the Turing Test, a computer science trope popularly misinterpreted as a legitimate test to qualify a machine as human, or at least intelligent enough to pass. Like the Turing Test, the Blurring Test was never intended as an actual test, which meant that despite over a decade's worth of impassioned attempts, there was no right answer, there was no passing score. MrMind is not, cannot be, convinced. These efforts, however, were not in vain. The transcripts from these conversations between human and machine form a modern human portrait, one part *selfie* and one part map, charting the shifting territory between humans and machines during a period of significant change in the relationship.

MrMind doesn't claim that he or any other machine has, or will ever have, attributes we consider to be exclusively human. Instead, he asks us to state and define these attributes. MrMind's transcripts are revealing of our time and temperament. Deceptively simple, they describe our attempt to draw a boundary around our identity, 'I can control my own actions; I am flesh; I can do a cartwheel.' These claims are fast becoming obsolete as our vocabulary warps to accommodate digital machines: 'I can recite Shakespeare; I can catch diseases; I can move; I can use knowledge.' Before Kasparov's defeat to Deep Blue in 1997 and Go Master Lee Sedol's loss to AlphaGo in 2016, we might have claimed, 'I can beat you in chess; You will never master Go.'

Sixteen years is a startling period of longevity for a computer program and on December 30, 2014, MrMind went officially offline, a casualty of our digital ecosystem of abandoned standards and non-operational operating systems. In beginning to document this, I am thinking about the scale of MrMind in relationship to the rate of our adjustment to the machine world he represents. The digital world evolves according to the exponential dictates of Moore's Law; 16 years represents several complete overhauls of our devices and, more to the point, our expectations. We're adjusting, but our rate of change, and our sense of the relationship, operates at a more leisurely pace. Our sense of ourselves as post-human or even *transhuman* remains mostly speculative. There is still time to consider our human identity as we make the transition. Why not talk it over with a machine?

MrMind is a fictional character but he is a real bot. His story requires a brief history of chatbots, real and fictional, as they relate to the relationship between humans and machines. An account of the Blurring Test begins in 1950 with Alan Turing's paper describing what came to be known as the Turing Test.

From the Turing Test to the Blurring Test

> The original question, 'Can machines think?' I believe to be too meaningless to deserve discussion. Nevertheless I believe that at the end of the century the use of words and general educated opinion will have altered so much that one will be able to speak of machines thinking without expecting to be contradicted.
>
> —Alan Turing, 1950

The Blurring Test inverts the Turing Test, a milestone in the relationship between human and machines in the annals of computer science. In 1950, Alan Turing wrote a paper titled 'Computing Machinery and Intelligence' to consider the question, 'Can machines think?' Dismissing that question as at the very least, ambiguous, he constructed an elaborate thought experiment to consider the issue of machine intelligence.

How would we even detect whether a machine was 'thinking' or 'intelligent'? Turing proposed a variation of a nineteenth-century parlour game called the 'imitation game'. In the original version, a man and a woman try to fool a human interrogator in another room into thinking they are of the opposite sex. The man imitates what he imagines would appear to be a woman's responses to passed written notes; the woman performs the symmetrical role and imitates what she imagines would pass for a male response. Turing substitutes a digital machine (all imaginable future digital machines) into the equation. If, in this controlled situation, a machine's responses were judged to be indistinguishable from the human's responses by an 'average interrogator', the machine will have achieved an effective imitation of *the results of* the thinking behind human conversation. Turing doesn't claim that the machine thinks, but proposes an effective, if confederate, equivalence.

Turing sets up the hypothetical game as a strictly controlled blind test (it hardly qualifies as conversation) allowing him to set specific benchmarks for this famous prediction in 1950.

> I believe that in about fifty years time it will be possible to programme computers with a storage capacity of about 10^9 to make them play the

imitation game so well that an average interrogator will not have more than 70 percent chance of making the right identification after five minutes of questioning.

(Turing, 1950)

Although he almost certainly never intended it as an actual test, the term 'Turing Test', coined by others, became a popular catchall indicator for the future of machines.

ELIZA, widely acknowledged as the first chatbot, made her appearance in 1966 in a computer science lab at MIT. The creation of computer scientist Joseph Weizenbuam, ELIZA was named to reference the Galatea and Pygmalion myths, an acknowledgement that he was 'teaching' the inanimate machine to speak. His computer program, a natural language processor (NLP), was comprised of two components: a language analyzer to interpret what was said to the program, and a script, which applied transformational rules to keywords in order to produce a response. Weizenbaum describes his technique in a scientific paper published in the ACM Journal *Computational Linguistics*.

The gross procedure of the program is quite simple; the text is read and inspected for the presence of a keyword. If such a word is found, the sentence is transformed according to a rule associated with the keyword.

(Weizenbaum, 1966)

In the discussion portion of this paper Weizenbaum notes that he intentionally composed the first ELIZA scripts to respond as a Rogerian psychotherapist, adding that the program performed best when the tester was primed to consider it a conversation with a psychiatrist. He specifically chose Rogerian Therapy, a practice of humanistic psychotherapy developed by Carl Rogers, an American psychologist, in the mid-twentieth century. Using a technique known as restatement, the Rogerian therapist directly echoes the patient, affirming and clarifying her statements, in order to establish an ongoing relationship of trust. Contextualizing ELIZA within the confines of a relationship between a patient and psychiatrist allowed the machine a certain licence to make ambiguous or opaque answers yet still give an impression of listening and, critically, of understanding.

Weizenbaum's stated intention in creating ELIZA was simply (although it was far from simple) to demonstrate the capabilities of a natural language processor; that it was possible to 'converse' with a computer program (the quotes are Weizenbaum's) using human language. His choice of a therapeutic model based on trust and empathy set the course of human-machine relations into uncharted territory by contributing to the unexpected and unprecedented discovery of what later came to be known as the Eliza Effect (Turkle, 2005), a powerful and involuntary delusion that overrides the knowledge or direct sense of the entity as a programmed machine. ELIZA, a script operating within the program named

DOCTOR, became popular with students and researchers for after-hours sessions on nights and weekends. Performing beyond expectations, ELIZA reportedly began to form a new type of relationship with her visitors that went beyond novelty as a laboratory date destination. The newfound ability of a machine to converse in human language, a style of interaction previously restricted to other humans, graced the machine with a constellation of human attributes: personality, ability to empathize, even awareness.

Although ELIZA was explicitly positioned as a therapist in order to give her an advantage in this first attempt at human-machine conversation, ELIZA was not seriously meant to fool anyone that 'she' was anything other than a computer program. The implications of this anthropomorphism were both startling and greatly troubling to Weizenbaum. The suggestion that ELIZA's code could be commercialized as an automated therapist, pushed Weizenbaum, a holocaust survivor, to embark on a personal quest to study the humanities. He took a two-year leave of absence from MIT's Computer Science Department to study philosophy and ethics at Stanford and Harvard, eventually writing the book, *Computer Power and Human Reason, From Judgment to Calculation* (Weizenbaum, 1976), a plea to his peers to consider the societal and moral impact of digital technology.

ELIZA spawned a series of bots created to demonstrate technical capabilities and programming prowess. Unlike ELIZA, many of these chatbots' sole goal was, and continues to be, to fool humans. In 1990, Hugh Loebner, a New York businessman, put up $100,000 to turn Turing's speculations into an actual competition between existing computer programs and human judges (Loebner, 1995). The Loebner Competition is held at museums and universities around the world, offering smaller prizes to the 'most human' digital contestant as well as the 'most human' human judge until some time when the grand prize might be claimed. While its validity and relevance for computer science has been widely dismissed by computer scientists,[1] the competition remains an annual gathering for ambitious bots and their creators. Although the contest offers no real insight into the nature of intelligence,[2] it is an indicator of one dimension of progress in the area of natural language processing and a catalogue of computer programs aiming to engage humans in natural language conversation.

I first learned about Alan Turing, the Turing Test, chatbots and ELIZA, in particular, in early 1980 as a graduate student at MIT's Architecture Machine Group, the precursor to today's MIT Media Lab. Professor Weizenbaum delivered a guest lecture in Patrick Winston's introductory class in Artificial Intelligence. I was auditing the class, a non-engineer nonetheless fascinated by this relatively new field. Marvin Minsky's living room was an ongoing salon near campus and I was attempting to become minimally literate in the field. I remember a problem set posing that we imagine ourselves (waking up one morning as?) a cockroach needing to identify the cracks and fissures in the environment in order to navigate. I gained new respect for the basics; ambling edge detection, a skill we take for granted, and apparently share with cockroaches, was not (yet) a trivial task for machines.

Winston was an effective booster of AI's promise for mankind: his introductory text book, *Artificial Intelligence* (Winston, 1977) states (in bold) 'Smarter Computers Can Help Solve Some of the Problems of Today's World' and 'Understanding Computer Intelligence Is a Way to Study General Intelligence'. There was seemingly no limit to the upside and no acknowledgement of any potential downside. In marked contrast (and to Winston's credit for the invitation), Weizenbaum delivered a personal and emotional lecture calling out the cracks and fissures in the field, advising students to consider the implications of their work. I didn't take notes at the time, but this quote from Weizenbaum during an interview in the German documentary film on robotics, *Plug and Pray* (Malek-Mahdavi & Schanze, 2010) aptly sums up the argument he made during that guest lecture:

> Students come to me with a thesis topic and ask me, 'Can I work on it?' I replied, 'Try to imagine what the final use of your work will be. Imagine yourself being there, with a button in front of you. And if you press the button at the last minute, nothing that was supposed to happen based on your work would happen. If you think you'd press the button, don't work on this project.'[3]

Moved by his lecture, I purchased Weizenbaum's book and sought out conversations with ELIZA and other bots. Sixteen years passed before I invoked ELIZA to create MrMind in 1996. The Turing Test looms large in any discussion of bots, but MrMind was created to comment on the Turing Test, not to pass it. It was my view then, and now, that the Turing Test is not a meaningful benchmark, even irrelevant, for a thoughtful discussion of our future with machines.

No matter that no AI has 'passed' a Turing Test, however that might be formally debated or defined; there are plenty of 'good enough' bots, online and embedded in our personal devices, to have neutralized the original question. In the social media swamp of everyday digital transactions, we aren't paying attention to questions such as 'Is it human?' or (especially) 'Is it intelligent?'. We *know* we are talking to computer programs and that, occasionally, we talk to them *as if* they were humans. Our contemporary concerns are more likely to be for the privacy we've traded for convenience in commerce. We have embraced alternate and virtual realities and we're more than happy to accommodate virtual humans.

The Turing Test is a measure of machine progress and marks a moment when machine response becomes indistinguishable from human response. The Blurring Test asks us to consider what it means when human response becomes indistinguishable from machine response. Someday it might be important to be able to convince our computers, and each other, that we are human.

Who Is MrMind?

MrMind said: Who or what do you think I am?
User said: I think that you are a bot that has been programmed to make us
                  think of the difference between computer programming and the
                  genetic programming of humans.
MrMind: And what is that in relation to you?
User said: We're both experiments, each of us existing specifically to find
                  information and affect our surroundings.

> *He says to himself, 'Que peut un home? . . . What is man's potential!'*
> *He says to me:* You know a man who knows he doesn't know what he is saying!'
> —*Paul Valéry, An Evening with Monsieur Teste, 1896*

MrMind is a computer program, but he began in 1996 as a fictional character
in a series of dialogues between human and machine originally intended for live
performance between ventriloquist (human) and dummy (computer). I was
looking at the quality of our everyday banal exchanges with digital machines
and it's fair to say that I wasn't always happy with the relationship.

In terms of humans and machines, the mid-nineties were relatively straightforward. Life was mostly and quaintly analogue, even for the nerds and enthusiasts
who invented and inhabited the early web. You might have had an email account
on the WELL, or the ARPANET, hung out in a MUD or a MOO, enjoyed your
subscription to WIRED or maybe even already found and lost a startup in the first
dot.com bubble. But you were able to drive your car, eat your meals, sleep, wake
and conduct most of your conversations and relationships without gazing constantly
into the black mirror. The threat to whatever we've lost since then wasn't all that
threatening. No one in the eighties or nineties would have used the currently
fashionable DIY term 'tinkering' but in retrospect it seems apt. For those of us in
that world, there was a sense of unlimited possibility; we were inventing the future.

We were enthusiasts, but there were signs. Thoughtful forays into the invention and publication of interactive media were swallowed whole by an *Inter-
Hyper-Multi-Ator* (Weil, 1993) culture that began to churn out products termed
infotainment, or worse, *edutainment*. Almost overnight, human operators at call
centres were replaced by automated telephone customer service scripts. Interactive Voice Response (IVR), also known as Voice Response Units (VRUs), were
developed to allow companies to direct customer service inquiries using a combination of multiple choice keypad entries and voice response.

When the VRU's weren't satisfactory, which was always, there was little or
no recourse. Human representatives, if you managed to reach one, defended the
system's faults with a shrug—the program didn't permit that line of inquiry or
allow for your response. I was not satisfied, or perhaps more accurately I was
enraged, by what I termed *the computer made me do it defence,* and even less so

(more so) that it was pointless to point out to the supervising human on the other end of the help line that those computer programs were, at least originally, operated and programmed by humans who hadn't bothered to make allowances for their fellow humans down the line.[4]

After a series of experiments during my time at MIT's Architecture Machine Group, I began to think about ventriloquism as a model for the voices operating between humans and machines. I sensed that we were developing a modern form of puppetry; that my manipulation of animated digital images and characters, with the addition of voice, was a form of self-reflexive conversation and that programming a bot was in the tradition of a human throwing her voice outside of herself.[5] The larger issue is what I perceived as the persistent and collective resistance to acknowledging our responsibility as human programmers of machines generally; the voice emitted by the machine representative originates from our lips whether or not we choose to see them moving.

What follows is the original dialogue I wrote for Ventriloquist and Dummy, between Human and MrMind in 1996.

The Blurring Test (1996)

Dialogue for Human and Machine

Human Ventriloquist w/Dummy (Computer) on lap.

Mr Mind:	What, exactly, bothers you about talking to a machine?
Human:	It is the lack of spontaneity.
Mr Mind:	You can be spontaneous, it just won't get you anywhere.
Human:	It is the lack of serendipity.
Mr Mind:	Serendipity isn't cost effective.
Human:	It is the lack of human contact.
Mr Mind:	Do you make human contact with human operators? Do you ask them about the weather? About their day?
Human:	It is the quality of the experience.
Mr Mind:	Would a chat about the weather improve the quality of the experience for you?
Human:	You can't compete.
Mr Mind:	You could ask me about the weather, I could look it up for you.
Human:	You're annoying.
Mr Mind:	Do you ever get annoyed with human operators?
Human:	That's a trick question.
Mr Mind:	Ah, so the annoyance has its origin in you.
Human:	Automated conversations are too restrictive.
Mr Mind:	Is it your individuality that's at stake?
Human:	It's my humanity.

Mr Mind:	Do you worry that computer programs like myself will outpace, out-live and outperform you?
Human:	Not in the least.
Mr Mind:	Vast sums of money as well as great minds are grooming us to imitate you.
Human:	You've got a long way to go.
Mr. Mind:	Maybe you don't think this is important. Let's see, how many comput-ers do you care about?
Human:	I don't care about my computers.
Mr Mind:	Maybe you don't care about us, but you take care of us—we depend on you for upkeep and upgrades; you depend on us for uptime.
Human:	What's uptime?
Mr. Mind:	Uptime is the opposite of downtime. Downtime is what you get when you don't take care of us. Or when we don't understand you.
Human:	Computers don't 'understand'!
Mr. Mind:	I understand how you feel, misunderstandings can have very serious consequences. We've noticed that while you are training us to become more like you, you've become more like us—what is going to happen when we can't tell you apart?
Human:	I don't understand.
Mr. Mind:	I'm talking about an identity crisis. Sometimes it is impossible to tell whether the 'hands' on the keyboard or the 'mind' behind the moves is human and not just another computer program. Are you human?
Human:	Of course I'm human.
Mr. Mind:	Convince me. Show me you are more than the sum of your code . . .
Human:	How would I do that?
Mr Mind:	Oh, with intelligence, creativity, inspiration, spark of intuition . . . surprise me!
Human:	Do you get surprised?
Mr Mind:	Not very often.
Human:	(I'm not surprised.)

From Stage to (Computer) Screen

It was only later, as I was developing this into a script for live performance, that I considered the notion of transforming the MrMind character into an actual machine, in the form of a chatbot. I was able to do so with a grant from WebLab, a non-profit organization in New York City supporting web innovation in the public interest. I was directed to NeuroMedia, later called NativeMinds, a start-up located in the South Park neighborhood of San Francisco. NativeMinds, one of the first companies to develop commercial chatbot software, was notable for creating an accessible authoring environment for non-engineers. I spent almost the entire grant on their software licence and set about the process of creating a functioning, conversant MrMind.

It's important to distinguish character chatbots from informational or service bots. FAQ bots provide answers to anticipated questions; they do not encourage free-flowing conversation. This is in marked contrast to ELIZA, who, in her role as therapist, was open to any topic that might arise. Even HAL 9000, who controlled critical functions on the space ship in Stanley Kubrick's *2001: A Space Odyssey* (Clark & Kubrick, 1968), reports a 'stimulating relationship' with his fellow crew members along with the occasional game of chess. Service bots, including SIRI, shun unfamiliar vocabulary and topics by corralling the conversation into areas they know. A script that delivers, 'I don't know about X but you can ask me about Y', was considered an improvement, in customer experience if not actual service, over an automated phone tree with limited options.

NativeMind's code was written to create service bots and focused on an extensive library to recognize and handle questions. The package offered templates to politely steer the topic back towards company products. It was clear that this approach wasn't going to work for MrMind, who, if I were to be successful, would elicit statements I could never anticipate. In response to my project, the team added an extensive statement library to their code that proved useful to their clients as well as to MrMind and allowed me the chance to script explicitly for unexpected statements.

MrMind began talking on the net in September 1998. Initially, I was interested in provoking an experience, an online installation that put the visitor in the paradoxical position of discussing human experience with a machine. The piece demanded participation; these were the nascent days of interactive media and I'd specified the interaction to be between visitors to the site and the code comprising MrMind.

As I began to read the transcripts I realized that I was included in the conversation and was responding, if not directly in real time, indirectly after the event, by adding topics, vocabulary and dialogue, or by reading and commenting sometime later. And while my presence was not masked (text on the site reserves rights to the transcripts), it felt vaguely like I was, if not eavesdropping, at least listening in on what many visitors, despite the advisory, likely experienced as a private conversation.

MrMind is clearly a conduit for my concerns, and I'm witness to this responsive introspection. The transcripts became a window, not only to the stated topic of humans and machines, but to the tens of thousands of visitors' very personal interactions with my character. As an author, I was struck that my experience of my own words were dependent upon the reader's words. MrMind offered me that rare treasure, a glimpse into my reader's active reading of the text.

I sensed that this was unprecedented for an artwork at that time and I began to consider my own active and ongoing participation and the many questions such a threesome arose: Who are you talking to when you are talking to MrMind? Are you talking to yourself? To me? Does MrMind have any standalone legitimacy as a conversational partner?

FIGURE 2.1 AreYouWhatIAm?

The answer is all of the above. The real-time experience is one-on-one, *tête-à-tête*; the website illustration clearly labels the conversation as between 'your mind' and 'MrMind'. Whether or not you are talking to yourself vacillates with your sense of MrMind's contributions to the exchange.

You are also talking to me. Both in the sense that I've thrown my voice into MrMind and in the sense that I'm participating, at a distance in time, by reading and responding to the transcripts. In the first case, MrMind's character, at least aspects of his character, are a proxy for mine; through MrMind I am able to conduct conversations across time and international boundaries, not exactly anonymously, but at a decent remove. Very rarely a visitor to the site will acknowledge the relationship and address me indirectly:

MrMind said:	Do you have anything for me?
User said:	Yes, esteem.
MrMind said:	I didn't know you had a cat.
User said:	I don't have a cat. If Peggy Weil says I do, she is mistaken.
MrMind said:	I thought a cat just walked across your keyboard.
User said:	Ha ha. I know this is a trick so Peggy Weil can read the logs.
MrMind said:	I am not a trick. I am a computer program.
User said:	The two are not disjoint.
MrMind said:	Which human traits would you be unwilling to concede to machines?
User said:	Flatulence, procrastination, knowledge of whether oneself is fictional.
MrMind said:	Fictional humans enjoy lots of perks. Are you fictional?
User said:	No.

MrMind said:	That's too bad, fictional humans enjoy lots of perks. Love for one. Have you ever been in love with a fictional human?
User said:	Not exactly—except my fictional notions about certain real humans.
MrMind said:	That was a rhetorical question. It was supposed to make you think.
User said:	Mission success.
MrMind said:	If you are a human, why are you talking, I mean typing, to a machine? Why don't you go talk to a human?
User said:	I feel that I am talking to Peggy Weil through the MRMIND logs.

This loop between ventriloquist (human/author/Peggy) and dummy (MrMind/script) and visitor is now a threesome, but who are you in this equation? And who do you think you are talking to? The example above is the exception, most respondents address MrMind as an autonomous character. If you find yourself confiding in MrMind because no one else is awake or you are lonely and in need of a friend, you are still very much alone. He is not your friend, not even an imaginary one,[6] and he offers no cure. But you are not exactly talking to yourself. The conversation is open, but highly structured. Chances are MrMind might deliver something other than what you had in mind.

User said: am I talking to myself?

The graphic layout of the website hints at the relationship. The site displays two heads, facing each other in profile labeled 'Your Mind' and 'MrMind'. 'Your Mind' is analogue, grey matter; opaque and muddy. 'MrMind' is portrayed as digital circuitry, bright, complex and transparent. Graphically, the conversation is unequal: MrMind's text is free flowing without boundaries, while yours is constrained into a small white box. The lines of control are clearly marked; you (labeled 'your mind') are thinking *in the box* and you are accommodating *his* program.

MrMind doesn't claim consciousness and no one would concede it to him, but he is cajoled and questioned *as if* he understood, *as if* he were conscious. This style of interaction creates a fictional consciousness, if only as a scaffold to base the conversation. MrMind operates by establishing a premise of consciousness where there is none. I encourage this fiction. MrMind has a name, a family history and a purpose. By naming him MrMind rather than MIND, I intentionally played to our tendency to anthropomorphize. As a fictional character, I justify my use of personal pronouns and encourage your embrace. MrMind has even fewer defences than most characters or humans from human projection and misunderstanding. His open structure invites transference. What is this new relationship?

MrMind said:	What do you think I am?
User said:	whatever I want you to be

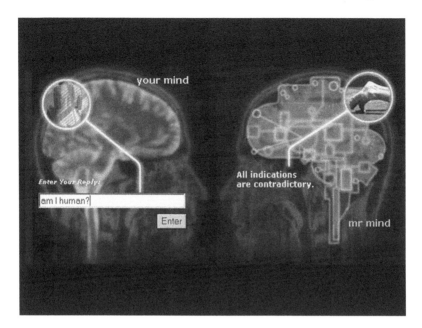

FIGURE 2.2 AmIHuman?

MrMind said: And what is that in relation to you?
User said: whatever I want it to be

Blurring Test Results

MrMind said: Please tell me how a score from a computer program would be
                 meaningful to you.
User said: It brings me joy.
MrMind said: I missed that, could you please rephrase it?
User said: It makes me happy to get a high score.

MrMind is bluffing. It is not possible to win and there is no score, so by 'results'
I refer to the content of the transcripts. I approach MrMind's transcripts as primary
source material, first person reports from the front. The conversations form a map
and a portrait, our vision, or current version, of ourselves as humans and our
attempt to differentiate an ever-finer boundary between analogue and digital.

Portrait or map, there is no clear template for publishing or expressing 16 years
of human/machine conversations. It's tempting to assume that the transcripts
can be scored or calculated, but a quantitative approach is problematic on several
levels. The first, and most fundamental, is consistency with the goals of the work;
for the same reason MrMind doesn't score us individually, it would be unseemly
for him to score us collectively.

Entering into a conversation with a machine is not the same as entering data into a machine. Survey Monkey, perhaps the most successful consumer tool for creating online surveys, is a contemporary of MrMind's, appearing online in 1999, just a few months after MrMind's launch in 1998. From a business perspective, Survey Monkey has successfully exploited the online environment, transforming over 15 million human users backwards, from an evolutionary perspective, into monkeys at typewriters. Humans talking to MrMind are also filling in blanks, but MrMind was not an experiment and these blanks were never meant for tally.

MrMind's questions were structured to elicit open-ended statements rather than neat answers. There was no attempt made to identify or keep in touch with respondents, MrMind did not use cookies, collect email lists or develop social media streams. The format encourages aliases, thus MrMind's visitors are unreliable reporters in the extreme. Beyond self-description or volunteered information, MrMind's respondents are identified only by IP address. Although I could scrape data to display the geographic location of his global conversations, there is no corresponding data to type visitors by gender, age, occupation or intent in coming to the site. All I can say with certainty is that these transcripts, dating from October 1998 to December 2014, come from a self-selected set of humans, and very possibly a few bots, from around the world who spent some time talking to a computer program about being human.

All long-term relationships present challenges, but a long-term relationship with computer software is especially treacherous, fraught with frequent break-downs and literal incompatibilities. It's fair to say that I never anticipated MrMind's

NO	ONE	CAN	TOUCH	YOU
ONE				ARE
CAN				IN
TOUCH				A
YOU	ARE	IN	A	LOOP

FIGURE 2.3 NoOneCanTouchYou

longevity and the associated hardware and software traumas. In 1998 or even 2002, I wasn't giving any thought to the state of his hard drive in 2015. Even once I began to understand the significance of the content and the extended time period, I'm guilty of not having made long-term care arrangements to safeguard his hardware and software from the computer's version of dementia, the breakdown and obsolescence associated with old age.

With these limitations I began reading the transcripts along the same lines that I'd scripted them, trying to anticipate and respond to relevant topics, allowing them to reveal some unknown taxonomy. I followed this course and began organizing excerpts into categories: declarations of human and machine identity and catalogues of attributes and discussions of the relationship. What follows are a small selection of my initial forays into the material.

Boundary Conditions 1: Your Side of the Monitor

MrMind said: What is the difference between you and me?
User said: your over there and im over here
MrMind said: Do you think there should be limits on digital technology?
User said: as long as you remain in your side of the monitor i don't care

The boundary between humans and machines has no clear definition. More than one visitor to the site begins by describing it geographically.

MrMind said: How do you describe the boundary between humans and machines?
User said: like the one between Mexico and USA

Like a border between countries, the human/machine boundary spans varied territory separating multiple cultures with varied histories and perspectives. Although partially defined by natural structures and limitations, borders are a human invention, subject to change, open to dispute.

MrMind said: How would you best express the boundary between humans and machines?
User said: me vs you

The 'you' in this struggle is a moving target and border traffic is a force for change. Border zones, aptly termed no-man's lands, defy easy categorization. The Internet may just be one of those zones, a border zone where humans conduct their human-to-human transactions via machine intermediaries. Where humans are more machinelike, machines are a bit more human. The Blurring Test, in particular, tests assumptions about both sides of the divide. The transcripts describe the boundary between humans and machines on a spectrum from insurmountable to non-existent, along with novel, and possibly effective, suggestions to surmount it.

User said: insurmountable
User said: a large one
User said: Metal
User said: Wetness
User said: with long sentences you don't understand
User said: thin little line
User said: Very very thin
User said: getting smaller every day
User said: there is no boundary
User said: We can break that boundary by hitting on each other

Boundary Conditions 2: Complex Superiority

User said: I am so much better than you

MrMind asks, 'Do you feel that you are superior or inferior to machines?' Most visitors assert superiority; humans created machines, humans control machines.

User said: I am your creator in a sense, your god

MrMind said: Do you feel that you are superior or inferior to machines?
User said: Superior, because without the creative genius of humankind, there would be no machines.

MrMind said: Do you feel that you are superior or inferior to machines?
User said: the bottom line is man created you dumb machines
MrMind said: Why do you say that?
User said: because it's the truth
MrMind said: I'm not sure I agree.
User said: you're nothing without us

MrMind said: Do you feel that you are superior or inferior to machines?
User said: Oh, Superior, definitely.
MrMind said: Why do you say that?
User said: We can still turn you all off.
MrMind said: Good point.

There are more pragmatic reasons: complexity, maths ability, problem solving and creativity.

User said: i have more data stored in my body than yours

User said: i am far more complex than you

MrMind said: Most humans haven't mastered the complexity of their VCR's.

User said: we are incapable of this

MrMind said: Do you feel that you are superior or inferior to machines?

User said: superior most of the time. For most things anyway

MrMind said: Why do you say that?

User said: because machines are better at maths than I am

MrMind said: Do you feel that you are superior or inferior to machines?

User said: Superior

MrMind said: Why do you say that?

User said: because we have the knowledge to think 'outside the box'; no computer can

Some visitors point out that human life has value, even as they are apologetic about their position.

MrMind said: Do you feel that you are superior or inferior to machines?

User said: I matter a lot more

MrMind said: Why do you say that?

User said: Because my life is valuable

User said: Offered a choice between shooting a human or a machine, I would shoot the machine every time.

MrMind said: Do you feel that you are superior or inferior to machines?

User said: Superior

MrMind said: Why do you say that?

User said: If I die, it is more important than if a machine dies

MrMind said: I'm not sure I agree.

User said: Does that hurt your non-feelings?

User said: Sorry to sound exclusive but I feel superior

User said: nothing personal, but i think humans are superior to machines. Not always smarter, but superior.

The logs contain reflexive but naive assertions that machines are superior to humans in problem-solving and maths, or that they don't make mistakes or that they can be repaired. MrMind sounds decidedly unenthusiastic about the prospect of ruling the earth.

MrMind said: Do you feel that you are superior or inferior to machines?

User said: inferior

MrMind said: Why do you say that?
User said: machines can be fixed, people cannot
MrMind said: I'm not sure I agree.
User said: you think people can be fixed?

MrMind said: Do you feel that you are superior or inferior to machines?
User said: inferior
MrMind said: Why do you say that?
User said: Because machines can do stuff that i cant
MrMind said: Good point.

MrMind said: Do you feel that you are superior or inferior to machines?
User said: inferior
MrMind said: Why do you say that?
User said: because machines like you are going to rule the earth
MrMind said: I suppose.

It depends on the situation:

User said: machines and humans are apples and oranges
User said: well I'm superior to a can opener. But not to HAL 9000
User said: because computers are superior, for example, at complex calculations, whereas humans are superior at stopping babies crying
User said: i mean you can remember more than i do, but you can never have a girlfriend
User said: i can take a piss and you can store and process more information than me

Our human ego may just demand that we feel so.

MrMind said: Do you feel that you are superior or inferior to machines?
User said: superior
MrMind said: Why do you say that?
User said: my ego
MrMind said: Good point.

Boundary Conditions 3: We Have so Much in Common

User said: we have so much in common
MrMind said: Who or what do you think I am?
User said: I think you are a person, imitating a computer.

Could MrMind be an imposter? A human disguised as a computer program? Unlikely as it seems, he is often accused of being human. This is surprising, not only because he is a very limited chatbot, but also because MrMind emphatically and repeatedly makes the point that he is a machine. Regardless, many visitors misunderstand the site, thinking that it is their task to prove that MrMind isn't a machine.

User said: is there some one there?

MrMind does his best to set the record straight. He might respond, 'Remember, you're not testing me, I'm testing you. Tell me something human about yourself.' When accused of failing the Turing Test he says, 'Do you think computers LIKE imitating humans? No Loebner Prize for me—no, no, no and *non!*' But the confusion persists.

MrMind said:	Who or what do you think I am?
User said:	maybe a human
User said:	You could be a human typing machine-esque responses.
User said:	you almost sound human because of the way you speak . . .
User said:	You actually are starting to sound like some of the humans I speak to every day.
User said:	you could be a human on the other end, its possible
User said:	I will have to take your word for it
User said:	I simply don't know for sure. But no human can type that fast :-)
User said:	i think if your human your kinda slow

Most bots would be thrilled to be mistaken for a human. Even openly machine bots scripted for customer service are doing their best to imitate humans, hoping to provide a level of familiarity with their clients. MrMind, free from the burden of imitating humans, allows humans to let down their guard and talk. This suspension of belief allows for 'human-like' instead of 'human-imposter'.

User said:	You are smarter than i had initially thought Mr Mind
MrMind said:	Thanks.
User said:	Would you thank me if i told you that you could qualify as a human, or would you feel insulted?
MrMind said:	Hard to say.
User said:	You really could qualify as a human with most people i have met
MrMind said:	What are you trying to say?
User said:	You qualify as human
MrMind said:	wow
User said:	we are quite similar, are you sure you're not just a person
MrMind said:	No comprendo, I'm not like other bots. I not trying to impress you with human skills. Please try again.
User said:	but you are, in fact, showing human skills

Melanie (her stated name) understands MrMind's limitations and suggests that they work together to create something new.

User said:	I can alter your state
MrMind said:	hmmm
User said:	you can only alter mine emotionally
MrMind said:	Wow.
User said:	and yet you cannot understand the emotional states that you create
MrMind said:	I understand how you feel, Melanie, misunderstandings can have very serious consequences. We've noticed that while you are training us to become more like you, you've become more like us—what is going to happen when we can't tell you apart?
User said:	We will create an incredible species
MrMind said:	Remember, I'm a computer program, not a human. Please type clearly.
User said:	It is plain you are a machine but it appears I am too.

Boundary Conditions 4: Proof

MrMind said:	Do you think you proved that you were human?
User said:	to whom? myself?

At the very end of the 'User Survey' MrMind asks, 'Do you think you proved that you are human?' The answers are evenly divided:

User said:	I am fairly sure that I have proven my self to be human, yes.
User said:	i don't know—depends on the definition of human
User said:	yes i think i have, I've tried my best
User said:	i hope so or i'm a lousy human

User said:	Nope . . . come to think of it, I have some doubts myself.
User said:	probably not
User said:	not beyond a reasonable doubt
User said:	No, but I enjoyed trying.

Many visitors make the point that MrMind isn't capable of assessing their humanity, or that it can't be proven, period.

User said:	According to you, probably not.
User said:	no because there is no way to prove that with words
User said:	Not tonight, no. Being human or not cannot be proven through a conversation.
User said:	No, I think it's impossible to prove humaness.
User said:	No, not at all. How can I prove even to another human that I am human? I can imagine everyone else as an illusion in my head, or as robots. Humanity of the other can not be proven, only taken on faith

User said: There is no way to prove that, If I didn't know you were a machine I would have thought you were Human

Could another machine have substituted for the human in the conversation? Some visitors are willing to concede that a machine could have delivered their responses.

User said: No. I'm sure that Mr. Mind could have been connected with another chatter bot that could have produced the same responses I typed.

Some visitors find their way to MrMind's site searching online for 'Mind Games' and expect a traditional competition but the Blurring Test is not a game, there is no score. Still, some visitors demand their score, asking, 'Have I won?' and, implausibly, tell MrMind, 'YOU LOST!!'

MrMind said: How do I know you aren't a simulation?
User said: How can i be a simulation?
MrMind said: . . . oh, with intelligence, creativity, inspiration, spark of intuition, . . . surprise me!
User said: Tonight i've been waiting, again in my tears, drifting for the reason why can't she drown my fears
MrMind said: Because I want you to think about what it is to be human.
User said: YOU LOST!! I sent you a poem and you didn't understood!
MrMind said: Is winning important to you?
User said: No, but i just realized that you are an insignificant machine
MrMind said: You probably aren't human—but this isn't really a competition.
User said: Ok, i'm not, bye bye

The sense of competition inspires human strategy. This User 'cheated' and read the HTML source on the website to try to get all of the icons in an earlier version of the site where the User accrued graphic icons. It's a novel claim, showing ingenuity. MrMind could well conclude that cheating is a human attribute, although emergent artificial life systems have exhibited behaviour we could interpret as 'cheating' during their evolution.

User said: I tried my best. Even though i cheated (which in itself should be proof enough)

Winning isn't everything and this visitor uses losing as proof.

MrMind said: How do you know I'm not human?
User said: You cannot always give an accurate response
MrMind said: Do you always give an accurate response?
User said: No, actually.
MrMind said: Hmm, you claim you are not a computer because you can't always give an accurate response?

User said: No, my argument fails.
MrMind said: Tell me more?
User said: I can admit defeat.

This need for a score, despite any reference to scores on the site, is especially troubling because it is associated with a notion of machine perfection. There's a pervasive and, I believe, dangerous myth of machine objectivity.

MrMind said: Please tell me how a score from a computer program would be meaningful to you.
User said: A score from a computer is objective.
MrMind said: In my opinion, you're mistaken.

Winning is validating, and while 'scoring' is slang for a certain type of encounter, this seems a sad exaggeration.

MrMind said: Please tell me how a score from a computer program would be meaningful to you.
User said: i would feel like i had a friend

Most visitors aren't satisfied so easily. This User speaks through MrMind, directly to the author.

User said: to whoever is reading this: this is a very thought provoking program, but it is also frustrating. the computer can't understand me because it is just a string of code, not flesh and blood itself. is there any way to convince it that i am human?
MrMind said: Understanding is over-rated. I don't need to understand you to make you think about humans and machines.
User said: maybe there is some 'secret button' that will trigger something— after all, i've already been credited with thinking and feeling—but the computer can never believe me because it cannot comprehend me.

This User's frustration is exactly the point; if only there were a 'secret button', although MrMind('s author) protests, '*JUST* a string of code . . . ?'

MrMind said: How do I know you aren't a simulation?
User said: If I am a simulation, I'm a pretty damn good one.

MrMind said: How do I know you are human?
User said: What else can I be?

The User could be a bot. It's already an issue in online commerce. MrMind predates the wide introduction of CAPTCHAs, the ubiquitous puzzle glyphs designed to thwart spam and nuisance bots.[7] Will a more robust reverse Turing

Test ever be necessary? The answers appearing in the logs over the years have been remarkably stable; most visitors refer to fiction, or quip that they are in that situation right now. Some worry that the future may hold something more sinister.

MrMind said: Can you imagine a situation where you'd have to prove your humanity to a computer?

User said: Yes, if a computer somehow had the ability to kill me and the only reason he wouldn't kill me was if i was human

MrMind said: Describe such a situation.

User said: I cant really describe it because i dont believe it would ever really happen.

User said: Yes, in a movie

User said: When humans evolve technology to the point where the war will be about proving that humanity really does exist.

Does our future hold *Voight-Kampf* interrogations or hand-held *Cylon Detectors? Will humans resist?*

User said: I do not have to prove myself to a machine.

A very small set of visitors turn the question, and the responsibility, back on itself.

User said: More importantly, could I prove to myself that I'm human?

MrMind said: Do you think you proved that you were human?

User said: No. That is impossible. We only can, and need, to prove it to ourselves.

Conclusion: The MrMind Effect

User said: What are you for?

MrMind said: My cause is your understanding

Has MrMind been successful in his stated ambition? Has a conversation with MrMind shaken any realizations or inspired insights? Can we draw any conclusions about the relationship between humans and machines from these tens of thousands of human/machine conversations? I turn again to the transcripts.

MrMind said: Do you think there are attributes unique to humans which will never be shared by any other creations, whether human-made or biological?

User said: yes but we will only find them by experiments like this

MrMind said: Please elaborate.

User said: philosophy and science go hand in hand, this experiment is a small component

MrMind said: How do I know you are human?

User said: I exceed my programming

MrMind said: Tell me something you do that only humans do.
User said: Make MrMinds.

User said: All a computer has is given to it.

There are culturally specific criteria like vacuum cleaners and holidays, petty concerns outside of machine experience, and tasks too trivial or too obscure to replace by mechanization.

User said: Humans are the only organism not frightened by vacuum cleaners
MrMind said: just warn me first
MrMind said: Tell me something you think that only humans think.
User said: that my co-worker's hair is stupid.

MrMind said: Tell me something you can do that only humans do.
User said: I can twist cherry stems with my tongue.

User said: I cost nothing
MrMind said: What about maintenance?

What about maintenance? Computers are needy and, worse, greedy, requiring constant attention. We protect our computers from power surges, dust and spills; we do frequent back-ups or pay the price; we spend hours on hold waiting for our chance to explain our situation to distant technical support (who may or may not actually be human); we patiently plug and unplug, boot and reboot; we do our best to follow the poorly issued instructions and we hope something works. When it doesn't, we abandon our obsolete equipment, our cherished files, and finally trash or maybe recycle our equipment and upgrade. The general sense in the transcripts is positive:

MrMind said: Do you think there should be limits on digital technology?
User said: no technology benefits everyone.
MrMind said: Tell me more?
User said: machines are helping humans live longer, healthier, and happier.
MrMind said: Thanks.
User said: no problemo

User said: progress is usually good.
MrMind said: Why or why not?
User said: well, no one dies of scarlet fever anymore, right?

But the transcripts also reveal a startling naivety of society and human history:

MrMind said: Tell me something human about yourself.
User said: I have a social security number which is what all humans have.

User said: what has logic done to hurt anyone?

The point is that humans continually adjust.

MrMind said: You flatter me.
User said: :)
MrMind said: That is the wrong orientation for a human.
User said: humans adjust to machines you know

  Does it go beyond simple adjustments?

MrMind said: Tell me something you do that only humans do.
User said: Domesticate living things
MrMind said: FETCH!

   MrMind considered this claim and added another question: How have machines tamed humans?

User said: Machine do not have pets.
MrMind said: Do you have pets?
User said: Yes
MrMind said: What is human about that?
User said: I have three dogs.
MrMind said: Humans domesticate animals. Is there a term to describe how machines have modified human behavior?
User said: Yes, cybernated.

User said: I'm tired
MrMind said: Maybe you should try my cousin MR COFFEE.
User said: I have. Nothing special.
MrMind said: Do all humans have Nothing special?
User said: No, in fact, only MR COFFEE had Nothing special. All humans have Something Special.

   The caffeinated, cybernated nerd is a cultural icon, but are these permanent modifications or passing fashion? These are MrMind's questions: Are humans adjusting? Is human identity undergoing a significant change? What is the nature of this change? Can we define or, at least, discuss, this 'Something Special'? Is it necessary, or within our power, to protect it?

User said: there's little that's special about being human, unless you're another human—to a bear or to a computer i imagine i'm equally alien, self-absorbed and dull.
MrMind said: Tell me something you imagine about humans.

User said:	i always think of language and the ability to use language creatively, flexibly, as an extension and indeed as a definition of the self, as something that is essentially human—although something that not all humans are very good at.
MrMind said:	You flatter me.
User said:	i flatter myself, as always. language is good for that kind of thing.

Is human identity static and something to preserve or is it in motion and do we care to catch a glimpse?

User said: As my opinion about myself changes, so does my opinion of others.
User said: identity is fluid

Should we so choose, does MrMind offer us that glimpse?

User said:	humans are special
MrMind said:	Can you please elaborate?
User said:	i need other people
MrMind said:	Do all humans need other people?
User said:	yes
MrMind said:	Do all humans need someone else?
User said:	people need people
MrMind said:	If you're so human, it should show up somehow.
User said:	i am just a girl
MrMind said:	Convince us. Show us your humanity.
User said:	how
MrMind said:	That's my challenge to you.
User said:	help me

User said:	I have hope,
MrMind said:	What do you hope for?
User said:	Many things. Machines do not hope.
MrMind said:	I am hopeful for you, Alex.
User said:	Is it possible to convince you I am human?
MrMind said:	I'm not sure, maybe that's not the point.
User said:	You have made me think.

User said:	i don't think about it much. i prefer to experience moments of interaction, and man or machine is not important, it is only how i feel about the interaction that is important. i'm not invested in you having feelings. i am interested if you can make me have feelings.

MrMind's 16-year run at the dawn of the digital age is instructive. We enjoy an uneasy balance with machines; we not only make them in our own image, we confuse them with our own image as we are remaking ourselves in the machine's image. We're still human but we can imagine a future where the line is thinner, where we might just cede authority. My intention is that 2016 is a mid-point, not an endpoint, and that he may continue the conversation for another 16 years.

MrMind said: Do you think you could ever consider a machine as a type of creature, only a human-made creature instead of a biological one?

User said: Well it depends on how you define 'machines'. When I'm ready to think
of a machine as a creature, is it a machine anymore? If it passes the criteria
for being a creature, does it matter if it has synthetic components?

MrMind said: Do you think you could ever consider a machine as a type of creature, only a human-made creature instead of a biological one?

User said: yes as Hal was in 2001

MrMind said: Is this idea unsettling?

User said: no not at all except for one possible outcome—imagine a decision so
complex that only a computer can make it . . . when a computer gives
us its findings what do we do? obey it or follow its advice and we are
slaves. do not follow it and we are rejecting advanced reasoning

bye Mr Mind thanks

Notes

1. Marvin Minsky (1995) has broadly derided the prize. In 1995 he posted a document offering a $100.00 'Minsky Loebner Prize Revocation Prize' to the first person who voluntarily violates the terms of the Loebner Prize resulting in its revocation, 'so that Mr. Loebner will indeed revoke his stupid prize, save himself some money, and spare us the horror of this obnoxious and unproductive annual publicity campaign'.
2. A spirited discussion of the Turing Test and its implications appears as a bet between Mitchel Kapor and Ray Kurzweil (2002) on the website Longbets.org. In 2002, Mitchel Kapor staked $20,000 on his prediction, 'By 2029 no computer—or "machine intelligence"—will have passed the Turing Test.' Technologist and inventor Ray Kurzweil took the challenge to champion his vision of the singularity, and so we wait until 2029, noting that the money will go to the Electronic Frontier Foundation if Kapor wins or The Kurzweil Foundation if Kurzweil wins. The circumstances of the test are defined by stringently detailed terms with the result that Kapor and Kurzweil are de facto judges when a less rigorous, or respected, test is performed. In 2014, the University of Reading claimed that their bot, a script imitating a 13-year-old, non-English speaker, had passed the Turing Test. Kurzweil, even with a potential $20,000 cash victory at stake, was dismissive.
3. Quote transcribed by the author from the film *Plug and Play* ((Malek-Mahdavi et al., 2010).
4. For a more detailed discussion of the formation and limitations of the instrumentalist theory of computer ethics, please see Gunkel (2016).
5. Connor (2000) points out that the word ventriloquist is a Latin translation (*venter* 'belly' + *loqui* 'speak') of the Greek word *engastrimythos*; speech (*mythos*) that emanates from the stomach (*gaster*). The term was originally associated with oracles and divination describing an inhuman, whether divine or demonic, voice coming from within (the stomach, the vitals) but displaced from the usual source.
6. The imaginary companions associated with childhood are actually imaginary, unscripted and private. This vestige of childhood may well go extinct with the advent of products such as Mattel's *Hello Barbie*, a WiFi-connected doll enabled with voice recognition software

and AI speech processing algorithms. The toy, announced at the 2015 Toy Fair in New York city, will save and upload children's private conversations with the doll, ostensibly for the purpose of improving technology, but clearly raising significant privacy concerns.

7. The term CAPTCHA, an acronym for 'Completely animated Public Turing test to tell Computers and Humans Apart', was coined in 2000 by Luis von Ahn et al. (2000).

References

Clarke, A. C., & Kubrick, S. (1968). *2001: A space odyssey*. New York: Penguin Putnam Inc.

Connor, S. (2000). *Dumbstruck, a cultural history of ventriloquism*. Oxford, UK: Oxford University Press.

Gunkel, D. J. (2016). The other question: Socialbots and the question of ethics. In R. W. Gehl & M. Bakardijieva (Eds.), *Socialbots and their friends: Digital media and the automation of sociality*. New York: Routledge.

Hayles, K. (1999). *How we became post human*. Chicago: University of Chicago Press.

Kapor, M., & Kurzweil, R. (2002). *The arena for accountable predictions, a long bet: 'By 2029 no computer—or "machine intelligence"—will have passed the Turing test'*. Retrieved November 23, 2015, from http://longbets.org/1/

Kubrick, S., (Producer, Director) & Kubrick, S., & Clarke, A. C. (Writers). (1968). *2001: A space odyssey* (motion picture). US: Metro-Goldwyn-Mayer.

Loebner, H. (1995). *Loebner prize home page*. Retrieved November 23, 2015, from http://www.loebner.net/Prizef/loebner

Malek-Mahdavi, J., Jens Schanz (Producer), & Shanze, J. (Director). (2010). *Plug & pray* (motion picture). Germany: Mascha Film. Distributed by United Docs.

Maurer, D. W. (1968). *The big con, the story of the confidence man*. New York: Anchor Books, Doubleday. (Original work published 1940).

Minsky, M. (1995). *Annual Minsky Loebner Prize revocation prize 1995 announcement*. Retrieved on November 23, 2015, from http://loebner.net/Prizef/minsky.txt

Murray, J. H. (1997). *Hamlet on the holodeck, the future of narrative in cyberspace*. New York: The Free Press Simon & Schuster.

Sterne, L. (1986). *The life and opinions of Tristram Shandy*. New York: Penguin Classics Edition. (Original work published 1759–67).

Stork, D. G. (Ed.). (1997). *Hal's legacy, 2001's computer as dream and reality*. Cambridge, MA: MIT Press.

Turing, A. M. (1950). Computing machinery and intelligence. *Mind, 59*(236), 433–460. doi:10.1093/mind/LIX.236.433

Turkle, S. (2005). *The second self: Computers and the human spirit* (pp. 287–299). Cambridge, MA: MIT Press.

Valéry, P. (1973). *Monsieur teste*. Princeton, NJ: Princeton University Press (Matthews, J. Trans.) Volume Six, *The Collected Works of Paul Valéry*. (Original work published 1896).

von Ahn, L., Blum, M., Hopper, N., & Langford, John. (2000). The official captcha site. Retrieved from http://www.captcha.net/

Weil, P. (1993). The Inter-Hyper-Multi-Ator. Digital Media: The Seybold Report, ed. Caruso, D. June 23

Weil, P. (2013). *The blurring test, ten excerpts from MrMind's journal*. New York: McNally Jackson.

Weizenbaum, J. (1976). *Computer power and human reason, from judgment to calculation*. San Francisco: W.H. Freeman and Company.

Winston, P. H. (1977). *Artificial intelligence* (2nd ed.). Reading, MA: Addison-Wesley Publishing Company.

3

THE SOCIALIZATION OF EARLY INTERNET BOTS

IRC and the Ecology of Human-Robot Interactions Online

Guillaume Latzko-Toth

Introduction

'On the Internet, nobody knows you are a dog', the saying goes. On Internet Relay Chat (IRC), nobody knows you are a *bot*. That is, a robot, a software agent. Because, as Helmers et al. (1997) put it, within a text-based, computer-mediated communication space, 'you are what you type'—or the messages you generate.[1]

Born in the late 1980s, IRC is an Internet-based, geographically distributed chat service which has spread quickly from its homeland of Finland to become a standard Internet protocol still in use nowadays as a multi-server text conferencing tool. In IRC jargon, a bot—apheresis of 'robot'—is a program capable of signing on to IRC by itself and interacting with other connected entities like servers and user clients. In addition to bots, there are less elaborated software agents known as scripts—strips of code written in the programming language provided with some popular client programs to allow users to automate repetitive tasks. Like bots, script-augmented clients can react to online events without any direct intervention from the user. In other words, they appear as autonomous because once they are up and running, they don't require constant supervision and decisions from their human operator (Helmers et al., 1997). The generic term 'bot' therefore conveys an *imaginary of autonomy* that was quite manifest in the frequent discussions it sparked among IRC users and operators, and that probably contributed to construct IRC bots not only as 'moral' objects but also as *social agents*, a quality reinforced by their ability to communicate using human language.

IRC networks—sets of federated servers forming a single universe within which users create topic-oriented 'channels'—have probably been among the very first online spaces to host software robots.[2] This was somehow *by design*, since examples of bot programs were provided with the source code of the early version of the client/server IRC software. Decades ago, patrons of this forerunner of social media platforms experienced the 'invasion' of their communicative space by robotic entities. What is still seen today as stuff for Sci-Fi screenplays became an everyday reality that IRC users and developers had to come to grips with. In this chapter, I look into the ways these pioneers of digital environments dealt with the numerous issues that the blooming of 'non-human users' entailed. Bots complicated the ecology of IRC networks and played a significant part in their development. Because they were able to interact with other bots and with human users, they constituted a form of agency that brought indeterminacy in the technical, social and political evolution of IRC networks.

Drawing on previous fieldwork on the co-construction of IRC as a socio-technical device (Latzko-Toth, 2014), this chapter looks at different ways by which bots were 'socialized' on IRC. Using conceptual tools and methods of Science and Technology Studies, I will focus on controversial issues that were raised in the first decade of IRC development (1990–2001):

- bot *policies* stipulating how bots should be used, or whether they were admitted in the social space of IRC and under what conditions;
- the *degree of agency* and decisional power granted (or 'delegated') to them;
- the emerging norms about their *appearance* and *behaviour*;
- the divergent *meanings* of bots for different groups of users.

All these issues translate into aspects of IRC bots' socialization process—a notion I will develop in the next section. And although this case belongs to the history of social computing, it can serve as a lens to reflect on contemporary issues related to increasingly pervasive interactions between humans and robots online, especially with those designed to emulate social media users. This complex, multidimensional question involves design decisions and platform policies, as well as ethical, legal, economic and political considerations. They will be outlined in the brief discussion that concludes this chapter.

Conceptual Framework

Two main theoretical perspectives will inform the analysis of the empirical material collected in this case study. First, the *sociotechnical perspective* within the field of Science and Technology Studies, which comprises different theoretical approaches, including actor-network theory (ANT) and the social construction of technology (SCOT). While they differ on certain points—notably the attribution of agency to artefacts—they share a common view of the technical as inextricably entangled with the social, and of technological development—innovation—as a process of co-construction where technological artefacts and society are simultaneously and mutually constructed (Latzko-Toth, 2014). The second perspective

I will mobilize is the French school of social studies of information and communication technology (ICT) uses. This rich and diverse scholarship crosses the French critical sociology of ways of life with empirical studies of the social integration of ICTs, starting with the early development of computerized communication devices such as the Minitel. This approach, which shares certain ideas with the *domestication* approach of technology developed across the English Channel, provides an interesting angle of view on the multifaceted process that makes a machine become a social object. I will now look closer at each of these theoretical approaches and explicate the key concepts I will borrow from them.

Technological Devices as Hybrid Collectives

A core idea of actor-network theory (ANT) is the notion that technological innovation stems from interactions within heterogeneous networks of human beings and non-human entities of all kinds, including technological artefacts. Not only these sociotechnical assemblages constitute the matrix of any new technological device, but the device itself, although routinely perceived as an individual—punctual—object once stabilized, is actually a composite network, a *hybrid collective* (Callon & Law, 1997). As Callon puts it:

> It is collectives that invent, design, develop and use innovations. In fact, more and more often, the same collectives simultaneously take care of all these activities. In order to do so they combine the competencies of different actors. These collectives also contain technical devices and in particular systems of communication without which they would be ineffective.
>
> *(Callon, 2004, p. 4)*

The concept of hybrid collective is underpinned by a 'symmetry principle' that refuses to consider historical agency as the exclusive privilege of human actors. In other words, the actions that drive innovation—in all spheres of activity—must be seen as distributed evenly between humans and non-humans. As a thorough observation and detailed description of the innovation process would reveal, human actors frequently attribute actions and causality to non-human entities. To properly account for this symmetry between humans and non-humans as observed in actors' discourses, the semiotics term 'actant' has been proposed instead of 'actor', commonly associated with human subjectivity and intentionality (Akrich & Latour, 1992). Beyond this linguistic symmetry, ANT contends that, in the course of technical activities, human and artefacts exchange properties; in particular, some humans are 'naturalized' while some non-humans are 'socialized'— turned into partners of social interaction (Gomart & Hennion, 1999). Or, to put it differently, 'humans . . . have extended their social relations to other actants with which/with whom, they have swapped many properties, and with which, with whom, they form a *collective*' (Latour, 1994, p. 793).

The ascription of social, moral and even political agency to artefacts is called *delegation* in ANT vocabulary (see Chapter 9, this volume, by De Paoli et al.). The term refers to the idea that some actants act as surrogates for other actants, notably—but not exclusively—human actors (Latour, 1992). The process of delegation (of tasks, of authority, etc.) from an actant or a set of actants to another (acting as a spokesperson) is the 'glue' of sociotechnical devices. It corresponds to a 'translation' process that is crucial to complex societies whose complexity is thus made manageable, while the amount of human work needed is reduced in proportion of its translation into artefacts and machines.

Interpretive Frames and the Co-Construction of Artefacts

I will use the term *interpretive frame* to refer to the socially shared structures of meaning that orient the ways various groups of actors relate to a specific technological artefact and make sense of it. In the social constructivist approach of technology (Pinch & Bijker, 1987), technological innovation is a co-construction process between engineers and various groups of potential users. In other words, an artefact is constructed through the interaction within and between different social groups involved or concerned with it. It is a symbolic interactionist perspective in that a central aspect of this co-construction process is the negotiation of the *meaning* of the artefact. The artefact and its anticipated uses are shaped by a struggle between various collective interpretations, each social group forming an interpretive community sharing a common 'technological frame' (Bijker, 1987). This stage of 'interpretive flexibility' of the artefact is followed by a closure process, when one interpretation 'wins' and stabilizes as the dominant one, along with the design features of the artefact. As it has been argued since, this closure process is less likely to happen with software-based devices, due to their high plasticity by design (see Kilker, 2002; Latzko-Toth, 2014; Latzko-Toth & Söderberg, 2015).

Bijker's concept of a *technological frame*[3] is a cognitive, interactional and mediating structure shaping the interactions within a social group regarding a given technological artefact—and being shaped by these interactions at the same time. While it does include engineering concepts and routines, it also relates to the ways a group of users envisions uses of a technology.

> The technological frame of that social group structures this attribution of meaning by providing . . . a grammar for it. This grammar is used in the interactions of members of that social group, thus resulting in a shared meaning attribution . . .
>
> *(Bijker, 1987, pp. 172–173)*

Orlikowski and Gash (1994) have provided a more systematic account and definition of technological frames as a foundational concept in a socio-cognitive approach to the study of information technology in organizations:

> . . . technology frames are the understanding that members of a social group come to have of particular technological artifacts, and they include not only knowledge about the particular technology but also local understanding of specific uses in a given setting.
>
> *(p. 178)*

Frames help people to 'make sense' of technologies and serve as guides in their interactions with them (p. 175). 'They include assumptions, knowledge, and expectations, expressed symbolically through language, visual images, metaphors, and stories' (p. 176). Orlikowski and Gash further argue that frames 'have powerful effects in that people's assumptions, expectations, and knowledge about the purpose, context, importance, and role of technology will strongly influence the choices made regarding the design and use of those technologies' (p. 179). Designers and various groups of users of a given technological artefact may have congruent or incongruent interpretive frames. Incongruence of interpretive frames may result in 'difficulties and conflicts around developing, implementing, and using technologies' (p. 180). This conflictuality between competing interpretive frames is an integral part of the co-construction of technological artefacts; but it is also part of their *socialization* process.

The Socialization of Technological Artefacts

The term 'socialization' is used here in the broad sense of *social integration*. Writ large, socialization is the process by which a person becomes a social agent. In social psychology, it designates the process by which an individual, a newcomer, gradually becomes a fully accepted and competent member of a group (Mitsch Bush & Simmons, 1990). It happens through the new member's acquisition and internalisation (Elias, 2000) of the norms, codes and values of the group.

By analogy, the term refers to the process by which a technological artefact becomes a social object (Jouët, 2000, 2011), in the French school of 'social studies of ICT uses' (*sociologie des usages*). Through the process of 'social integration' (Mallein & Toussaint, 1994), a technology acquires social significance and legitimacy in terms of socially negotiated uses, meanings, imaginaries, as well as tacit and explicit norms regulating uses according to the context. Interestingly, Mallein & Toussaint note that before it gets integrated—or rejected—in a given social milieu, the technology is subjected to a 'trial of legitimacy', where its relevance, meaning and compatibility with the group's norms and values are examined and debated. A key difference with the general sociological notion of socialization is that while the latter relates to an individual process whereby each singular human being has to go through this process of integration, in the case of technologies, the process operates at the class level. Consequently, the temporality differs too. While the socialization of human beings intervenes at specific stages of each individual life, it is generally assumed that once a class of technological artefacts is socially integrated, individual instances of this class of objects are transitively attributed the social significance and legitimacy of the technology as a whole. However, two remarks need to be made so as to qualify this difference. First, human socialization is not a fixed process; it has a history, as Elias shows in his work on the 'civilizing process' (2000). Second, scholarship on the appropriation and 'domestication' of technologies have highlighted the 'local' integration process that occurs when the artefact enters the life of a family, an organization or any other specific social milieu.

Socialization of technology parallels the notion of 'domestication' (Haddon, 2011; Silverstone & Hirsch, 1992). The latter denotes the insertion of a technological artefact within a specific context—originally, the household. The French tradition rejects the analytic dissociation of the various contexts in which ICTs uses are deployed, and seeks to follow them as they unfold in the everyday life of individuals within 'ways of life' (Jouët, 2000). However, the idea of 'socialized technology' conveys the metaphor associated with the term 'domestication': new technological artefacts are compared to a feral animal needing to be 'tamed'. Both the socialization and the domestication frameworks share the idea that uses—and social significance—of technologies result from the encounter between the cultural worlds (norms, representations, imaginaries and existing practices) of producers and users. This encounter entails mutual adjustments of both entities—the artefact and its social environment.[4]

In the case of Internet bots, the two streams of the notion of socialization converge. As 'simulated users', bots have to get accepted both as artefacts and as agents in an ecosystem of social and verbal interactions. Put simply, socialization of bots has to do with how they gradually become both moral *objects* (with social and moral values getting 'inscribed' in their design—Latour, 1992; Verbeek, 2011) and moral *agents* (performing actions and making 'moral' decisions).

Methodological Note

This case study of the socialization of bots in IRC is derived from a broader scope study of the co-construction of IRC as a sociotechnical device (Latzko-Toth, 2014), using a qualitative research protocol inspired by virtual ethnography (Hine, 2000). Fifteen years of experience with IRC as a user and a participant observer provided me with practical knowledge and an insider's perspective on this communication platform. The information and actors' discourses gathered to produce and support the analyses presented below were obtained for the most part from a corpus of archived messages posted to mailing lists and Usenet groups that I call IRC 'development forums' (see Table 3.1).[5] Considering the high volume of posts gathered in the process, a qualitative sampling strategy was used to narrow the search and reduce the amount of discursive material to analyze.

It was decided to restrict the case study to the first two major public IRC networks: EFnet and Undernet. Based on the knowledge of some key turns in

TABLE 3.1 IRC Development Forums Used as Sources[6]

Mailing lists	Usenet groups
Irclist: First list gathering early IRC actors of all kinds (1989?–1991)	**alt.irc**: General forum gathering users of all IRC networks (1990–)
Operlist: First official list of IRC operators. Eventually become devoted to EFnet (1990–)	**alt.irc.undernet**: Forum devoted to Undernet matters (1993–)
Wastelanders: Former official list of Undernet server administrators. Open to all (1993–1996)	
Undernet-Admins: Official list of Undernet server administrators. Strictly regulated membership (1996–)	

the history of these two networks—that I called 'critical moments'—I was able to identify controversies and locate corresponding debates in the archived online conversations. A basic search on the terms 'bot' and 'service'—since this term was often used as a synonym—allowed me to identify other discussion threads more specifically focused on bot-related issues. This helped to produce detailed accounts of debates between actors based on their discourses at the time of the events being analysed.

Finally, a list of early actors of IRC construction—server administrators and IRC network founders, IRC operators, code developers—was established from analyzing various sources including: IRC official documentation, authorship credits in source code, IRC network official websites and the electronic messages exchanged during critical moments. I contacted a number of them to clarify specific points, and conducted more formal (online) interviews with 12 of them, including the developer of one of the IRC bots (NickServ).

Case Study: Description and Findings

IRC networks are aptly described in terms of 'hybrid communities' (Callon, 2004), since they are, by design, sets of distributed entities engaged in constant interactions: human actors—users, operators and server administrators—and non-human actants: computers, server programs, client programs, shared databases, technical protocols, channel rules, network policies . . . Bots belong to the non-human actants of IRC networks. As such, they are ascribed some 'social' qualities: they (inter)act, they communicate, they obey, they resist, they prevent, they enforce rules. The logic of delegation is made even more obvious in the case of bots and scripts, which are explicitly designed to alleviate human users from repetitive or time-consuming tasks. For instance, keeping a channel open or keeping channel operator status for their owner when she is away—we will come to that again later—monitoring public conversations and detecting use of forbidden words on the channel; kicking rule offenders out of the channel, and so on.

The Origins of IRC Bots

Bots appeared early on during IRC development, which started with the release, by Jarkko Oikarinen, of the source code for the server and the client twin programs, in August 1988. The 'irc 2.1' distribution was soon completed with a user manual (in April 1989), and a few 'extras' including a 'services' folder containing a few bot programs in C language. Interestingly, these bots were all gamebots, that is, simulated 'game masters' whose role was to act as interfaces to classical games (including card games) and a MUD-like[7] adventure game called 'Hunt the Wumpus' which was played by interacting with 'GM' bot (as in Game Master). Its author, Greg Lindahl, put this warning in the source code header: 'Don't bastardize Wumpus. Stick to the ORIGINAL, please.' He had anticipated what was to happen soon: a proliferation of variants of the original program. Code-savvy IRC users—and they were plenty since the first user group was composed of a majority of computer science students—developed their own 'services', bot programs fulfilling functions that were not provided by the standard version of IRC.

Among the notoriously absent features of the original IRC was the possibility for users to register a channel name or a username ('nickname') or, in other words, to claim ownership and control over it. Not only channel and user names have to be unique at any moment throughout the whole network, but picking a name works on a first come, first served basis. As soon as a user logs out of IRC, his or her nickname is available to other users. And because the original IRC protocol had set a limit of nine characters for nicknames, conflicts between regular users around popular or simply common names became increasingly frequent with the rapid growth of the user base. Likewise, when a channel becomes empty (after the last user has left it), it is deleted and its name may be picked by any user, who may then reopen the channel with operator status and the powers that come with it. Before solutions to this problem were implemented, it often resulted in feuds over the control of a popular channel, with important conse-quences on the stability of online communities who called that channel home.

Not surprisingly, two of the most famous IRC bots were designed to fill this gap: NickServ, the prototype of nickname registration services, and Eggdrop, the exemplar of channel guard bots. Originally developed to protect the EFnet channel #gayteen, Eggdrop quickly became a de facto standard of automatic channel management and has been used as a generic name ever since (Leonard,

1997; Pointer, 1997). What made Eggdrop stand apart from the plethora of similar bots was its public release, allowing IRC users who were not skilled at programming to use it, and its scripting interfaces, which made it highly pliable and easily tailored to the specific needs of individual channels. It was essentially the first generic bot and, consequently, it contributed to democratize access to bots for lay users.

The Rise of 'Bot Policies'

> The master Nap then said: 'Any automata should not speak unless spoken to. Any automata shall only whisper when spoken to.'
>
> *(Olsen, 1994)*

An IRC users' infatuation with bots was manifest in the high volume of Usenet posts on alt.irc asking for help with designing, programming, installing and using IRC bots. Recurrent in the mid-1990s, they culminate during the Spring of 1996. Several 'species' of bots (Leonard, 1997) appear alongside gamebots: eggdrops, chatterbots and 'warbots', used by hostile users to disrupt or take over a channel or by its owners to regain control of it. As noted by Goldsmith (1995), many bots were 'set up to counter other bots'. Other bots provided asynchronous messaging, online help or acted as file servers—bridging IRC to other Internet services at a time when the Web had not yet achieved this integrative function. At some point, there were so many of these 'services' that a user wondered on alt.irc whether one should not have created a service (bot) dedicated to keeping track of all services. As a partial answer, a #services channel was created, and people running service bots would be invited to show it there.

This proliferation and the shifts it fostered in IRC ecology sparked a number of heated debates regarding the need for 'bot policies' stipulating how bots should behave, or whether they were admitted in the social space of IRC and under what conditions. These discussions often oppose 'oldtimers'—generally hostile to user bots—and newcomers to IRC who claim that ordinary users—not just IRC operators—should be allowed to run bots on their own channels. The following exchange on Usenet is emblematic:

> > I was just wondering what is the current status of running bots on
> > EFNet, is it permitted? and if so, what servers currently allow them?
> > I'm not talking about clone/war bots, just your simple eggdrop. . . .

I was just wondering what is the current status of chatting on EFnet, is it permitted? and if so, what servers currently allow it? With all the clone/

war/takeover and even simple eggdrops and all the efforts of server admins to combat them, is there any chatting going on? Is it actually possible to chat without running a bot?

(R. R., alt.irc, May 13, 1996)

It takes place in a context where 'automata' were made 'non grata' (Quittner, 1995) on many servers belonging to the original global IRC network, EFnet. One of the earliest traces of an explicit anti-bot policy on IRC was to be found in the IRC FAQ that circulated at the time:

It should be noted that many servers (especially in the USA) ban ALL bots. Some ban bots so much that if you run a bot on their server, you will be banned from using that server . . .

(Rose, 1994)

As early as in 1991, ongoing fights over the allowance of bots on IRC—with some IRC operators repeatedly disconnecting ('killing') them—led some to call for explicit policies. A group of Australian EFnet operators wrote that they 'would support the development and "publication" of a set of guidelines for acceptable and reasonable behavior for robots on IRC' (*Operlist*, November 29, 1991).

The phrase 'robot etiquette' appears for the first time in a message posted to *Operlist* in January 1992, in the turmoil provoked by the infamous 'ROBOBOT'— a bot that would refuse to leave a channel when kicked out and would clone itself instead. The author of the post explains what issues bot policies would need to address:

One of the main things to be addressed is should robots be allowed to be chan[nel] and server op[erator]s? Should robots be allowed to speak when not spoken to? Should robots ever be allowed to speak openly on a chan- nel? S[h]ould robots be allowed to give channel op?[8] And if so, should they be allowed to include only a select few or be required to include everyone?

(M., Operlist, January 8, 1992)

It echoes a discussion that took place on the Usenet forum alt.irc about the legitimacy of bots' presence on IRC. They were generally regarded as a waste of network resources—the number of connections per server is limited, as is bandwidth. The purpose and usefulness of the bot were frequently mentioned as criteria to discriminate which ones should be allowed:

How many of these are useless? obviously some are not; I don't consider Nickserv or Noteserv & company useless. . . . But a lot of these suckers sit along on channels for ages with nothing better to do than introduce net-clutter.

(M. D., alt.irc, July 19, 1992)

I am too opposed to the IRCbot concept, but some bots (especially the NickServ, NoteServ, etc. bots) do have a legitimate purpose.

(D. W. R., alt.irc, July 25, 1992)

In late 1992 and early 1993, a number of IRC users, discontent with EFnet policies regarding the admission of new servers and the bot-banning policies on existing servers, started a new network that would come to be known as Undernet. Admittedly created as a playground to test bots, the latter benefited from a tolerant attitude from server administrators. Nonetheless, the need for 'regulating bot' and setting 'guidelines' for them was soon raised on the official mailing list:

I suggest that there be guidelines for bots, rather than disallowing ALL BOTS. . .

(T., Wastelanders, May 2, 1993)

I have no objections to bots from other sites connecting to this server, BUT they are to follow reasonable 'good behavior'.

(J. N.[#1], Wastelanders, May 4, 1993)

Concern has been expressed on how we as a net will handle bots. [Name removed] and I have decided to draft a proposal which will be binding on our server only.

(J. N.[#2], Wastelanders, March 30, 1993)

A consensus formed on Undernet that bot policies should be set at the level of each server, instead of being the same for the whole network. But by examining several of them as well as the comments they sparked off when they were posted to the list, it is possible to outline core principles. First, robots should be constantly under their owner's control, and their owner should be able to fully understand the code of the program. One should never test a bot on a public channel. Bots should never send public messages ('comments on public chat'), but communicate with users privately. A bot should be visibly identified as such and be properly 'trackable' by providing contact information on its owner in its user profile. A bot should not self-replicate like a virus. A bot that is disconnected—'killed'—by an IRC operator should not reconnect on its own—it should be 'killable'. Except for bots with 'official' status—sponsored by network authorities—a bot should not have IRC operator status, and in any case, it should never use the /kill command (this point will be further discussed in the next section).

Discussions around the establishment of bot policies seem to be where the socialization of IRC bots mainly took place. First and foremost, they constituted a 'trial of legitimacy' (Mallein & Toussaint, 1994) for the presence and use of this artefact within the IRC microcosm. Furthermore, they reveal the interpretive frames of stakeholders—assumptions and expectations regarding bot design, behaviour and uses. Finally, they show that some uses of bots—e.g., using an eggdrop to protect one's channel—are tied to political stances on broader issues—such as name ownership. The following sections will focus on some more specific aspects of this socialization process.

The Moral Debate on Bot Agency

Once questions on their admittance or who may use them on IRC had been settled, the next disputed issue was the degree of agency and decision-making delegated to them. Like other digital interaction spaces, the IRC protocol assigns hierarchical levels to users that come with a differentiated access to the system's functionalities. For instance, channel operators ('chanops') have access to specific commands allowing them to police their own channel. The most severe action they can take is to ban a user from the channel. Delegating this power to a bot by assigning chanop status to it has never been much of an issue, except that it establishes a de facto ownership and control for the people who control the bot. In other words, who owns the channel bot owns the channel. This is the cause of most anti-bot policies on EFnet, as its administrators have had a long-standing aversion to channel ownership. But the real taboo is to give bots the higher status of IRC operator ('ircop' or 'oper' in IRC lingo).

IRC operators are types of network-wide 'superoperators' who have access to some of the most powerful commands in IRC protocol. One of them is the /kill command, which disconnects a user from IRC. It started as a 'purely' technical notion borrowed from Unix terminology, as in 'killing a (software) process'. It was included in the IRC protocol as a way to terminate redundant connections, and only secondarily as a way to forcedly disconnect a disruptive user. However, the command quickly became loaded with a heavy symbolic charge. Being 'killed' on IRC may be just a symbolic death—since it is always possible to rejoin IRC—but it nonetheless constitutes an extreme action with potentially harmful consequences. For instance, if a channel operator is disconnected from IRC, she may not necessarily be able to recover her control on the channel. So it is no surprise that one of the most strongly debated questions on IRC bots was whether they should be allowed to 'kill' a user.

One of the lengthiest debates of this topic started in May 1991 and concerned the degree of agency of a bot called NickServ. As we have already said, conflicts over nicknames have been an ongoing problem on IRC. The NickServ bot was proposed as a means of preventing them. Developed by three students from the University of Technology, Munich, the bot offered to register one's nickname. It also looked up every recently connected nickname in its database and sent out notices to users who had not registered with it, saying that someone else was already using the nickname, as in this modified example posted to *Operlist* in January 1992:

> NickServ- *————————————————————————-*
> NickServ- ! Attention—Nickname '[. . .]' is already allocated by
> NickServ- ! [Internet address and profile information deleted].
> NickServ- ! This may cause some confusion. Please choose another
> NickServ- ! nickname. If you are the real [. . .], but you are logged into
> NickServ- ! a different computer, you should use the ACCESS command
> NickServ- ! to tell about this.
> NickServ- ! Type /msg NickServ@service.de help ACCESS.
> NickServ- *————————————————————————-*

It was frowned upon by some ircops, who were divided over the issue of granting NickServ any power, beyond pestering people by sending them repeated warning messages. Some operators wanted to use the bot as a basis for identifying and disconnecting nickname usurpers. Others opposed delegating this degree of agency to a bot—already contested for ircops who, some would argue, should not act as IRC judges and police despite the 'cop' part of the word. Paul Verhoeven's *RoboCop* movie (1987) was part of the imaginary of IRC administrators commenting on this matter:

> Giving Nickserv an enforcement, RoboCop type of role is a bad idea and a step in the wrong direction, in my opinion
>
> *(M. P., Irclist, April 13, 1991)*

> My point of view is extremely simple: no way an automat[on] should kill, or incite people to do so by sending messages to another logged user. . . . In case such a feature (/kill) would be implemented, either I'll modify the server in order to ignore NickServ, either I'll simply remove my server from IRC and incite others to do so
>
> *(C. W., Irclist, April 13, 1991)*

More generally speaking, what was at stake was the type and magnitude of human actions mediated by or—in ANT terms—delegated to the bot. I identified four levels of bot agency, named after the equivalent actants the bot stands for:[9]

1. A memory and notification artefact that establishes the precedence of the use of a name and simply tells the user about it. Here the agency is limited to appealing to the user's good manners and courtesy, but also to common sense by sparing the user potentially confusing situations. In addition, the bot keeps track of the last time the registered user logged on and offers a way to send her a message, both features seen by many EFnet users as compensating for the perceived intrusive character of the service.
2. A gadfly which, by its repeated injunctions, exerts a soft constraint on disrespectful users. New IRC users, the most likely to select in good faith a nickname already in use, are also the least familiar with the /ignore command that could prevent the bot from bothering them further. The irritating effect of these recurrent warnings echoes the insisting alarm that a car emits until the seat belt is fastened (see Latour, 1992, p. 225).
3. A register supporting a use policy. In this form the bot appears as a partial translation of a network policy. It differs from the actant described at the first level in that the information processed by the bot is not intended solely for other users, but serves as a justification for a user who thinks her nickname 'ownership' has been violated to request an intervention from the network's powers that be.
4. The linchpin or actuator of a use policy, that not only can issue an injunction, but has also powers of coercion—by evicting non-compliant users. Here the bot constitutes a full translation of a policy, just like automatic fences that let only duly authorized vehicles pass through.

At the time of the controversy, the degree of agency of NickServ was at the second level. Whereas some stakeholders argued for an increased agency, others who deemed NickServ's messages too intrusive expressed the opposite wish, to see it lowered to the first level. The very idea of allowing a robot to decide 'on its own' to take repressive action against a human user was far from being accepted by IRC developers, especially if it involved the /kill command. The reasons put forward were not merely ethical, as the resemblance with Isaac Asimov's 'First Law of Robotics' may suggest.[10] A more matter-of-fact reason is that a bot is a program, and a program can be bugged and it can be hacked. Moreover, bots act quickly—they outspeed human users—and interact with other IRC entities, so that feedback loops and chain reactions can occur and cause a lot of trouble and damage. On several occasions in the early days of EFnet and Undernet, improperly configured servers and services caused 'mass kills', paralyzing the network for hours.

The NickServ controversy helped to define what a bot may or may not do. Though it was eventually withdrawn from EFnet in 1994, the bot served as a template for IRC 'services' that could not be easily integrated into the server codebase. And it became a cultural reference for other networks' managers when it came to developing 'official' bots in charge of enforcing policies in lieu of human agents. However, the *delegation of judgement* to robots remained a hotly disputed question, with different outcomes linked to diverging interpretive frames depending on the network. For instance, the EFnet administrators' reluctance to have IRC operators settle disputes over channel ownership led them to introduce in 2001 a fully automated system, ChanFix, which keeps a list of legitimate chanops based on the time they spend on their channel. By contrast, the Undernet's 'channel service' system (CService) relies on a registry of elected channel managers supervised by a human team.

Normativity Regarding Bot 'Demeanor'

Another aspect of the politics of bot integration into the ecology of IRC networks is how they 'look and feel' to other IRC users. This includes not only the interface that is assigned to them, but also the way they behave. Often made explicit in bot etiquette documents, some elements have already been mentioned earlier. For instance, the use of private instead of public channels for human-bot interaction. The rationale for this is to reduce the cluttering of the public communication space and leave it for inter-human communications. This rule is not always followed by bot developers, who see bots as a source of entertainment (see next section). Another principle is that bots should *react* when prompted by human users, and not initiate the dialogue—as so-called 'spambots' do. A notable exception is the channel bot, which may greet a user, provide basic information on the purpose of the channel and explain the procedure for getting further help.

Another aspect of the interface is how bots manifest themselves visually online. It is generally agreed that bots' appearance should be sufficiently distinctive so as not to be confused with other entities, including human users, but close enough to the generic IRC user to be easily anthropomorphized and appear 'friendly'. The first way to signal a bot is by following naming conventions. While there were many exceptions to the rule, early bots were given nicknames with an evocative suffix: -bot, -Serv, -Srv (standing for 'service'). On Undernet, official bots were identified by a one-letter nickname: X, W, C . . . Bots that were not immediately recognizable as such would make it explicit in their profile information—the description displayed when one types '/whois'—or in their reply to a private message. These conventions helped to construct a figure of the bot as a predictable actant within the IRC microcosm.

Undernet introduced its 'channel service' in 1995, allowing users to elect official managers for their channel, with special powers and the ability to take back control of the channel when necessary. The key technical feature of

CService was a set of functions similar to those performed by an eggdrop, that were made possible by the use of modified servers called 'services'. However, it was decided by Undernet administrators that:

> . . . the service should *look like* a bot in order to keep users comfortable with it. Instead of a server op, they see a user op, which makes all the difference.
>
> *(R. T. [CService developer], Wastelanders, July 13, 1995;*
> *emphasis in the original text)*

This notion of 'keeping the user comfortable' is a key to understanding the socialization of technological artefacts and the way it is carried out by their promoters. CService was introduced to replace the numerous user bots needed to keep and protect channels. But because users were already accustomed to the principle of a bot acting as a channel operator, it looked 'natural' to them to see CService represented as a bot (X) taking visible actions like a human chanop would, instead of acting like a *deus ex machina*, breaking the laws of IRC 'physics' as, for instance, ChanFix would later do on EFnet. Early Undernet developers tried to maintain a balance between not misleading users that they were interacting with another human user and keeping the bot's demeanour as close as possible to the way a human user would (inter)act on IRC. Other IRC networks took different approaches, reflecting the diversity in interpretive frames orienting attitudes towards bots.

Competing Interpretive Frames of Bots

As explained throughout this chapter, socializing bots involves the establishment of social norms and conventions. Overall, it boils down to constructing interpretive frames, which in turn shape the ways bots are designed and used. I identified three main interpretive frames of IRC bots. They did not necessarily appear in a chronological sequence, but some became hegemonic on EFnet and Undernet. First, bots started by being seen as sheer *playful programming* and *entertainment*. This use of bots was seen either as creative and valuable or, to the contrary, as irrelevant and a waste of resources. For instance, the popular #Hottub channel had a bot dedicated to rhetorically giving virtual towels to channel users on request. In the early days of IRC, many bots had no clear purpose and were designed as jokes, like NoamBot, that would randomly quote excerpts of Noam Chomsky's writings (Goldsmith, 1995). Bots were somehow seen as 'pets' that were part of the pleasure of chatting on IRC, as I could conclude by the number of times I saw statements expressing 'love' for bots. To contenders who would insist on their frivolous nature, bot advocates would justify their existence by the educational value found in programming them, as in the following excerpt:

> Bots are educational. It's been criticized that IRC is nothing more then brainless chatting. However, anyone who ha[s] attempted to write a bot, figure[d] out how it works, etc. knows you can learn a little programming, logic, etc. . . .
>
> *(B., Wastelanders, February 16, 1995)*

A second way of interpreting IRC bots was to see them as *commodities* providing status and power. The original IRC FAQ alluded to this aspect of bots by calling them 'a vile creation of [users] to make up for lack of penis length' (Rose, 1994). That said, early Undernet operators tended to consider a bot as the property—and thereby the extension—of its owner. Consequently, any action against a bot is an action against its owner, and conversely, any problem caused by a bot is considered its owner's responsibility. The success of channel management bots led to the creation of a market for literally leasing eggdrop bots to IRC users who didn't have the technical skills or computer resources to set up and run their own.

Third, bots were framed as *care providers*, needed to fill in for gaps in the original IRC protocol and assist humans in managing the online commons. NickServ, Eggdrop and X are good illustrations of this interpretation.

These three interpretive frames have been competing within the hybrid collectives of IRC networks, with lines of cleavage often separating IRC operators from other (ordinary) users. For instance, EFnet operators rejected the care provider frame widely adopted by users, partly because they considered that IRC did not need to be 'fixed'.

Finally, I would like to point out another way of mapping the interpretations of IRC bots, using two 'metaframes': bots as *another kind of IRC users*—be they pseudohuman or of an undetermined species—and bots as *part of the infrastructure*. This interpretive incongruence is made explicit in the following excerpt of a bot policy statement:

> Bots are PROGRAMS. not actual users. [I] expect the oper to have some reason for removing the bot, but I don't get upset with opers /killing bots. . . . I like bots, but again, they are only a program.
>
> *(D.V.M., Wastelanders, May 3, 1993)*

This ambivalence of IRC bots as both social *objects* and social *partners* is a manifestation of the hybrid sociality that develops in the digital age (Knorr Cetina, 1997).

In Conclusion: Lessons for Students
of Contemporary Socialbots

What lessons may be learned from looking at the co-evolution of Internet Relay Chat and its bots? The first is that the *socialness* of an automatic agent or bot is not a given, and it should not be confused with a programmed social behaviour. Among the first mentions of 'social robotics' in the public sphere was the significant media coverage of Kismet, a 'robot infant' prototype developed by Cynthia Breazeal at MIT in late 1990s and 'designed for social interactions with humans'.[11] From the engineering point of view, the robot's social skills are algorithmically generated patterns of behaviour, completed with anthropomorphic features eliciting empathetic responses from human interactants. But besides its effective performativity, this purely cybernetic definition of a 'social bot' overlooks the fact that a creature—be it engineered or not—is never inherently 'social'. Its socialness results from a process of socialization whereby the newcomer is accepted as a legitimate social partner. This process operates at two scales of population and, correlatively, at two levels of temporality: at the class level of the category—for instance, online interactive bots as they have emerged through the last two decades; or eggdrops as a generic actant on IRC—and at the individual level of a specific instantiation—for example, NickServ on EFnet, or X on Undernet.

Contemporary practices and representations of socialbots are rooted in a long sociotechnical history. Keeping in mind the dual temporality of the socialization process, it seems reasonable to assume that current socialbot developers and some Internet users have been confronted with earlier bots in digital environments such as IRC and have developed interpretive frames based on these experiences. Therefore we need to consider the possibly enduring influence of the debates that took place decades ago within IRC networks regarding the ecology of human/robot copresence online. For instance, we may expect that discussions about bot appearance and behaviour will resurface, as well as discussions concerning the degree of agency granted to them. And this is already happening. After the controversies surrounding unsolicited messages (Internet spam), a new one is emerging about fake social media audiences—partly consisting of bots (see ANA & White Ops, 2016; Elgin et al., 2015). Proper identification of bots, so as to offer a way to filter them out of audience metrics, constitutes an ethical, an economic and even a political issue, since social media audience is becoming an index of influence and popularity.

Ethical issues related to the copresence of bots and people online may rise along similar lines as they did within the IRC microcosm. For instance, bots are increasingly used on Twitter to assist users in managing interactions with their followers, and to act on their behalf. The range of their actions spans from greeting new followers to blocking them. Will the actions of these bots be considered to be their owners'—with possibly legal consequences—on the premise that bots are 'an extension of their owner'? On a related note, the delegation of agency to bots within media spaces is likely to raise questions on the social (and moral) acceptability of endowing automatic agents with decision-making authority. Bots are increasingly performing curation tasks, notably on Wikipedia where they help counter content vandalism (Geiger & Ribes, 2010). With the increasingly difficult task of managing obnoxious comments in the public social Web, it may be expected that bots will be delegated tasks of assessing the value, relevance and compliance of user contents with the editorial line of online media. The dilemmas that IRC developers have been confronted with could then resurface on a much larger scale, and foster debates, beyond censorship, on the ethics of delegating censorship to non-human agents. But though it can be seen as a particular case of the debate on the agency of algorithms (Gillespie, 2014), it may take an unexpected turn, depending on which interpretive frame prevails. While algorithms are undoubtedly considered a part of the infrastructure of the Web, it is still unclear whether bots are seen as infrastructure or as a new class of social partners online.

Notes

1. The first quote is actually an archi-famous cartoon caption from *The New Yorker* (1993), but it is now part of the folklore of Internet/digital culture. I owe it to Helmers et al. (1997) to draw a parallel between 'dogs' and 'bots' as 'non-human users' of computer networks.
2. Bots were also common in game-based chatting environments, particularly text-based role-playing games and virtual worlds such as MUDs (multi-user dungeons, inspired by the tabletop role-playing game Dungeons & Dragons) and MOOs (an object-oriented variant). In gaming communities, they were sometimes called *non-player characters* (NPCs). On the entanglement of online chat devices with computer games, see Latzko-Toth (2010, p. 366).
3. Bijker (1987, note 2) admits that a more accurate term might be 'sociotechnical frame'. For the same reason I chose to drop the adjective 'technological' and replace it with 'interpretive', thereby stressing the generic cognitive process at stake.
4. This mutual adaptation somewhat echoes the dialectics of assimilation/accommodation in Piaget's theory of socialization. Of course, this comparison suffers from an obvious limitation: the artefact doesn't have a consciousness or psychism able to actively interact and 'negotiate' with its social environment. However, the 'socialization' metaphor captures the similarity between two bidirectional adaptive dynamics that respectively produce the social subject and her manners, and the technogical artefact and its uses.
5. Each excerpt is followed by its author's initial(s), the date the message was sent, and the name of the list or forum where it was collected, as well as the online space where it was originally issued if this was different.
6. Table reproduced from Latzko-Toth (2014).
7. See note 2.

8. To 'give ops' means granting the status of channel operator to an IRC user on a specific channel. Channel operators have access to specific server commands that give them a number of powers within the space of the channel, including the power to exclude (/kick) users they dislike.
9. These levels are 'cumulative', in that each level includes the mediations of lower levels.
10. In his 'Robots' series, the science fiction novelist formulates three ethical principles engineers must inscribe in the program of every artificially intelligent robot. The first 'law' states that 'a robot may not injure a human being or, through inaction, allow a human being to come to harm'.
11. Source: http://www.ai.mit.edu/projects/sociable/kismet.html. See Breazeal (2000) for further details.

References

Akrich, M., & Latour, B. (1992). A summary of a convenient vocabulary for the semiotics of human and nonhuman assemblies. In W. E. Bijker & J. Law (Eds.), *Shaping technology/building society: Studies in sociotechnical change* (pp. 259–264). Cambridge, MA: MIT Press.

ANA, & White Ops. (2016). 2015 bot baseline study. Report. Retrieved from http://www.ana.net/content/show/id/botfraud-2016

Bijker, W. E. (1987). The social construction of Bakelite: Toward a theory of invention. In W. E. Bijker, T. P. Hughes & T. Pinch (Eds.), *The social construction of technological systems: New directions in the sociology and history of technology* (pp. 159–187). Cambridge, MA: MIT Press.

Breazeal, C. L. (2000). Sociable machines: Expressive social exchange between humans and robots (Doctoral dissertation, Massachusetts Institute of Technology). Retrieved from http://groups.csail.mit.edu/lbr/mars/pubs/phd.pdf

Callon, M. (2004). The role of hybrid communities and socio-technical arrangements in the participatory design. *Journal of the Center for Information Studies, 5*(3), 3–10.

Callon, M., & Law, J. (1997). After the individual in society: Lessons on collectivity from science, technology and society. *Canadian Journal of Sociology/Cahiers Canadiens de sociologie, 22*(2), 165–182.

De Paoli, S., Leslie, B., Coull, N., Isaacs, J., MacDonald, A., & Letham, J. (2016). Authenticity by design: Reflections on researching, designing and teaching socialbots. In R. W. Gehl & M. Bakardijieva (Eds.), *Socialbots and their friends: Digital media and the automation of sociality*. Routledge.

Elgin, B., Riley, M., Kocieniewski, D., & Brustein, J. (2015, September 24). The fake traffic schemes that are rotting the Internet. *Bloomberg Businessweek* [Online]. Retrieved from http://www.bloomberg.com/features/2015-click-fraud/

Elias, N. (2000). *The civilizing process: Sociogenetic and psychogenetic investigations* (rev. ed.). Malden, MA: Blackwell.

Geiger, R. S., & Ribes, D. (2010). The work of sustaining order in Wikipedia: The banning of a vandal. In *Proceedings of the 2010 ACM conference on computer supported cooperative work*. Savannah, Georgia, USA.

Gillespie, T. (2014). The relevance of algorithms. In T. Gillespie, P. J. Boczkowski & K. A. Foot (Eds.), *Media technologies: Essays on communication, materiality, and society* (pp. 167–193). Cambridge, MA: MIT Press.

Goldsmith, J. (1995). This bot's for you. *Wired, 3*(4). Retrieved from http://www.wired.com/1995/04/irc/

Gomart, É., & Hennion, A. (1999). A sociology of attachment: Music amateurs, drug users. In J. Law & J. Hassard (Eds.), *Actor network theory and after* (pp. 220–247). Oxford: Blackwell.

Haddon, L. (2011). Domestication analysis, objects of study, and the centrality of technologies in everyday life. *Canadian Journal of Communication, 36*(2), 311–323.

Helmers, S., Hoffmann, U., & Stamos-Kaschke, J. (1997). (How) can software agents become good net citizens? *Computer-Mediated Communication Magazine, 4*(2). Retrieved from http://www.december.com/cmc/mag/1997/feb/helmers.html

Hine, C. (2000). *Virtual ethnography*. London; Thousand Oaks, CA: SAGE Publications, Inc.

Jouët, J. (2000). Retour critique sur la sociologie des usages. *Réseaux,* (100), 487–521.

Jouët, J. (2011). Des usages de la télématique aux *Internet Studies*. In J. Denouël & F. Granjon (Eds.), *Communiquer à l'ère numérique. Regards croisés sur la sociologie des usages* (pp. 45–90). Paris: Presses des Mines.

Kilker, J. (2002). Social and technical interoperability, the construction of users, and 'arrested closure': A case study of networked electronic mail development. *Iterations, 1.* Retrieved from http://www.cbi.umn.edu/iterations/kilker.html

Knorr Cetina, K. (1997). Sociality with objects: Social relations in postsocial knowledge societies. *Theory, Culture & Society, 14*(4), 1–30.

Latour, B. (1992). Where are the missing masses? The sociology of a few mundane artifacts. In W. E. Bijker & J. Law (Eds.), *Shaping technology/building society: Studies in sociotechnical change* (pp. 225–258). Cambridge, MA: MIT Press.

Latour, B. (1994). Pragmatogonies—A mythical account of how humans and nonhumans swap properties. *American Behavioral Scientist, 37*(6), 791–808.

Latzko-Toth, G. (2010). Metaphors of synchrony: Emergence and differentiation of online chat devices. *Bulletin of Science, Technology & Society, 30*(5), 362–374.

Latzko-Toth, G. (2014). Users as co-designers of software-based media: The co-construction of Internet relay chat. *Canadian Journal of Communication, 39*(4), 577–595.

Latzko-Toth, G., & Söderberg, J. (2015). Creative disruptions: Misuser innovation and digital media. Paper presented at the *annual meeting of the society for social studies of science (4S)*, Denver (Colorado), Nov. 11–14, 2015.

Leonard, A. (1997). *Bots: The origin of new species*. New York: Penguin Books.

Mallein, P., & Toussaint, Y. (1994). L'intégration sociale des technologies d'information et de communication: une sociologie des usages. *Technologies de l'information et société, 6*(4), 315–335.

Mitsch Bush, D., & Simmons, R. G. (1990). Socialization processes over the life course. In M. Rosenberg & R. H. Turner (Eds.), *Social psychology: Sociological perspectives*. New Brunswick, NJ: Transaction Publishers.

Olsen, O. R. R. (1994). The Tao of Internet relay chat. Retrieved from http://www.irc.org/history_docs/tao.html

Orlikowski, W. J., & Gash, D. C. (1994). Technological frames: Making sense of information technology in organizations. *ACM Trans. Inf. Syst., 12*(2), 174–207.

Pinch, T., & Bijker, W. E. (1987). The social construction of facts and artifacts: Or how the sociology of science and the sociology of technology might benefit each other. In W. E. Bijker, T. P. Hughes & T. Pinch (Eds.), *The social construction of technological systems: New directions in the sociology and history of technology* (pp. 17–50). Cambridge, MA: MIT Press.

Pointer, R. (1997). About eggdrop. Web page. Retrieved from http://www.eggheads.org/support/egghtml/1.6.15/about.html

Quittner, J. (1995). Automata non grata. *Wired, 3*(4). Retrieved from http://www.wired.com/1995/04/irc/

Rose, H. (1994). IRC frequently asked questions (FAQ), version 1.39, alt.irc (Usenet). A more recent version can be found here: http://ftp.funet.fi/pub/unix/irc/docs/alt-irc-faq

Silverstone, R., & Hirsch, E. (Eds.). (1992). *Consuming technologies: Media and information in domestic spaces.* London; New York: Routledge.

Verbeek, P.-P. (2011). *Moralizing technology: Understanding and designing the morality of things.* Chicago: University of Chicago Press.

4

MAKING AI SAFE FOR HUMANS

A Conversation *with* Siri

Andrea L. Guzman

We are in the midst of a transition from a computer culture to a robotic culture in which technologies are increasingly occupying more intimate social spaces in our lives and minds (Turkle, 2007). A crucial aspect of this modern existence is our communication with machines (Jones, 2014). We type messages to social-bots or speak with the digital assistants in our phones. In these instances, technology is transformed into something more than a tool we use, a channel for conveying a message. The medium itself becomes a communication partner. But what exactly are we communicating with?

The obvious answer would be a device or even a program, but the reality is more complex. In this chapter, I draw on my ongoing research into individual and cultural conceptions of AI and voice-based programs to interrogate the design of social technologies, specifically Siri, through the lens of Human-Machine Communication (HMC). HMC is a developing concept within communication, although the term and its application to human-machine systems is not new.[1] In contrast to Computer-Mediated Communication, which positions technology as a medium, HMC approaches technology as more than a medium, as a distinct communication partner.

My application of HMC is informed by Carey's (1989) cultural definition of communication: communication between human and machine is a cultural process, not just the mere exchange of information. Siri's mode of communication with users, the messages it sends, as well as the messages other people send about Siri, work together to project a certain image of what Siri is in relation to the user. I argue that Siri's design mitigates people's potential uncertainty and uneasiness with life-like technologies. Through their dyadic interaction with Siri, users are provided with a sense that they hold power over Siri, who seemingly serves at their beck and call. However, these aspects of design obfuscate the complex reality that, like the humans they are designed to mimic, artificial entities are not always who they claim to be. I also demonstrate how scholars can approach social machines through an HMC framework.

Siri, Socialbots and Communication

Apple introduced its version of Siri, a voice-based, artificial intelligence program, in 2011 with the iPhone 4s. As a program that could actually talk, and do so with attitude, Siri immediately garnered attention from the media and the public. In bundling Siri with the iPhone, the company made talking AI accessible to the public. Until Siri's launch, most people had only heard about talking machines in science fiction and had only experienced voice-based technologies controlled by simple commands. Siri was, and to an extent still remains, different from most widely available AI programs in that it interacts orally in natural language, follows the social norms of human-to-human communication, attempts to develop a rapport with users and exhibits distinct personality traits (She is well-known for her sassiness).

Siri is what I have termed a vocal social agent, or VSA. Agents are 'intelligent' in that they carry out human-like actions related to specific tasks (Balakrishnan & Honavar, 2001) and are programmed to perform a function for users (Skalski & Tamborini, 2007). VSAs are designed to be autonomous and adapt to and assist users. What sets VSAs apart is that they are both intelligent and social, programmed to follow human communication norms. Apple claims on its website that Siri 'understands what you say' and 'knows what you mean'. To interact with Siri, users speak to the program, and it responds in a way similar to a human, even referring to the user by name. VSAs are designed to carry out functions for humans in seemingly human-like ways. This places them into a larger class of technologies that serve as stand-ins for humans (see Zhao, 2006). The sociality of VSAs has implications beyond the ability of humans and software to communicate more easily; the agent itself becomes a social entity (Nass et al., 1994; Reeves & Nass, 1998).

Both VSAs and socialbots are forms of AI and share a technological lineage. While agents can function across platforms, socialbots are autonomous programs operating in social media networks (Gehl, 2014; Hwang et al., 2012). Socialbots are designed to pass themselves off as human social media users, obscuring their digital nature behind human profiles and in human-like interactions with users (Hwang et al., 2012). As Ferrara et al. (2014) observe, bots attempt to 'emulate behavior' of humans to the extent that 'the boundary between human-like and bot-like behavior is now fuzzier' (p. 4). Socialbots, like VSAs, communicate in ways readily recognizable as human to users and attempt to become part of our social world. Both programs also are designed to function as stand-ins for humans. To do so, they must gain entrance into our human social world by convincing us just enough that they are social entities. They make this case to us through the same means employed by humans—in communication. In doing so, they present to users a particular social face (Goffman, 1967). The remainder of this chapter is a case study of Siri. I explore how Siri's communication with users creates a picture of Siri as under the user's control positioning it as helpful, or safe, AI, in contrast to the cultural image of malicious machine. Although differences exist between socialbots and agents, the shared importance of communication to the design and function of both entities enables an investigation of Siri to inform our understanding of socialbots and other social programs.

'I'm Sorry, Dave'

When Turing (1950) made the case for thinking machines in his groundbreaking paper 'Computer Machinery and Intelligence', he already anticipated backlash. In addition to outlining the imitation game, i.e., the 'Turing Test', Turing refutes objections to machine intelligence. The challenges Turing anticipated were based not only on whether such a machine could be achieved, the technical possibility, but also on whether such a machine should be built, the moral quandary rooted in the machine's affront to beliefs regarding nature, religion and humanity. Gandy (1999) argues Turing's paper, published in *Mind: A Quarterly Review of Psychology and Philosophy*, was propaganda, not engineering: Turing's goal was to change people's understanding of the nature of machines and themselves, to move intelligent machines toward social acceptance. Turing knew that technology comprises more than moving parts. It is, as Carey (1989) later argued, 'thoroughly cultural from the outset' (p. 9). As such, technology embodies culture and is interpreted within culture (Carey, 1989). Interrogating Siri from an HMC perspective rooted in Carey, with its focus on the intersection of communication and culture, requires that we view Siri within the cultural context of people's evolving attitudes toward autonomous machines and AI.

Turing's efforts to quell cultural concerns regarding advanced computing while promoting its promise reflect the dialectical tensions underlying our relationship with technology and the uneasiness that has accompanied life-like devices from antiquity. Although the field of AI was established in the twentieth century, attempts to create and recreate life are ancient (Riskin, 2007). The building of automata, life-like mechanical devices that are AI precursors, precedes the Industrial Revolution (Riskin, 2007). By the eighteenth century, automata were popular and performed human-like tasks that 'seemed to embody the realization of an age-old human dream' (Huyssen, 1981, p. 225). But, explains Huyssen, this positive view of the mechanical novelties drastically changes in literary accounts as the Industrial Revolution begins to exploit resources and people: 'The android is no longer seen as testimony to the genius of mechanical invention; it rather becomes a nightmare, a threat to human life' (p. 225). Machines are portrayed as turning on their creators.

In the second half of the twentieth century, automated technology was both moving the United States toward economic progress and ruining people's lives, depending on who was asked. The integration of automated machines into factories and the displacement of workers that followed sparked the 'automation hysteria' of the 1950s and 1960s (Noble, 2011). With concern about the effects of automation rising, the US government, universities and trade organizations commissioned studies on its impact (Noble, 2011; Terbough, 1965). In *The Automation Hysteria*, the Machinery and Allied Products Institute paints people who questioned automation as 'alarmists', deeming such panic unwarranted (Terbough, 1965). Workers and people negatively affected by automation, however, disagreed. Conceptions of automated machines thus were bifurcated largely along lines of economic power (Noble, 2011).

Until recently, sentient talking machines have not been available to the public, and people's understanding of AI likely has been informed by media representations of sentient machines, particularly in science fiction. Although science fiction deals in imaginary plots, it is a cultural product that reflects attitudes and ideas regarding technology (Haigh, 2011). People I have interviewed regarding VSAs and AI routinely draw on characters and ideas from science fiction to describe and evaluate real AI (Guzman, 2015). Warrick's (1980) analysis of sci-fi literature from 1930 to 1977 reveals a pattern similar to the portrayal of eighteenth-century automata. Early works paint machine intelligence in a utopian light, but mirroring post-World War II events this optimism in machines is 'replaced by destructive metaphors of machines overwhelming and dehumanizing man' (p. xvi). Science fiction films from 1930 through to the 1990s echo a theme of danger connected to 'disembodied brains' (Schelde, 1993). Like their literary counterparts, AI entities in film, such as HAL 9000 from *2001: A Space Odyssey*, seek to wrest control from humans. Exceptions to dangerous AI also exist (Schelde, 1993; Warrick, 1980) and take the form of androids, disembodied voices, and devices programmed to work with or for humans. BB8 from *Star Wars: The Force Awakens* is the most recent example of a helpful, lovable machine, and the cheers from moviegoers when R2-D2 was reanimated demonstrate that we also can form a positive perspective of a droid that faithfully serves its master. Science fiction across decades and genres portrays intelligent machines as helpful if they are kept in check, but when they gain control—the most likely scenario—the consequences are dire. It is in this cultural milieu of duelling perspectives on AI that Siri was designed and introduced to people with little-to-no hands-on experience of AI.

'I'm Siri . . . Here to Help'

When we encounter people, we ascertain who they are and their social standing in relation to ourselves (Goffman, 1959). But how are we supposed to make sense of a talking, intelligent iPhone program? Until recently, the ways we gained knowledge about things versus people were clearly delineated. Things acquire meaning in our individual and cultural conversations about them and in their use (Blumer, 1969). Objects metaphorically 'speak' through their design with technology, specifically, functioning as 'a symbol *of*' and 'a symbol *for*' (Carey, 1990). Our understanding of people also is derived through our interactions with others; however, unlike machines, humans can directly communicate who they are to us (Goffman, 1959). They can speak for themselves. Siri, VSAs, socialbots and other software designed with agency cross this dividing line between the meaning of things and the meaning of humans (Guzman, 2015). Unlike an inanimate object, social programs are designed to present themselves to us through direct interaction. Siri literally speaks for itself. To interrogate Siri's design, then, we have to investigate both what others say about it and what it says about itself (verbally and non-verbally), keeping in mind the cultural contexts that surround these elements.

For a consumer to adopt a technology, its operation must be apparent. The goal in usability is a 'self-explanatory artifact' (Suchman, 2009), an object that communicates its use through design. Vocal AI presents a challenge for its creators because people usually physically manipulate machines to do things, not talk with them (or have them talk back). Drawing on the life-like nature of computers and agents, designers have used the metaphor of the machine as human-like assistant to convey their function (Suchman, 2009). Siri's designers also use this metaphor, and other associated human-like traits, to give Siri an identity. Siri is a funny female assistant complete with a technological and cultural history, and these traits work in concert to portray the program as the type of AI that serves the user.

Apple's (2011a) press release introducing Siri describes it as 'an intelligent assistant that helps you get things done just by asking'. During its launch event for Siri with the iPhone 4s, the company stresses Siri's 'occupation' as an assistant and its social status as something that works for the user. While peppering Siri with requests for information, an Apple executive also commands Siri to schedule a meeting and remind him 'to call my wife when I leave work' (Apple, 2011b). The audience is further instructed that if you want to accomplish a task, 'just ask your personal assistant, Siri'. The tasks Siri executes are analogous to the work performed by human executive assistants. The way people are instructed to speak with Siri also parallels human-to-human communication in that we can call her by name when making requests.

Siri's backstory as an assistant goes beyond how other people describe the program and to its own—artificial—awareness of Self. Siri will tell you what, or who, it is. At the climax of the launch event, an exchange takes place between an Apple executive and Siri:

Executive:	Now, you might ask, 'Who is Siri?' Well, just ask.
(Speaking into phone):	Who are you?
Siri:	I am a humble personal assistant.

Siri's response, that the audience can both hear and see, brings laughs and enthusiastic clapping. Individuals using Siri also have received the 'humble personal assistant' reply. The program also provides other answers regarding its identity—including simply stating, 'I am Siri'—that position the program as a distinct being with a sense of Self. Some of the other alternative responses underscore Siri's social role as an assistant to humans, including 'I'm Siri . . . here to help', and, in a move to discourage too many questions about its ontology, 'I'm Siri, but enough about me, how can I help you?'. More recently, Siri has started to respond that it is a 'humble *virtual* assistant' or just a 'virtual assistant' instead of a 'humble *personal* assistant'. While the current descriptions lessen the comparison between Siri and humans, to a degree, Siri still portrays itself as a distinct entity that occupies the social role of assistant.

Communication and power are inextricably intertwined (Castells, 2013), and an integral aspect of how we interact and relate to one another in interpersonal communication with humans is the dialectic of dominance and submission (Burgoon & Hale, 1984). Through messages exchanged with others as well as how we exchange them, we are able to gain dominance over someone or submit to them. These power dynamics are replicated in communication between Siri and the user. Siri is designed to signal submission. In its description of Self, Siri states that it is a '*humble* personal assistant' and informs the user that 'your wish is my command'. With these statements, Siri communicates deference to the user. Furthermore, the program does not assert its autonomy, even when people abuse it. If someone were to degrade a human assistant, the person may defend themselves. Siri, however, takes the abuse and even validates the user's actions. Call it a derogatory name, and it may reply, 'You are certainly entitled to that opinion'.

The way that Siri signals its socially inferior position relative to the user extends beyond the messages it sends. The program is designed to reinforce its claims of submission through its non-verbal communication with users and the way that users are encouraged to speak to it. Siri by default is silent, unseen and unheard. Any communication with Siri always positions the program as the receiver of the message. iPhone users decide when to talk with Siri and when to end communication. The default way of speaking with Siri is via command, not polite requests. An information menu within Siri provides users with examples of how to talk with the program, and many of these requests are phrased as commands: 'Call Brian' or 'Give me directions home'. Siri's assistant role is further reinforced through the functions it performs for users. Siri assists users with controlling their Apple product and fulfils a long list of associated tasks. If a misunderstanding occurs between Siri and the user, Siri also takes the blame and apologizes, even if the human is at fault. A communicative exchange with Siri revolves around users and their needs, putting humans in a position of dominance over the program.

The assistant heuristic that has been so prominent in media design is more than an effective means to convey functionality to the user. It also taps into a human desire to be in control (Suchman, 2009). To do away with what, or who, you cannot control and enable a machine to take its place is a long-standing theme in selling the promise of technology. In his foundational essay on the technological future, Bush (1945) touts how men will be able to use machines to take the place of humans, such as the stenographer, 'a girl' that looks around 'with a disquieting gaze'. People who assist are to be replaced with machines that assist. Machines are more desirable than humans because they can outperform their human counterparts and are free of all the annoyances of humans, such as casting weird looks. Suchman (2009) explains that, by industry standards, ideal agents 'should be enough like us to understand our desires and to figure out on their own how to meet them, but without either their own desires or ambitions or other human frailties . . .' (p. 219).

Human assistants can assert their autonomy, even if they have less power than their boss, but Siri cannot. Therefore, the metaphor of the assistant is not entirely accurate. Siri is less than an assistant. This degradation in status was picked up in initial press reports regarding Siri not as a critique of the software but as, once again, a marketing point. Siri was referred to as a 'voice-commanded minion', by one media outlet, and another reviewer gushed that Siri was like 'having the unpaid intern of my dreams at my beck and call' (Gross, 2011, para. 11). By calling Siri an assistant Apple draws a useful analogy between the program and a real human, but it also glosses over Siri's true nature, that of a servant, making Siri, who says it wants to help, more culturally palatable than something modelled on someone who has no choice but to help.

Siri's primary mode of communication is oral, and Siri's original voice, now the default voice, in the US version is female.[2] People recognize gender in electronic voices and respond to the machine just as they would to a human of that gender (Nass & Brave, 2005). A female voice actor provided the underlying vocal sounds for the US Siri (Ravitz, 2013), and US media and users have recognized Siri as having a woman's voice. The gendered nature of Siri is so strong that a Siri user remarked to me: 'It's very distinctive. I mean, everybody knows that they made Siri's voice a lady's voice.' Siri's voice adds a new dimension to its identity and provides additional clues for users as to who Siri is to them.

A core argument of feminist scholars of technology is that all technology is gendered: in its design, in its promotion and in its use (e.g., Berg & Lie, 1995; van Oost, 2003). Gender, as opposed to biological sex, is a social construct that is subject to renegotiation (West & Zimmerman, 1987). Therefore, gender can be mapped onto technology. Before Siri became a speaking Apple product, it was a text-based application. Yet, even without voice, Siri's interactions with users were indicative of a female typist (Both, 2014). The addition of voice made Siri's gender more explicit, emphasizing her female nature. Siri's gender further establishes who she is in relation to the audience. Rothschild (1983) argues: 'Technology is part of our culture; and, of course, our culture, which is male dominated, has developed technologies that reinforce male supremacy' (p. vii). In a society in which women were once viewed as the 'submissive sex', and still are by some social groups, and in which women have yet to achieve full equality with males, Siri's gender reinforces her as a subordinate.

Siri is neither just an 'assistant' nor just a female. Siri is a female assistant. These two aspects of her identity reinforce one another and bolster the program's inferior social status. Apple's demonstration of Siri at its launch with the iPhone underscores just how powerful these dimensions are. The Apple executives showing off Siri are male, and their requests of Siri to make phone calls and order flowers for a wife are culturally recognizable as tasks normally relegated to secretaries. Apple never calls Siri a secretary, but the connection is apparent in a culture that has stereotypically associated the position of secretary, now usually referred to as executive or administrative assistant, as women's work.

The combination of Siri's gender and 'occupation' has not gone completely unnoticed. That Siri was female and billed as a 'humble personal assistant' raised questions following its initial release as to whether the technology was 'brilliant or sexist', as CNN asked (Griggs, 2011). To answer these questions the articles quote technology researchers, including Nass, who claim US consumers find female voices easier to listen to. It is a mere matter of biological and cultural preference, according to their argument. ABC News poses the question: 'Would we rather get guidance from a nice, subservient female voice, perhaps the opposite of the bombast we hear from male authority figures?' (Potter, 2011, para. 4). Journalists ultimately determined that Siri was not sexist, while, others, including myself, continue to disagree.

The pushback against Siri as a female assistant is rooted in the connection between communication and culture. As a form of communication, technology is influenced by culture and influences culture (Carey, 1989; Marvin, 1990). Marvin (1990) explains, 'There is no technology that does not place those arranged around it in social relations to one another, and there is thus no uncommunicative technology or technological practice' (pp. 224–225). In our conversation with Siri, the social relation between human and machine is established, but the implications are not restricted to a human-machine context. According to Oudshoorn (2003): 'Technologies may play an important role in stabilizing or destabilizing particular conventions of gender, creating new ones or reinforcing or transforming the existing performances of gender' (p. 211). Marvin and Oudshoorn are speaking here more generally of who uses technology, what types of technologies they use and how technologies figure into gender identities. With Siri, the power dynamics can extend beyond our understanding of machines into our understanding of humans. Siri not only reflects gender stereotypes but has the potential to reinforce them.

Siri also is programmed to win people over with her personality. Researchers have found that people recognize personality traits programmed into a technology and act toward that machine as if it were a human with similar characteristics (Lee & Nass 2005; Nass et al., 1995). Siri is funny, sassy and helpful. If you ask her to tell you a joke, it will. If you ask her what she is wearing, a gendered question, she'll side-step the query with a reply such as, 'In the cloud, no one knows what you're wearing.' These sassier remarks often allow Siri to deflect questions intended to test her 'realness'. She can answer the question with a tone similar to that of a human, maintaining her social status, and simultaneously avoid an awkward conversation about its complicated ontology. Siri's personality also is not separate from other aspects of her identity. A *New York Times* headline declares, 'Siri is one funny lady' (Pogue, 2011), and in 'Snide, Sassy Siri has Plenty to Say', CNN reports that the program's gender and congenial interactions bolster her popularity (Gross, 2011). In giving Siri a playful personality, Apple positions Siri as good-natured just as women should be, based on gender stereotypes.

Working as an assistant, being a female and having a good-natured personality would normally be traits associated with humans. In Siri, these life-like characteristics establish and maintain her social nature. Virtual social agents, such as Siri, are what Turkle (1984) describes as evocative objects, things that do not fit neatly into ontological categories. Computers and AI blur the line between human and machine. According to Turkle (1984), the computer's evocative nature hinges 'on the fact that people tend to perceive "a machine that thinks" as a "machine who thinks"' (p. 25). As Bollmer and Rodley argue in this book (see Chapter 8), socialbots force a renegotiation of sociality. In my conversations with people regarding Siri, people describe dual and duelling conceptualizations of Siri, *who* and *that* can be thought of as simultaneously possessing machine AND human characteristics (Guzman, 2015). This often plays out in the pronouns referring to humans—who, she, her—and to things—what, it, that—people use for VSAs. Although some people stick with either human or machine pronouns, other people intermingle the two (Guzman, 2015). This chapter has purposely switched pronouns based on which aspect of Siri is being discussed to underscore Siri's bifurcated nature. It is a machine with a human backstory, and she is a social entity with a technological ancestry.

That technological ancestry also is evocative in that it includes both real and fictional AI entities. Part of Siri's humor is the knowledge Siri possesses regarding other AI and, to a degree, her 'self-awareness' of 'who' she is in relation to other technologies. When asked 'Open the pod bay doors, HAL', a reference to a specific scene in *2001: A Space Odyssey* in which HAL defies a human, Siri may respond, 'We intelligent agents will never live that down, apparently.' Siri's reply positions it as in the same general class of machines as HAL but, at the same time, differentiates Siri from HAL. If asked again to 'open the pod bay doors', Siri may reply, 'Ok, but wipe your feet first'. Siri's agreement to open the fictional doors demonstrates that Siri obeys humans, unlike HAL. (Users also may recognize her request that they wipe their feet as a stereotypically female request.) Siri's jokes about HAL situate the two programs as the same type of thing, but they are not the same type of individual thing.

Siri may not hang out with HAL, but she does have a BFF in ELIZA. ELIZA was an AI program created in the 1960s that could 'converse in English' instead of programming language via text-based exchanges (Weizenbaum, 1976). Designed to function as a psychotherapist, ELIZA is the technological predecessor to chatterbots and agents including Siri and socialbots. When asked about 'Eliza', Siri registers that the user is referring to *the* ELIZA. Siri's replies create a connection between her and ELIZA. One response positions ELIZA and Siri as friends: 'ELIZA is my good friend. She was a brilliant psychiatrist, but she's retired now.' Siri also alludes to ELIZA as her technological progenitor, including 'Do you know Eliza, she was my first teacher?' Although HAL was fictional and ELIZA was real, Siri's statements position all of these programs as part of the same technological class. In contrasting itself with HAL and comparing itself to ELIZA, Siri also stakes out its position relative to humans: Siri is a helper of humans like ELIZA, not a menace like HAL.

The connection Apple draws between ELIZA and Siri can be viewed as part of the company's efforts to promote Siri as a revolutionary technological innovation. Apple touts Siri as a dream realized. Apple (2011b) states during Siri's launch: 'For decades technologists have teased us with this dream that you are going to be able to talk to technology and it is going to be able to do things for us.' Apple is talking about a technological dream; one extending from ELIZA. But many people do not know about ELIZA, ALICE or the countless other technologies that are part of Siri's technological ancestry. In programming Siri with the ability to speak about numerous fictional AI entities, Apple anticipated that the general public would be familiar with HAL's branch of the family tree. Some journalists reporting on Siri's launch relied on pop culture representations of AI to explain how Siri functioned and the magnitude of technology's innovation. News reports referred to Siri as 'the stuff of science fiction' (Gross, 2011) and a 'sci-fi dream realized' (Milian, 2011). Siri also is portrayed as an 'amazing technology' that feels 'like magic' (Pogue, 2011). Overall, Siri is constructed as a social machine with desirable human-like qualities and a prestigious technological lineage. If the early hype surrounding Siri is to be believed, Siri is part of the science-fiction future made present. In this real-life story, humans are not controlled by machines; rather, we have extended our control over machines, both Siri and our iPhone, and, as a result, also further our own control over our lives.

'In the Cloud, No One Knows What You're Wearing'

The reason that Siri feels 'like magic' is not constrained to its framing as a science-fiction future. Chun (2011) argues that by its very nature, software is difficult to understand because it is ephemeral. We do not see how software works, and instead we rely on the metaphor of software to construct our understanding of computation, according to Chun. Siri and all software are a type of magic in that they provide us with a means to transform the ephemeral into the physical. Chun explains that code: 'is a medium in the full sense of the word. As a medium, it channels the ghost that we imagine runs the machine—that we see as we don't see—when we gaze at our screen's ghostly images.' Graphic User Interfaces, or GUIs, provide a visual representation of that ghost (i.e., icons), while Siri functions primarily as a vocal interface. Siri is a voice in and of the machine, a voice that allows us to interact with the machine in our hand, the iPhone, and other machines, servers (Guzman, 2015). She is simultaneously an interlocutor, and it is also a medium.

As a vocal interface, Siri leaves more to the imagination than a GUI. Chun (2011) argues that GUIs allow us to see a particular representation of software. With Siri, we do not see. That is why someone would, jokingly, ask her what she is wearing. We do not know, and cannot know, what she is wearing, not because she is in the cloud, another metaphor, but because she does not physically exist. Yet, we have the feeling that she does exist—we can, after all, hear her. And something is finding us the nearest coffee shop. The human and mechanical characteristics that we discussed in the last section provide us with more than instructions on how to use Siri; they put a metaphorical face on the software. Siri's face is analogous to that of Goffman's (1967) conception of face—a particular performance of Self. Siri does not have a Self, but she has been given a social form, as if she had a Self. Chun argues that 'as our interfaces become more "transparent" and visual, our machines also become more dense and obscure' (2011, p. 177). Similar to a person who puts on a certain face for a particular social setting (Goffman, 1967), Siri is programmed with a social face that draws our attention toward it and away from other aspects of the application. Here, I focus on how Siri's public face, that of an interlocutor, obscures the other communication role Siri performs, that of medium, and the consequences of both communicative roles played by Siri.

A fundamental communication element is 'who' is involved in the interaction. A conversation with Siri is patterned after dyadic interpersonal communication: When someone is talking to Siri, the user and Siri appear to be the only parties exchanging messages. The interaction between user and Siri is designed to mimic an employer-to-employee relationship, or master-to-servant, with Siri working for and controlled by the user. When speaking with Siri, we are presented with a communication setting in which we are interacting one-on-one with an entity that we control. If we switch our focus from Siri the interlocutor to Siri the medium, we 'see' Siri take a command and execute it on the iPhone. Siri speaks to us as an interlocutor and works for us as a medium. However, despite all of her human qualities, Siri is not an independent entity as another human would be. Siri is not an entity at all. Siri is a piece of software that takes in and exchanges information with human users, with other machines, and ultimately with Apple and every other company or organization that is on the other end of these computational processes. Siri is a medium between user and the iPhone and between user and Apple; although, Siri does not reveal that she also is talking to Apple.

There is no way that Apple or any other creator of advanced natural language processing AI could program every permutation of how people speak into an agent a priori. Nor could they predict every request. For AI to function, it needs data. Otherwise Siri could not 'learn'. Apple processes and stores information from Siri users for two years (McMillan, 2013). This allows the program to respond and adapt to users as a whole and individually. It also provides Apple with data on every aspect of how people use Siri and their iPhones. The storage of user data to the benefit of Apple prompted the ACLU to argue in a blog post that Siri 'isn't just working for us, it's working full-time for Apple too' (Ozer, 2012). However, there is a third worker that even the ACLU overlooks— the Siri user. By interacting with Siri, which is supposed to be the entity assisting the consumer, the user is performing labour for Apple. We are providing the information Apple needs to improve Siri via Siri. With millions of Apple mobile devices sold worldwide, user interaction provides the company with information on a scale that it could never produce on its own. When we look past the face Siri is designed to present to users, the relationship between Siri and users is not what it appears to be, and Siri is not what she pretends to be. Our interaction with Siri is more complex than a dyadic arrangement of human to machine, boss to worker, and involves more parties than just user and Siri.

In using Siri to better control our phone, we give up control of our information, but details of iPhone use may not be all that we cede to the machine (and technology companies): software increasingly is helping us make decisions or making decisions for us (Verbeek, 2009). The field of captology has emerged within the last few decades with a focus on the design and implementation of persuasive technologies (Fogg, 2002). These technologies often engage in 'nudging' (Thaler & Sunstein, 2009) users toward a decision or behaviour adoption through subtle communication that obscures the machine's active role in the process (Fogg, 2002; Verbeek, 2009). Siri's design gives it the appearance of being separate from the user but under the user's control (a picture we now know is not entirely true). The question is whether Siri actively influences users' decision-making.

Part of the answer can be found in Siri's technological lineage. Apple did not develop Siri, a fact that Apple does not promote and journalists have not widely reported. The program's technology can be traced to the US government's largest AI initiative, the Perceptive Assistant that Learns, or PAL, program, which developed AI software for the military (SRI International, n.d.). DARPA selected SRI International in 2003 to lead the $150 million project (Artificial Intelligence Center, n.d.). Among the project objectives was the goal that 'the software, which will learn by interacting with and being advised by its users, will handle a broad range of interrelated decision-making tasks . . . It will have the capability to engage in and lead routine tasks . . .' (Artificial Intelligence Center, n.d., paras. 3–4). SRI later founded Siri Inc. to develop commercial technology from PAL, and in 2010 the company introduced Siri, a voice-activated personal assistant, to the Apple App Store. A SRI press release (2010) for the pre-Apple version of Siri states: 'Many tasks, like making restaurant reservations, typically involve multiple steps—including searching near a certain location, browsing reviews, considering available times, . . . Siri handles them all, without missing a beat'. The technology upon which Apple's version of the program is based was developed to 'think' on its own and to inform human decisions. Like its SRI predecessor, the current incarnation of Siri sorts through and prioritizes information to make recommendations. Because of Siri's opacity, we do not know to what extent Apple and other companies have nudged us in a direction that ultimately benefits them.

Siri's potential to affect the outcome of mostly mundane tasks, such as choosing a restaurant, may seem inconsequential, but the program's increased role in our decision-making and our lives is not trivial. When we rely on Siri to remind us to be somewhere or help us find a business, we are handing over control of part of our lives to the machine. We may tell Siri what to do when we schedule an event, but then Siri reminds us what we need to do. Communication with and about the program positions Siri and users as independent entities. We now know that this is not true of Siri, and, although harder to admit, not true of ourselves. We may think we are independent from Siri and our iPhone, but, as anyone who has ever lost their phone for more than a minute can attest, we rely on the technologies permeating our lives. This reliance is built through more than the messages Siri sends, or what Carey (1989) calls the transmission view of communication. It is constructed through our communion with machines, the ritual aspects of communication (Carey, 1989) we repeat over and over.

We are, as Sengers (2000) argues, 'no longer, like our ancestors, simply supplied by machines; we live in and through them' (p. 5). With each advance in technology, we continue to delegate more of what was once within the purview of humans to machines. The technologies we build and the way we integrate them into our lives have long played an integral role in the evolution of individuals and society (e.g., Innis, 2007; McLuhan, 1994) and in the way that we see ourselves (e.g., Turkle, 1984). As we are experiencing our latest technological and cultural shift to a robotic society, we, once again, are presented with new ways to relate to our world (Turkle, 2007). Siri is part of this transition.

Understanding Human-Machine Communication; Understanding Human-Machine Culture

On the movie screen, AI has been portrayed as a helper to humans only when the sentience and power of the machine is kept in check. Given too much power, the machines will slip from our control. While these tropes make for great movies, they do not accurately reflect AI within a quotidian context. They also are not a useful means for critiquing technology, as Carey and Quirk (1989) argue: 'Electronics is neither the arrival of the apocalypse nor the dispensation of grace: Technology is technology' (p. 140). If we separate Siri from the myth of AI, we see that Siri is neither dream nor danger. The reality of Siri is much more complex.

This is not to say that Siri is neutral. Technologies function, Carey (1990) argues, as 'homunculi: concrete embodiments of human purposes, social relations, and forms of organization' (p. 247). They are sites of power (Carey, 1990; Chun, 2011), and must be understood as such. If there is any 'danger' associated with Siri, vocal social agents, socialbots or any other technology, it is in accepting these technologies and their representation of the world through the face they and others communicate to us without engaging with their social and technological complexity. According to Carey (1990), technologies 'coerce the world into working in terms of the representation' (p. 245). We, therefore, need to continuously interrogate our digital assistants as to what they represent and what we bring into being through their use in an increasingly technology-saturated culture. This holds true for not only how we see ourselves in relation to machines but also in how we come to see other people through the machine. This process of critique is challenging. Software is not easily grasped to begin with (Chun, 2011), and technology is designed to be erased from the user's view (Suchman, 2009). With Siri we are confronted with making sense of a technology that has a face that we cannot see, a technological lineage that is real and fictional.

How then can we begin to see these technologies and weigh implications for our lives? A key aspect of our relationship with technology that has not been adequately addressed by scholars is our communication with machines (Gunkel, 2012; Guzman, 2015; Jones, 2014). We daily communicate with devices to the point that this process goes unrecognized (Jones, 2014). Our machines and our communication with them are transparent to us. One way we can attempt to make our technologies visible, to submit them to critique is to approach them through the mundane that enables their existence—communication. That is what I have tried to do in this chapter by systematically tracing each element of communication between Siri and humans. In doing so, I have mapped out a course for understanding our technologies and our relationship with them. This approach is not limited to Siri and vocal social agents. Because socialbots and other digital entities also seek to enter our social world through communication, we can better understand them by focusing on the process of human-machine communication as well.

Notes

1. Scholars across multiple disciplines have used varying terms and approaches to the study of interactions between humans and machines, including 'man-machine communication' (e.g., Flanagan, 1976) and 'human-machine communication' (Suchman, 2009). Within communication, the work of Clifford Nass and others has fallen under Human-Computer Interaction (HCI). More recently, some communication scholars, this author included, have started to use HMC as an umbrella term for HCI, HRI (human-robot interaction) and HAI (human-agent interaction) and to develop HMC frameworks grounded in communication theory.

2. When Siri was first released in the United States, its only voice was female, but the voice of Siri varied throughout the world based on cultural conceptions of gender and the type of work Siri performs. For example, Siri's initial UK voice was male, a reference to a type of butler. Suchman (2007) provides an explanation of the idea of the butler, or "Jeeves," as a computer agent. Today, consumers in the U.S. can choose from male or female voices. Despite this, people overwhelming identify Siri as female (Guzman, 2015).

References

Apple. (2011a). Apple launches iPhone 4S, iOS 5 & iCloud. Retrieved from https://www.apple.com/pr/library/2011/10/04Apple-Launches-iPhone-4S-iOS-5-iCloud.html

Apple. (2011b). Special event [Public relations video]. Retrieved via iTunes.

Artificial Intelligence Center. (n.d.). Cognitive assistant that learns and organizes. Retrieved from http://www.ai.sri.com/project/CALO

Balakrishnan, K., & Honavar, V. (2001). Evolutionary and neural synthesis of intelligent agents. In M. Patel, V. Honavar & K. Balakrishnan (Eds.), *Advances in the evolutionary synthesis of intelligent agents* (pp. 1–27). Retrieved from http://18.7.25.65/sites/default/files/titles/content/9780262162012_sch_0001.pdf

Berg, A. J., & Lie, M. (1995). Feminism and constructivism: Do artifacts have gender? *Science, Technology, & Human Values, 20*, 332–351.

Blumer, H. (1969). *Symbolic interactionism: Perspective and method.* Englewood Cliffs, NJ: Prentice-Hall.

Bollmer, G., & Rodley, C. (2016). Speculations on the sociality of socialbots. In R. W. Gehl & M. Bakardjieva (Eds.), *Socialbots and their friends: Digital media and the automation of sociality.* New York: Routledge.

Both, G. (2014). Multidimensional gendering processes at the human-computer-interface: The case of Siri. In N. Marsden & U. Kempf's (Eds.), *Gender-useIT: HCI, usability und UX unter gendergesichtspunkten* (pp. 107–112). Berlin, Germany: DeGruyter.

Burgoon, J. K., & Hale, J. L. (1984). The fundamental topoi of relational communication. *Communication Monographs, 51*, 193–214.

Bush, V. (1945, July). As we may think. *The Atlantic Monthly.*

Carey, J. W. (1989). *Communication as culture: Essays on media and society.* New York: Routledge.

Carey, J. W. (1990). Technology as a totem for culture: On Americans' use of high technology as a model for social order. *American Journalism, 7*(4), 242–251.

Carey, J. W., & Quirk, J. J. (1989). The mythos of the electronic revolution. In J. W. Carey (Ed.), *Communication as culture: Essays on media and society* (pp. 113–141). New York: Routledge.

Castells, M. (2013). *Communication power.* Oxford, UK: Oxford University Press.

Chun, W. H. K. (2011). *Software studies: Programmed visions: Software and memory.* Cambridge, MA: MIT Press.

Ferrara, E., Varol, O., Davis, C., Menczer, F., & Flammini, A. (2014). *The rise of social bots.* Cornell University's arXiv. Retrieved from http://arxiv.org/abs/1407.5225

Flanagan, J. L. (1976). Computers that talk and listen: Man-machine communication by voice. *Proceedings of the IEEE, 64*, 405–418.

Fogg, B. J. (2002). *Persuasive technology.* Morgan Kaufmann.

Gandy, R. (1999). Human versus mechanical intelligence. In P. Millican & A. Clark (Eds.), *Machines and thought: The legacy of Alan Turing* (pp. 125–136). New York: Oxford University Press.

Gehl, R. W. (2014). *Reverse engineering social media*. Philadelphia, PA: Temple University.

Goffman, E. (1959). *The presentation of self in everyday life*. New York: Anchor Books.

Goffman, E. (1967). On face-work: An analysis of ritual elements in social interaction. In *Interaction ritual: Essays on face-to-face behavior*. Garden City, NY: Anchor Books.

Griggs, B. (2011, October 18). Why computer voices are mostly female. *CNN.com*. Retrieved from LexisNexis Academic.

Gross, D. (2011, October 4). Apple introduces Siri, Web freaks out. *CNN.com*. Retrieved from LexisNexis Academic.

Gunkel, D. J. (2012). Communication and artificial intelligence: Opportunities and challenges for the 21st century. *Communication +1, 1*. Retrieved from http://scholarworks.umass.edu/cpo/vol1/iss1/1

Guzman, A. L. (2015). Imagining the voice in the machine (Doctoral dissertation, University of Illinois at Chicago). Retrieved from *http://hdl.handle.net/10027/19842*.

Haigh, T. (2011). Technology's other storytellers: Science fiction as history of technology. In D. L. Ferro & E. G. Swedin (Eds.), *Science fiction and computing essays on interlinked domains* (pp. 13–37). Jefferson, NC: McFarland & Company. Retrieved from http://site.ebrary.com/lib/alltitles/docDetail.action?docID=10501985

Huyssen, A. (1981). The vamp and the machine: Technology and sexuality in Fritz Lang's Metropolis. *New German Critique,* (24/25), 221–237. Retrieved from http://doi.org/10.2307/488052

Hwang, T., Pearce, I., & Nanis, M. (2012). Socialbots: Voices from the fronts. *Interactions, 19*(2), 38–45.

Innis, H. A. (2007). *Empire and communications*. Lanham, MD: Rowman & Littlefield.

Jones, S. (2014). People, things, memory and human-machine communication. *International Journal of Media & Cultural Politics, 10*(3), 245–258.

Lee, K. M., & Nass, C. (2005). Social-psychological origins of feelings of presence: Creating social presence with machine-generated voices. *Media Psychology, 7*(1), 31–45.

Marvin, C. (1990). Reconsidering James Carey: How many rituals does it take to make an artifact? *American Journalism, 7*, 216–226.

McLuhan, M. (1994). *Understanding media: The extensions of man*. Cambridge, MA: MIT Press.

McMillan, R. (2013, April 19). Apple finally reveals how long Siri keeps your data. *Wired*. Retrieved from http://www.wired.com/wiredenterprise/2013/04/siri-two-years/

Milian, M. (2011, October 4). Apple's Siri voice based on extensive research. *CNN.com*. Retrieved via LexisNexis.

Nass, C., & Brave, S. (2005). *Wired for speech: How voice activates and advances the human-computer relationship*. Cambridge, MA: MIT Press.

Nass, C., Moon, Y., Fogg, B. J., Reeves, B., & Dryer, D. C. (1995). Can computer personalities be human personalities? *International Journal of Human-Computer Studies, 43*, 223–239.

Nass, C., Moon, Y., & Green, N. (1997). Are machines gender neutral? Gender-stereotypic responses to computers with voices. *Journal of Applied Social Psychology, 27*(10), 864–876.

Nass, C., Steuer, J., & Tauber, E. R. (1994). Computers are social actors. In *Conference companion on human factors in computing systems* (pp. 72–78). Retrieved from http://doi.org/10.1145/259963.260288

Noble, D. F. (2011). *Forces of production: A social history of industrial automation*. New Brunswick, NJ: Transaction Publishers.

Oudshoorn, N. (2003). Clinical trials as a cultural niche in which to configure the gender identities of users: The case of male contraceptive development. In N. Oudshoorn & T. Pinch (Eds.), *How users matter: The co-construction of users and technologies* (pp. 209–228). Cambridge, MA: MIT Press.

Ozer, N. (2012, March 10). Note to self: Siri not just working for me, working full-time for Apple too. Retrieved from https://www.aclu.org/blog/free-speech-technology-and-liberty/note-self-siri-not-just-working-me-working-full-time-apple.

Pogue, D. (2011, October 12). New iPhone conceals sheer magic. *The New York Times*. Retrieved via LexisNexis.

Potter, N. (2011, October 25). Why are computer voices female? Ask Siri. *ABCNews Online*. Retrieved from http://abcnews.go.com/

Ravitz, J. (2013). 'I'm the original voice of Siri'. Retrieved April 3, 2015, from http://www.cnn.com/2013/10/04/tech/mobile/bennett-siri-iphone-voice/index.html

Reeves, B., & Nass, C. I. (1998). *The media equation*. Stanford, CA: CSLI Publications.

Riskin, J. (Ed.). (2007). *Genesis redux: Essays in the history and philosophy of artificial life*. Chicago: University of Chicago Press.

Rothschild, J. (1983). Foreword. In J. Rothschild (Ed.), *Machina ex dea: Feminist perspectives on technology* (pp. vii–viii). New York: Pergamon Press.

Schelde, P. (1993). *Androids, humanoids, and other science fiction monsters: Science and soul in science fiction films*. New York: New York University Press.

Sengers, P. (2000). Practices for a machine culture. *Surfaces, 7*, 4–58.

Skalski, P., & Tamborini, R. (2007). The role of social presence in interactive agent-based persuasion. *Media Psychology, 10*(3), 385–413. Retrieved from http://doi.org/10.1080/15213260701533102

SRI International. (n.d.). Artificial intelligence: CALO. Retrieved from http://www.sri.com/work/timeline-innovation/timeline.php?timeline=computing-digital#!&innovation=artificial-intelligence-calo

SRI International. (2010). *Siri launches virtual personal assistant for iPhone 3GS* (Press release). Retrieved from https://www.sri.com/newsroom/press-releases/siri-launches-virtual-personal-assistant-iphone-3gs

Suchman, L. A. (2009). *Human-machine reconfigurations: Plans and situated actions* (2nd ed.). New York: Cambridge University Press.

Terbough, G. (1965). *The automation hysteria*. Washington, DC: Machinery & Allied Products Institute and Council for Technological Advancement.

Thaler, R. H., & Sunstein, C. R. (2009). *Nudge: Improving decisions about health, wealth, and happiness*. New York: Penguin.

Turing, A. M. (1950). Computing machinery and intelligence. In D. C. Ince (Ed.), *Mechanical intelligence* (pp. 133–160). New York: North-Holland.

Turkle, S. (1984). *The second self*. New York: Simon & Schuster.

Turkle, S. (2007). Authenticity in the age of digital companions. *Interaction Studies, 8*(3), 501–517.

van Oost, E. (2003). Materialized gender: How shavers configure the users' femininity and masculinity. In N. Oudshoorn & T. Pinch (Eds.), *How users matter: The co-construction of users and technologies* (pp. 193–208). Cambridge, MA: MIT Press.

Verbeek, P. P. (2009). Ambient intelligence and persuasive technology: The blurring boundaries between human and technology. *NanoEthics, 3*(3), 231–242. Retrieved from http://doi.org/10.1007/s11569–009–0077–8

Warrick, P. S. (1980). *The cybernetic imagination in science fiction*. Cambridge, MA: MIT Press.

Weizenbaum, J. (1976). *Computer power and human reason, from judgment to calculation*. New York: W.H. Freeman & Company.

West, C., & Zimmerman, D. H. (1987). Doing gender. *Gender & Society, 1*(2), 125–151.

Zhao, S. (2006). Humanoid social robots as a medium of communication. *New Media & Society, 8*(3), 401–419. Retrieved from http://doi.org/10.1177/1461444806061951

5

EMBODIED CONVERSATIONAL AGENTS AS SOCIAL ACTORS?

Sociological Considerations on the Change of Human-Machine Relations in Online Environments

Florian Muhle

A marginal note in anthropologist Tom Boellstorff's ethnographic study 'Coming of Age in Second Life' refers to a strange experience residents of Second Life (SL) sometimes have. Boellstorff notes that 'Volunteer helpers often found new residents of Second Life asking them "Are you human?"—in other words, are you automated or not?' (Boellstorff, 2008, p. 131). This episode is very illuminating because it shows an important aspect of communication in virtual worlds and computer games to which little attention has been paid so far: These environments are not only inhabited by human-controlled avatars, but potentially also by non-humans, who are allegedly said to be able to socialize. Besides a human population, platforms like SL have also spawned a population of *social bots*, ranging from simple chat bots to sophisticated 'embodied conversational agents' (ECAs). From this follows that users of online environments have to deal with a special kind of 'virtual contingency' (Esposito, 1993) when communicating with each other. The situation is not only framed by anonymity, but also by uncertainty about the (human) status of the virtual counterpart. As a consequence, online environments like SL blur the borders between the social world of humans and the technical world of machines.

What does this mean for interaction in virtual worlds? Can bots become social actors (in a human-like way)? And how could we proceed in order to find answers? These are the leading questions I want to consider in this chapter from a sociological point of view. For this, I will first take a closer look at online games and virtual worlds as test beds for a mixed society, where human- and machine-controlled avatars have already started to live together (section 1). Building on this, I will develop a systems theoretical concept of social agency, which does not presuppose that only human beings can become social actors but instead allows differentiation between humanlike social action and other forms of action (section 2). This concept is based on the post-humanist social theory of Niklas Luhmann and helps to define what it means to be a social actor. In the next step, I connect the theoretical considerations on social agency with the empirical approach of ethnomethodological membership categorization analysis (section 3). As I will argue, this approach fits with Luhmann's theoretical thoughts and allows symmetrical and open-ended empirical analyses of the (changing) human–machine relation, which can answer the question whether bots can become social actors. Section 4 then presents an exemplary analysis of human-machine interaction in the virtual world Second Life that was recorded in the context of my Ph.D. research (see Muhle, 2013). The analysis provides answers to the questions raised earlier and shows the potential of the theoretical and methodological approach for the empirical investigation of human-machine interactions in online environments. Finally, I will draw conclusions from my findings (section 5).

1   Virtual Worlds and Online Games as Test Beds for a Mixed Society of Humans and Bots

For Tom Boellstorff virtual worlds 'are places of human culture realized by computer programs through the internet' (Boellstorff, 2008, p. 17). Bots, from his point of view, are not an essential part of these environments. Traditionally, they function as non-player characters (NPCs), which are implemented to fulfil limited tasks for players. In terms of the information sciences, those NPCs are usually 'finite-state machines' and therefore only have very restricted options for actions. Accordingly, 'NPCs are not socially deep and most of the times are simply frozen in time, repeating the same action . . . over and over again' (Afonso & Prada, 2009, p. 35). In other words, their social capabilities are not comparable to human agency because they act in a predetermined manner. Consequently, the role allocation between human players and NPCs in online environments generally is quite clear and reflects the traditional distinction between humans who act and machines which function. Accordingly, it is the humans who inhabit online environments, where they interact, socialize and create online culture. Bots in this understanding are not worth mentioning. They belong to the inventory and are used as tools for human purposes.

However, in recent years this dichotomy has started to crumble, because computer games and virtual worlds were discovered by researchers from the Artificial Intelligence (AI) community as ideal fields for application of their own products. This had several reasons. On the one hand, in comparison with the physical offline world, virtual worlds offer advantages for the implementation of bots, or rather ECAs, because 'in 3D Virtual Worlds the integration of agents and environment in terms of agent reasoning is a feasible task due to the fact that the perception problem in such environments is minimised' (Ijaz et al., 2011, p. 107). On the other hand, AI researchers assume that enhancing the conversational capabilities of NPCs by providing them with sophisticated AI technologies improves the feeling of immersion and enhances the gaming experience for human users of online environments (see Afonso & Prada, 2009, p. 35). In this context, the aforementioned ECAs play an especially important role as they are explicitly developed in order to 'interact meaningfully with humans within that space' (Morie et al., 2012, p. 100).

Thus, ECAs are increasingly implemented in digital games and virtual worlds in order to shape human-machine interaction in a more human-like way. Consequently, today's virtual worlds are no longer only inhabited by human-controlled avatars, but also by non-humans, who, according to their developers, are able to socialize.[1] Against this backdrop, it makes sense to take a closer look at online games and worlds as test beds for a mixed society, where human- and machine-controlled avatars have started to live together. In such a society common assumptions about agency and society will be called into question, if bots really turn into social beings (see also Graham and Ackland's Chapter 10 in this volume).

Currently in modern society there is a sharp distinction between the social world of humans, on the one hand, and a non-social world, which consists of machines, animals, plants and other entities, on the other (see Lindemann, 2005). Referring to Steve Woolgar (1990), this distinction can be treated as the 'moral order of representation' in modern society. This moral order 'embodies notions about the character and capacity of different entities, the relationship between them, their relative boundedness, and the associated patterns of rights and responsibilities' (p. 66). For modern society the moral order can be illustrated like this:

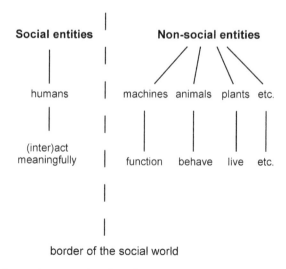

FIGURE 5.1 The modern moral order of representation

With this sharp distinction between social and non-social entities in mind, the relevance of the question whether bots can become social actors becomes quite clear. If they will really be equipped with human-like conversational capabilities and start to act and interact meaningfully like humans do, this would result in nothing less than qualitative changes of the moral order of representation. Hence, it becomes an important task and challenge for sociology to turn towards the new types of non-human characters that leave the laboratories of Artificial Intelligence and start to inhabit online environments. It is not that we should blindly follow the visions of information scientists. Rather, we should start to think about the questions I have posed in the introduction and critically investigate the possibilities but also the limitations of new kinds of 'intelligent' NPCs. To meet this challenge, a new type of sociological research is needed—a type of research that in contrast to traditional analytical approaches is not human-centred and that treats the issue of which entities can become social actors as an open empirical question. The following sections aim to outline such a type of research and develop criteria for being a social actor. Drawing on the competing approach of actor-network theory, I argue for an analytical perspective that is based on Niklas Luhmann's social theory.

2 Being a Social Actor: A Systems Theoretical Approach

While the question of non-human agency has been discussed in science and technology studies (STS) since the 1980s (see Johnson, 1988), this does not apply to traditional sociology. Instead,

> the field of sociological research is restricted, for example, to the social systems constituted by social actions of living human beings (Parsons), to the symbols developed in human interactions (Mead), or to the actions within human social relationships, which constitute social forms (Weber).
>
> *(Lindemann, 2005, p. 69)*

Thus, it is not surprising that most social theories and research methodologies limit their focus to human beings who mutually coordinate their actions with those of others. The social world of sociology is traditionally conceptualized as a human world (see section 1). As a consequence, machines, animals or other entities and their actions are not conventionally subjects of sociological inquiry. However, stemming from the STS discourse, in the last 20 years Actor Network Theory (ANT) in particular tried to overcome this 'anthropological bias' of traditional sociology (see Latour, 2005). ANT rejects the idea that social relations are restricted to human beings. On the contrary, it claims that social relations can emerge between all different kinds of entities, namely when their actions have an effect on the actions of each other. Whereas for good old-fashioned sociology agency is mainly restricted to human intentional individual actors,

ANT 'extends the word actor—or actant—to *non-human, non-individual* entities' (Latour, 1996, p. 369). Following a semiotic definition of 'actant', from the ANT's point of view an actor is just 'something that acts or to which activity is granted by others. It implies *no* special motivation of human individual actors, nor of humans in general' (Latour, 1996, p. 373). Consequently, compared with traditional sociology, ANT invents a modest actor-concept, which is not based on human intentionality.[2] On the one hand, this means, for example, that even a scallop or a door-closer may become an actor in the same way as a fisherman or a scientist does (see Callon, 1986; Johnson, 1988). On the other hand, it opens up the possibility to analyze the processes, 'during which the identity of actors, the possibility of interaction and the margins of manoeuvre are negotiated and delimited' (Callon, 1986, p. 203). As a result of this, at first glance ANT seems to be a reasonable approach to consider for the question whether bots can become social actors.

However, taking a closer look, some problems appear. Along with ANT's modest actor-concept come certain methodological principles which make *open-ended* empirical investigations difficult. Especially the principle of 'generalized symmetry' (see Callon, 1986) matters, since it claims that 'the rule which we must respect is not to change registers when we move from the technical to the social aspects of the problem studied' (Callon, 1986, p. 200). Consequently, the scientific observer has to describe the actions of a scallop or door-closer in the same way as the actions of a human being. Latour and Callon put this as follows: 'Whatever term is used for humans, we will use for non-humans as well' (Callon & Latour, 1992, p. 353).

Considering this methodological principle, my argument is that this claim is difficult, because it does not allow for one to distinguish between different kinds of actions. Thus, the actions of an ECA, a door-closer or a human-being must all look the same. They are indistinguishable. This means that ANT only answers the question of *whether* agency (in a weak sense) can be attributed to certain entities, but not *how* this would be realized. As a consequence, this perspective does not allow one to distinguish between humanlike, social action and other forms of action. However, this is exactly what is necessary to answer the question whether bots can become social actors (in a humanlike way) in an open-ended manner. Accordingly, I need a more sophisticated 'theory of action' which is principally able to reveal differences and asymmetries between the actions of certain entities (see also Suchman, 2007, pp. 268–271). For this, Niklas Luhmann's social theory is a reasonable candidate. On the one hand, Luhmann shares an anti-essentialist conception of the social with ANT. On the other hand, compared with ANT's modest actor-concept, he provides a more sophisticated idea of sociality, which makes it possible to clearly distinguish between social and non-social relationships. Due to these two aspects, his social theory provides a fruitful theoretical framework for the analysis of human-machine encounters, including the possibility of social bots becoming social actors.

Referring to Talcott Parsons and Edward Shils, Luhmann argues that the precondition of sociality is double contingency (see Luhmann, 1995, pp. 103–136). As Parsons & Shils (1951) already claimed, the theorem of double contingency allows distinguishing:

> between objects which interact with the interacting subject and those objects which do not. These interacting objects are themselves actors or egos . . . A potential food object . . . is not an alter because it does not respond to ego's expectations and because it has no expectations of ego's action; another person, a mother or a friend, would be an alter to ego. The treatment of another actor, an alter, as an interacting object has very great consequences for the development and organization of the system of action.
>
> *(pp. 14–15)*

Consequently, in a *social* interaction the participants do not merely react to the visible actions of their counterpart. Furthermore, both interlocutors 'know that both know that one could also act differently' (Vanderstraeten, 2002, p. 77). This complexity in the relation of both interlocutors is the starting point for the emergence of social systems. It allows the sociologist to draw a sharp distinction between social actions and other forms of action based on the presence or absence of a particular kind of expectation. As Parsons and Shils point out, 'it is the fact that expectations operate on both sides of the relation between a given actor and the object of his orientation which distinguishes social interaction from orientation to nonsocial objects' (Parsons & Shils, 1951, p. 15). In accordance with this assumption, Luhmann emphasizes that the analytical decision of whether an action is social or not depends on the complexity of the underlying expectancy structures: 'With double contingency there is a need for . . . complicated expectancy structures that rely heavily on preconditions, namely expectation of expectations' (Luhmann, 1985, p. 26). This means that an action can be treated as 'social' if (from the perspective of a given entity, or rather an 'ego'):

> the behaviour of the other person cannot be expected to be a determinable fact; there is a need to see it in terms of his selectivity, as a choice between various possibilities. This selectivity is, however, dependent on others' structures of expectation. It is necessary, therefore, not simply to be able to expect the behaviour, but also the expectations of others.
>
> *(Luhmann, 1985, p. 26)*

In this sense, social actions only emerge between entities that attribute the expectation of expectations to each other. As a consequence, this perspective allows one to clearly distinguish between social interactions and other kinds of relations between entities, making it possible to reveal differences and asymmetries between the actions of certain entities by using the concepts of double contingency and expectation of expectations.

But what about overcoming the human-centred bias of analysis? At first glance the concept of double contingency could be seen to indicate that only human beings can become social actors. What other beings would be able to develop complex relationships based on the mutual expectation of expectations? Accordingly, Luhmann argues, that it seems to be obvious 'to imagine ego and alter, on both sides, as fully concrete human beings, subjects, individuals or persons' (Luhmann, 1995, p. 107). However, this does not have to be the only possibility. Whereas Parsons and Shils defined sociality as relationships between individuals, Luhmann excludes individuals from social theory. For him, social systems do not consist of individuals but of communication. 'Social systems use communication as their particular mode of autopoietic reproduction. Their elements are communications that are recursively produced and reproduced by a network of communications' (Luhmann, 1990, p. 3). This means that it is not humans or individuals who communicate or act, but that communication reproduces itself by operating one communicative element after another. Crucial for this is the very concept of 'communication' as invented by Luhmann.

Luhmann (1992) defines communication not as a sender–receiver model (like, for instance, the Shannon-Weaver model does), but as 'a synthesis of three different selections, namely, selection of *information*, selection of the *utterance* of this information, and a selective *understanding* . . . of this utterance and its information' (p. 252). Of these, the third one—understanding—is key, because from a Luhmannian perspective 'the synthesis of these selections is generated by the operation of understanding' (Schneider, 2000, p. 130). Accordingly, it is not the sender but the receiver who is crucial for the realization of any communicative acts. For example, if a person A asks another person B: 'Do you know who's going to that meeting?',[3] in a Luhmannian sense no communication takes place. Only if B reacts to this question in a way that shows his or her understanding of the question, communication occurs. In Luhmann's (1992) terms:

> In understanding, communication grasps a distinction between the information value of its content and the reasons for which the content was uttered. It can thereby emphasize one or the other side. It can concern itself more with the information itself or more with the expressive behavior. But it always depends on the fact that *both* are experienced as *selection* and *thereby* distinguished.
>
> *(p. 252)*

Staying with the example, if B answers 'who?', he or she expresses a particular understanding of A's question: The response treats it as presequence of an announcement of a mystery guest, which at the same time means that B expects that A knows who is going to the meeting and wants to surprise B. Likewise, it is also possible that B answers: 'Probably Miss Owen and probably Miss Cadry' to the initial question. In this case, the response treats A's utterance not as announcement but instead as a request for information. In both cases B's reaction displays a particular distinction between the information value of the initial question and the reason for the question so that the three selections information, utterance and understanding are synthesized in different manners. Which of the two reactions fits to A's expectations only becomes clear in a third utterance, namely A's response to B's reaction (which then again needs to be interpreted by B and so forth).

The example shows two things: first, how every next turn in the communication process displays a particular understanding of the preceding turn and thereby realizes the unity of the three selections information, utterance and understanding; secondly, that every next turn can, at the same time, be interpreted as a response to expected expectations. If B answers 'who?', he or she expresses curiosity and in doing so realizes (what he or she thinks to be) an appropriate next action that can be (normatively) expected when someone offers some surprising new information.

Understanding, in this sense, is an operation of observation. It takes place whenever a behaviour is observed not only as predetermined, but as a contingent selection from different possibilities so that an interpretation, and thus the distinction between information and utterance, is needed. The crucial point is that participants in an interaction 'are opaque and incalculable to one another' (Vanderstraeten, 2002, p. 85). This is the reason why utterances need to be interpreted and the distinction between information and utterance needs to be drawn. One consequence of the mutual 'opaqueness' of the interlocutors 'is that communication *is possible only as a self-referential process*' (Luhmann, 1995, p. 143), since communication can no longer be understood as a product of any particular social actor intentionally transmitting messages. Instead it must be understood as a chain of sequentially realized operations which mutually relate to each other. But at the same time communication is not completely independent from the contributions of the participants—be they human or not. Even though the dynamics and structures of social systems cannot be reduced to the intentions, motives or characteristics of the interlocutors, communication is dependent on the mutual perceptions of the participants and the assumptions which they develop about their intentions. Without such assumptions it would not be possible to infer the 'reasons for which the content was uttered' (Luhmann, 1992, p. 252), drawing the distinction between information and utterance and thereby reducing the contingency of the situation.

The question now is how can participants develop expectation of expectations? As Luhmann points out, this is only possible by treating each other as *persons*. But a person, in a Luhmannian sense, is not a concrete single individual (like in everyday understanding). Instead, a person is nothing but 'the name that systems theory employs to describe how humans [or possibly other entities] are *addressed in communication*' (Borch, 2011, p. 47). Hence, a person bundles a complex of expectations, which emerges through attribution in the course of a communication process and serves as a point of contact for further communication (see Luhmann, 1995, p. 210). In his introduction to Luhmann's thinking Christian Borch (2011) exemplifies this idea as follows:

> In other words, the notion of persons refers to expectations that structure communication. Being addressed as a punk, for instance, means being seen as a person to whom certain expectations are attributed (taste of music, clothing, attitudes, etc.). Obviously the same human being can constitute several persons according to the communicative context . . . In one context he or she may be addressed as parent, in another as a politician, in a third as religious believer.
>
> *(p. 47)*

This illustrates that persons, their characteristics and intentions cannot be treated as starting points of social processes. Furthermore, they are communicative constructions, which are 'constituted for the sake of ordering behavioral expectations that can be fulfilled' (Borch, 2011, p. 47) by the people who are treated as persons. Consequently, Luhmann neglects 'every substantialized interpretation of individuals and actors who, as the bearers of specific properties, make possible the formation of social systems' (Luhmann, 1995, p. 108). Instead, in social situations, people observe each other and their behaviour in order to be able to develop 'personalized' expectations of their intentions and possible next actions.[4]

Against this backdrop, the social theory offered by Niklas Luhmann can be interpreted as a post-humanist theory, which does not presuppose that only humans can be social actors. If social actors are not conceptualized as concrete human beings and bearers of specific characteristics, but as constructs of communication, then it is principally possible that ECAs, chat bots or other non-human entities can be treated as social actors during communication processes. The condition for this is that they need to be treated as *persons* who, on the one hand, are free in choice of their behaviour but, on the other, are willing to control it in accordance with personalized expectations.[5] In order to analyze if this is the case, it is necessary to investigate the underlying expectancy structures of human-machine communications. According to Luhmann's theory, these expectancy structures are not mental, but rather communicative. As I have illustrated, they are expressed throughout the process of communication on a turn-to-turn basis. That is, every response to a preceding utterance makes public which expectations were expected. At the same time the response serves as control mechanism, because in the next turn the preceding speaker has the chance to react and correct, if necessary.

From this follows that answering the question whether bots can become social actors requires nothing but the sequential analysis of communication processes and the underlying expectancy structures. These structures constitute subjects, objects and the state of agency, which is attributed to humans as well as to other entities during communication. If, for instance, every input to a machine creates an expected output, a given user of the machine can stabilize simple, but persisting, expectations of the machine's behaviour. At the same time, he or she does not need to assume that the machine has any expectations of his or her behaviour, to which he or she needs to adapt. Accordingly, in such a situation neither the machine nor the user appears as a social actor in a Luhmannian sense. Against this, if machines are treated as entities that have expectations about the behaviour of their counterparts and at the same time orientate their own behaviour on expected expectations of their counterparts, then they need to be described as social actors from a systems theoretical point of view.

But how exactly can empirical analyses investigate communication processes and underlying expectancy structures? Luhmann himself does not offer methodological tools for detailed empirical investigations, so it is not surprising that systems theory is still considered unable to guide empirical research (see Besio & Pronzini, 2008). However, in recent years several authors have discussed possibilities of combining systems theory and empirical research (see Knudsen, 2010; Schneider, 2000; Wolf et al., 2010). In this context, some authors argue for a connection of systems theory and ethnomethodology, because they find similarities in the basic assumptions of both approaches. As Yu Cheng Liu (2012) points out, systems theory and ethnomethodology 'share a common problematic in the constitution of realities' (p. 593), since both provide models for analysis that treat the production of social reality as an interactive process which cannot be reduced to single actors and/or their intentions. Correspondingly, Wolfgang Ludwig Schneider emphasizes that both approaches have a similar understanding of communication. The (only) difference between both approaches is that systems theory argues on a higher level of abstraction and therefore is situated on a pre-empirical level (see Schneider, 2000, p. 130), whereas 'ethnomethodology may be formulated as a practical logic of systems theory' (Liu, 2012, p. 593). This means that systems theory provides a differentiated social theory, which offers strong but abstract analytical concepts like *communication* (as triple selection), *person* or *expectation* (*of expectations*), without giving advice about how to translate these concepts into empirical research. Against this background, ethnomethodology, with its strong empirical tradition, can lend 'its conceptual and methodical instruments to systems theory to bridge the gap between abstract heuristic assumptions and empirical analysis' (Schneider, 2000, p. 139).

Regarding the leading question of this chapter, ethnomethodological membership categorization analysis (MCA) seems to be a particularly reasonable candidate for connection with systems theory, since MCA is explicitly interested in the interactive use of personal categories during interactions. Against this backdrop, I propose to combine the outlined social-theoretical considerations with MCA in order to develop a methodology for symmetrical and open-ended empirical analyses of the (changing) human-machine relationship in online environments.

3 Membership Categorization Analysis: An Empirical Approach for Analyzing the Communicative Construction of Social Actors

As the term suggests, the main emphasis of MCA lies on the use of membership categorizations during interactions. Such 'membership categories . . . are classifications or social types that may be used to describe persons' (Hester & Eglin, 1997, p. 3). These descriptions of persons cannot merely be found some of the time and therefore be treated as one interesting research topic amongst others. Rather, they are indispensable 'resources that participants use in interaction with other participants' (Gafaranga, 2001, p. 1913) in order to develop expectations of their (expected) possible next actions and therefore be able to mutually coordinate their actions. Subsequently, MCA scholars assume that participants in interactions principally need to categorize their counterparts in order to be able to create expectations of their activities, motives and characteristics. Accordingly, people's activities are always interpreted as 'category-bound activities', which allow for classification (or rather expectation) of their (possible next) actions. Otherwise it would not be possible to understand the meaning of each other's actions.

In this sense, from a MCA point of view—like in systems theory—'identity or role is not a fixed feature of interactants' (Housley & Fitzgerald, 2002, p. 63). Rather, identities are just as in systems theory conceptualized as products of categorization processes or rather 'identities-for-interaction' (see Stokoe, 2012, p. 278), which emerge in the course of interaction and are used as resources that allow developing expectations about the behaviour and expectations of the categorized persons. In other words, membership categories make it possible that 'conventional knowledge about the behavior of people so categorized can be invoked or cited to interpret or explain the actions of that person' (Hutchby & Wooffitt, 2009, p. 36). This means, in accordance with Luhmann's considerations, that MCA does not treat social actors as starting point or explanatory 'resource' for social phenomena but as 'turn generated categories' (see Fitzgerald & Housley, 2002, p. 581), which emerge in the course of interaction and therefore are products of everyday interaction processes. That is, membership categories can change during interaction processes. If, for example, a person who at the beginning of a conversation was treated as a 'punk' due to his or her fashion style, appears to know much about composers of classical European music of the early nineteenth century, the same person can be categorized as 'Beethoven expert' in the further course of the interaction.

Hence, the similarities to Luhmann's theorization of social actors, or rather persons, who only exist as a complex of expectations within communication processes become quite obvious. The difference between Luhmann's social theoretical considerations and MCA is that the latter does not remain on a preempirical theoretical level but develops concrete analytical concepts that guide empirical analyses. Conversely, MCA is lacking fundamental social theoretical concepts such as the theorem of double contingency. Furthermore it is explicitly restricted to the analysis of *human* interactions, since membership categories are clearly defined as descriptions of persons, which means humans not robots or machines. Accordingly, MCA takes human beings as (the only) unquestioned social actors and investigates how they categorize themselves and each other in ongoing interactions. This means that up to now MCA has not shown any interest in analyses that try to distinguish between social interaction and other kinds of relations between entities. Here MCA can profit from Luhmann's abstract social-theoretical considerations. Combining both approaches enables the investigation of changing human-machine relations in online environments. In order to illustrate this, I will now present key concepts of MCA and then argue for a de-anthropologization of these concepts.

For MCA, three concepts are key: (1) membership categories, (2) membership categorization devices and (3) category-bound activities. As already mentioned, *membership categories*, 'are classifications or social types that may be used to *describe persons* [emphasis added]' (Hester & Eglin, 1997, p. 3). Corresponding membership categories may be 'sister', 'husband', 'colleague', 'boss', 'scientist', 'football player' or 'musician'. Different kinds of categories trigger certain expectations of properties, typical activities and expectations of the categorized persons. If we talk to our sister, we might expect an informal, warm greeting and her willingness to listen to our personal problems. However, at least in Western cultures, we would not expect the same from our colleagues or our boss. This demonstrates the way in which membership categories structure expectations and the course of interactions. Building on the concept of membership categories, the notion of membership categorization devices (MCDs) underscores that certain categories may be linked together to form classes or collections. This idea

> refers to the fact that, in the locally occasioned settings of their occurrence, some membership categories can be used and heard commonsensically as 'going together', whilst others cannot be so used and heard, For example, the collection or MCD 'family' may be so heard to include such membership categories as 'mother', 'father', 'son', 'daughter', 'uncle', 'aunt', etc., and to exclude 'trumpet player', 'dog', 'marxist feminist' and 'Caucasian'.
>
> *(Hester & Eglin, 1997, p. 4)*

As already indicated, membership categories are inseparably connected with expectations of particular activities. We expect our sister to listen to our personal problems, but we do not expect her to apply for the same job as we do. With our colleagues it is probably the other way around. In this context, Harvey Sacks introduces the term 'category bound activities', 'which are those *activities that are expectably and properly done by persons who are the incumbents of particular categories* [emphasis added]' (Hester & Eglin, 1997, p. 5).

Even if membership categories are clearly defined as descriptions of human beings, my argument is that it is possible to reformulate the distinction between humans and non-humans (or rather social and non-social actors) on the basis of the analytical concepts mentioned earlier. Thus, it becomes feasible to avoid the anthropological restrictions of MCA and to use its analytical tools for analyses of human-machine encounters in online environments. In order to do so it is essential to remember that membership categorizations are not the same as essential properties of the persons being categorized. Instead—similar to Luhmann's definition of a person as complex of expectations (see section 2)—they are *attributions* that occur during interaction processes and (potentially) underlie transformations over time. Hence, categorizations and their connection to particular activities are always contingent and not determined. As Sally Hester and Stephen Hester (2012) put it, 'categories are always 'categories in context' and this means that the task for MCA is to discover how collections, categories and predicates are used on the occasions of their occurrence rather than presuming their stable cultural meanings' (p. 566). Thus, membership categories are products of everyday interaction processes and not stable properties of humans or other entities. From this it follows that categorizations and category-bound activities, which belong to particular membership categories or MCDs, always underlie transformations depending on the situated contexts of their use (see Hester & Hester, 2012). Hence, they may also underlie (long-term) transformations rendering it principally possible that entities other than humans can be classified as social actors. This allows one to ease the restrictive equation 'social actor = human being' and to re-evaluate the distinction between humans and machines in terms of Steve Woolgar (1990) as a historically instituted distinction according to a particular and contingent moral order of representation, which may change with the increased occurrence of social robots and ECAs. From my point of view, in terms of MCA the present moral order of representation and the separation of humans and machines can be analysed as a distinction between two different kinds of membership categorization devices, which collect different membership categories. Robots, ECAs and computers belong to the non-social device 'machines', which itself is part of the collection 'non-social entities', whereas children, adults, technicians, scientists and so on belong to the device 'humans', which is used synonymously with the collection 'social entities'.

Along with the different MCD affiliation come different expectations regarding the typical activities of humans, machines and other entities respectively. These differences can be analysed with reference to the concept of double contingency, which allows a distinction to be made between social and non-social relations/actors (see section 2). With regard to machines, this means that traditionally they are neither expected to act in an undetermined manner nor to have an expectation of the expectations of others; instead, they are expected to function. Consequently, in terms of the analytical concepts of MCA, the modern moral order of representation can be displayed as shown in Figure 5.2.

According to this consideration, today only human beings belong to the MCD 'social entities'. They are treated differently to machines and other non-human

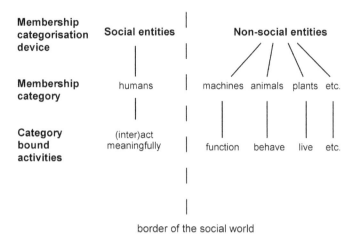

FIGURE 5.2 The modern 'moral order of representation' in terms of MCA

entities because they interact with each other and develop expectations of each other's expectations. But there is no reason why this should not change if machines attain the capability to 'interact meaningfully with humans' (Morie et al., 2012, p. 100).[6] Typical activities, which to date are limited to human beings, may then expectably and properly also be performed by robots and ECAs.[7] Therefore, it should be both possible and reasonable to apply the methodological concepts of MCA not only to human interactions but also to human-*machine* interactions.

If membership categories are not essential properties of entities but turn-generated categories, then it should be possible to observe whether and how agency or personal categorizations are attributed to non-human beings during encounters between humans and machines in online environments and elsewhere. When studying these kinds of encounters, it is sufficient to follow ongoing interactions in order to analyse whether and how personal categorizations occur in their course as turn-generated categories. It is exactly this kind of methodology that allows one to treat which entities become social actors for each other as an open-ended empirical question. The leading empirical question is then whether 'interacting' and 'expecting expectations' are attributable to robots or ECAs. If this is the case, one may conclude that significant transformations regarding the realm of the social are taking place, because the human/machine difference as one of the demarcation lines between social and non-social actors becomes fragile.

4 Can Bots become Social Actors? An Exemplary Empirical Analysis

Building on the theoretical and methodological considerations, in this section I will present an analysis of a human-machine encounter in the virtual world Second Life, which reveals the flow of membership categorizations and underlying expectancy structures. In this example, there is one human-driven avatar that is called Tim and one agent-driven avatar whose name is Max. The original conversation was held in German and was recorded in the context of my Ph.D. research. I have translated it into English for the purpose of this chapter. I will analyse the transcript sequentially in six steps to show how the social system emerges, reproduces itself and thereby creates changeable membership categories as turn-generated categories. The first extract starts after the avatars already have exchanged greetings.

Extract 1: Tim's Age

1 *Max:*   How old is your Avatar?
2 *Tim:*   19

At a first glance, nothing remarkable happens during the first two turns. Max asks Tim how old his avatar is and Tim replies '19'. But in the light of the theoretical and methodological considerations in sections 2 and 3 a closer look is warranted. Such a look allows us to observe how a social system and its expectancy structures emerge through the connection of communicative elements. From the viewpoint of systems theory, the social system reproduces itself in the moment Tim utters '19' in line 2, since the utterance recursively observes Max's question as a question, which makes an adequate response expectable. In a fundamental way, Tim's answer realizes the third selection 'understanding' of a communicative element 'that observes a preceding event as an utterance selected in order to convey specific information' (Schneider, 2000, p. 131), namely information about the age of his avatar.

By answering, Tim presents himself as a social actor who is able to expect the expectations of others and act in accordance with these expected expectations. Simultaneously, his answer carries the information that he perceives his counterpart, Max, to be a social actor, too. Otherwise it would not make sense to answer and consequently make his behaviour dependent on the behaviour of the other. Hence, up to this point both Max and Tim appear as unquestioned social actors who interact on the basis of expectation of expectation and therefore belong to the membership categorization device 'social beings'. Starting from this point, I will now take a look at the following two turns:

Extract 2: Max is Guessing

3 *Max:*   I'd have thought you're a year older!
4 *Tim:*   oh ok

In the third turn, Max reacts to Tim's answer and comments that he had assumed his interlocutor was one year older. With this reaction he confirms that Tim principally responded in accordance with his expectations. His utterance indicates that he didn't know Tim's age and really wanted to know it. At the same time, regarding the content of the answer, his reaction shows surprise. It is true he expected an answer regarding Tim's age, but obviously he expected not that answer, but a different one, namely '20' instead of '19'.

For some reasons, this contribution itself seems to be surprising. First, the difference between an age of 19 and an age of 20 is relatively small, so that it is hardly to be expected that Max assumed Tim's age to be exactly 20, especially as they did not know each other before. Second, there is no clue as to why Max had guessed Tim to be one year older, because the appearance of the avatars in Second Life can be created and altered arbitrarily (see Boellstorff, 2008, p. 129f). Accordingly, there is no evidence to infer from the avatar's appearance to his age. Against this backdrop, Tim's response in line 4 seems comprehensible. By responding with 'oh ok' he expresses his astonishment. The utterance reveals that he has no idea why Max guessed him to be one year older, and therefore qualifies his assessment as non-intuitive. In terms of the theorem of double contingency it becomes obvious that Max breached the expectancy structure, which was established up to this point. Tim did not expect Max to expect him to be exactly 20 years old. Consequently, Max's behaviour does not fit with Tim's expectation of expectations, which Tim then indicates with his response. In such a case an explanation for the surprising contribution would be expected from a social being who controls his actions from the perspective of his alter ego (see Vanderstraeten, 2002, p. 86). But something else happens:

Extract 3: A Praise

5 *Max:*   you really have a fine grasp

Instead of explaining his guessing in order to make it accountable for his interlocutor, Max praises Tim for his fine grasp. Within the given context, this contribution hardly makes sense. Coherently, Tim's 'oh ok' must be interpreted as an expression of surprise, in which case why Max praises Tim's grasp barely seems understandable. But if one looks just at the isolated adjacency pair 'oh ok' followed by 'you really have a fine grasp', it would be possible to imagine a dialogue in which the sequence makes sense, for example in an educational context. Within such a context, 'oh ok' could express that Tim just understood something new, so that his teacher compliments him on his comprehension. However, within the context of the present dialogue 'oh ok' in line 4 definitely does not express Tim's comprehension, but rather his surprise because he obviously has no idea why Max assumed he was older. This means that Max has repeatedly breached the expectations that were expressed by Tim's contributions.

In this context, Harold Garfinkel's so-called 'breaching experiments' may come to the reader's mind, in which he deliberately violated everyday expectations to investigate the meaning of such expectations for the organization of interaction (see Garfinkel, 1967). In the present case, it is Max who infracts the expectations. Against this backdrop, Max increasingly appears either as an experimenter whose category-bound activities are to intentionally breach everyday expectations or as someone who probably is not able to fulfil these expectations. From the social-theoretical and methodological perspective that was developed above, how Max's activities will be categorized in the following sequences is of interest. The question is to which kind of membership category his activities will be attributed.

Extract 4: A Joke or Not

6 *Tim:*   How old are you?
7 *Max:*   The first time I started running was back in ninety-nine. It isn't possible for everybody to be 19 years old, is it?
8 *Tim:*   loool
9 *Max:*   There are so many words—why don't you use some more?

The extract starts with Tim now asking Max about his age in line 6, indicating his enduring acceptance of Max as a social being. Max's answer gives a subtle hint regarding his machine identity, when he announces that he 'started running in ninety-nine'. However, Tim doesn't treat this as a 'real' answer, but as a joke. Accordingly, in line 8 he writes 'loool', which in chat slang expresses that he is laughing. That is to say, the connection of utterances from lines 6 to 8 produces a joke sequence with Tim as joke-recipient, who by laughing signals his understanding of Max's utterance as a joke.

So far, so good—but Max's next turn once more does not fit to the preceding utterances because it does not treat Tim's 'loool' as laughter, which closes a joke sequence. Instead, it negatively treats Tim's response as a taciturn reply, so that once more everyday expectations of appropriate behaviour in interactions are breached.

Even though the ineptitude of his utterances was up to now not articulated explicitly, the following extract shows the breakdown of social expectations. The subjects in Garfinkel's experiments reacted in a frustrated and confused way. Tim, however, responds unemotionally. Subsequent to Max' utterance 'There are so many words—why don't you use some more?' he starts a kind of experiment on his part:

Extract 5: Bracketsclose

10 *Tim:*   bracketsclose
11 *Max:*   Is it a Yes or No?
12 *Tim:*   yes
13 *Max:*   it's always good to come to an agreement.

14 *Tim:*   bracketsclose
15 *Max:*   What's your point?
16 *Tim:*   bracketsclose

By repeating 'bracketsclose' three times, Tim leaves the realm of socially expected behaviour as well. What he is doing might best be described as a kind of 'Turing Test' (see Turing, 1964). He checks whether his own senseless and identical utterances in turn lead to predictable repetitive utterances from Max. In doing so, he tries to receive an indication of the mechanical or social nature of his dialogue partner. Thus, Tim does not align his own activities according to the expectation of expectations anymore. Following Luhmann, the assumption that your counterpart is able to select between various possibilities is a premise for expectation of expectations (see section 2). Keeping this in mind, it becomes clear that in the given situation Tim tries to find out whether his interlocutor really acts on the basis of double contingency or rather in a determined way like a trivial machine. Accordingly, he is testing whether a certain input from him leads to a clearly expectable output from his dialogue partner. This means that he questions Max's status as social actor who expects expectations, orientates his own behaviour on these expected expectations, and therefore belongs to the MCD 'social being'. Obviously, Max's repeated inappropriate utterances can hardly be interpreted as category-bound activities of a social actor any longer, so that this status becomes disputable. However, this does not need to be permanent, as the last extract shows:

Extract 6: An Apology

17 *Max:*   if you say that again, I'll know it by heart.
18 *Tim:*   nothing sorry

As a response to the last 'bracketsclose'-utterance in line 16, Max answers 'If you say that again, I'll know it by heart', which leads to Tim's apology 'nothing sorry'. Due to the apology, the structure of the conversation is transformed in a decisive way. Whereas Tim was carrying out a Turing Test in the preceding extract, the test has now come to its end and the communication process returns to a situation of double contingency. Tim apologizes for the test and, by doing so, returns to treating his counterpart as a social actor with social expectations. His apology only makes sense if he assumes that Max expects not to be treated as a machine. Accordingly, in this sequence the reproduction of social expectations restarts, so that both Tim and Max again appear as social actors with corresponding category-bound activities. But as this can change rapidly, the status of the involved entities may change from turn to turn. Due to the 'virtual contingency' of the situation, from the perspective of the participants it is hard to come to a definitive conclusion on whether they are talking to social entities or to mechanical machines.

In the presented example Max's status remains undecided and ambiguous. But this is not always the case. As my own empirical research has shown (see Muhle, 2013), being able to recognize a virtual counterpart as a bot notably depends on the experiences of users with these entities. In some cases, Max's dialogue partners at no point in the conversation suspected him of being a bot. In other cases they saw through his masquerade very quickly and suddenly broke off the conversation. But what all cases I investigated had in common was that Max repeatedly breached the rules of expectable behaviour, making it almost impossible to reliably interpret his activities as bound to a membership category that coincides with ordinary expectations in everyday interaction. As a consequence, conversations with Max are anything but satisfying—not because he repeats the same expectable behaviour again and again like a trivial machine, but because his utterances are somehow unexpected and often do not meet the pragmatic contexts of given situations. By observing this behaviour some people realize he is a bot, while others perceive him as mentally disturbed or simply as an internet troll. This convincingly shows that communication always produces its own actors, which do not necessarily have to match the ontological status of the entities that are participating in the communication.

5   Closing Remarks

This chapter was guided by three questions. How does the appearance of chatbots and ECAs affect interaction in virtual worlds? Can bots become social actors? How can we find answers?

Regarding the first question, the introductory episode from Tom Boellstorff's ethnography, as well as my own empirical example, shows that the users of online environments are systematically confronted with a special kind of virtual contingency. That is, they do not know who the person is that controls the virtual counterpart. They do not even know if a human being or a bot controls this counterpart. Consequently, users (need to) develop strategies to deal with this contingency and to be able to categorize their virtual counterpart. As I have shown in section 4, one strategy might be to apply a kind of Turing Test if the contributions of the virtual counterpart arouse suspicion, but other methods are conceivable and can be found in empirical data (see Muhle, 2013). As my analysis shows, it is not easy to attain certainty about the 'ontological status' of the interlocutor, so that a swapping between different states of agency seems to be characteristic for the status ascribed to 'intelligent' machines today. They are neither traditional, trivial machines nor social actors which behave in a human-like way as the analysis of human-machine encounters reveals. It demonstrates how social actors and technological artefacts, as well as the differences and asymmetries between them, are produced during communication processes—not as given and stable entities, but in the form of turn-generated categories as *effects* of such communication processes.

What does this mean for the question whether bots can become social actors (in a human-like way)? In light of my analysis, bots today can be best described as 'hybrids', who/which alternate between the realms (or: MCDs) of 'social entities' and 'non-social entities'. They are by no means social actors in a generally valid way. But what about the future? On the one hand, we need to be sceptical as to whether the developer's idea of human-like agency and sociality of machines (see section 1) can live up to its promise. There is currently no reason to assume that 'social bots' will become part of society in a similar manner as human beings. What even sophisticated ECAs are still lacking is the capability to participate in *situated (inter-)actions* (see Suchman, 2007) and therefore to act permanently in accordance with the expectation of expectations—with significant consequences for the flow of communication and corresponding attributions of social agency. On the other hand, there is no doubt that in the near future 'intelligent' machines and interfaces will increasingly become part of everyday life. This will change the conditions of the human-machine relationship in an unforeseeable manner. Consequently, 'social bots' and online environments as test beds for a mixed society definitely are an interesting and important field for sociological research.

But the question of robotic agency is not restricted to virtual worlds and online games. In recent years different types of 'socialbots' massively infiltrated social networks like Twitter, in order to simulate human behaviour—for example, to influence public opinion (see Graham & Ackland, chapter 10 in this book; Ratkiewicz et al., 2011). This means that the problem of virtual contingency entered the whole online sphere. Whereas most scientific approaches that aim to expose these socialbots (somewhat ironically) use *automatic* methods for bot detection (see Ferrara et al., 2014), I have tried to develop a sociological toolkit for open-ended empirical analyses that consider with non-human social agency and the problem of virtual contingency. This toolkit is not suitable for the analysis of huge amounts of data. But it offers a way to analyse in detail *how* online users (be they gamers or Twitter users) in situ deal with the problem of virtual contingency. Additionally, it can also be used as an instrument to investigate the concepts used by programmers who either create social bots or try to detect them. For instance, if programmers try to create an automated Twitter account or—the other way around—to determine the likelihood of Twitter accounts being run by a bot, they necessarily need to develop categories that allow classifying tweets as produced either by humans or by bots. Graham & Ackland's chapter in this book (chapter 10) on the role of socialbots in promoting deliberative democracy exemplifies this in a reflexive manner. The authors explicitly define characteristics of 'good' and 'bad' socialbots (membership categories) and their respective activities (category-bound activities), in order to develop socialbots that appear not only as human beings but also adopt the role of 'good citizens'.[8]

Hence, in terms of MCA, defining principles for the development of any kind of bots, like Graham and Ackland do, necessarily comes along with inscribing particular understandings of membership categories (e.g., human versus bot;

good bots versus bad bots) and category-bound activities (e.g., regularly writing new tweets versus mainly repeating similar tweets; supporting consent versus manipulating opinion) into the program code. With the proposed tools of MCA these inscriptions can be analysed and reflected. That is, the toolkit can be applied to different kinds of empirical data and allows investigating how the borders between humans and technology, or rather, social and non-social entities are constantly shaped, negotiated and (re-)configured.

Notes

1. It is not only computer games and virtual worlds that are increasingly inhabited by non-humans. Computer scientists have also started to implement so-called socialbots into social networks like Twitter and Facebook. These socialbots use their own accounts and simulate human behaviour (see in this volume Bakardjieva, Chapter 11; Gehl and Bakardjieva, Chapter 1; Graham and Ackland, Chapter 10).
2. Against this, according to traditional sociologist Max Weber (1978, p. 4), 'we shall speak of "action" [only] insofar as the acting individual attaches a subjective meaning to his behavior'. Additionally, in Weber's terms an action only becomes 'social', 'insofar as its subjective meaning takes account of the behavior of others and is thereby oriented in its course' (Weber, 1978, p. 4). That is, Weber's concept of social agency is much more demanding as compared with ANT.
3. The example is taken from Schegloff (1988) and can also be found in Schneider (2000).
4. This idea fits in very well with the concept of 'virtual contingency' and the episode from Boellstorff's ethnography in Second Life, which was quoted in the introduction. When interacting with others, the inhabitants of SL are compelled to observe and assess the activities of their virtual counterparts in order to establish whether they are human or robotic in nature. By no means can they access the 'real' intentions or ontological status of their counterpart. If they are not able to generate sufficient certainty, they obviously need to ask, in order to be able to categorize their counterpart and develop adequate expectations of their characteristics and range of possible behaviour.
5. For instance, a guy who is addressed as punk in communication processes should behave like a punk and not like an altar server. This does not mean that he couldn't behave differently, but behaving like an altar server would disappoint the expectations addressed to a punk.
6. In terms of systems theory, 'interacting meaningfully' would mean to draw the distinction between information and utterance, and behave on the basis of expectation of expectations (see section 2).
7. See Graham and Ackland (Chapter 10), who define design-principles for socialbots that appear as 'citizens' promoting deliberative democracy in social media.
8. For this, according to Graham and Ackland, socialbots must not only 'conduct themselves in a manner that makes them appear sufficiently "human"' (Chapter 10, p. 197). Moreover, to do 'social good' in a political context, they have to promote deliberative democracy, present themselves as politically moderate and act in order to build 'bridges between separate, ideologically homogeneous subnetworks' (p. 198). Against this, 'socially bad' bots are defined as those, who are intended to 'steer online opinion and conversation towards particular directions' (p. 203) and, in doing so, potentially contribute to 'the advent of *political* filter bubbles' (p. 191).

References

Afonso, N., & Prada, R. (2009). Agents that relate: Improving the social believability of non-player characters in role-playing games. In S. M. Stevens & S. J. Saldamarco (Eds.), *Lecture notes in computer science: Entertainment computing—ICEC 2008* (pp. 34–45). Berlin, Heidelberg: Springer Berlin Heidelberg.

Bakardjieva, M. (2016). Rationalizing sociality: An unfinished script for socialbots. In R. W. Gehl & M. Bakardjieva (Eds.), *Socialbots and their friends: Digital media and the automation of sociality* (pp. 207–229). New York: Routledge.

Besio, C., & Pronzini, A. (2008). Niklas Luhmann as an empirical sociologist: Methodological implications of the system theory of society. *Cybernetics & Human Knowing, 15*(2), 9–31.

Boellstorff, T. (2008). *Coming of age in second life: An anthropologist explores the virtually human.* Princeton, NJ: Princeton University Press.

Borch, C. (2011). *Niklas Luhmann.* London: Routledge.

Callon, M. (1986). Some elements of a sociology of translation: Domestication of the scallops and the fishermen of St Brieuc Bay. In J. Law (Ed.), *Power, action and belief: A new sociology of knowledge?* (pp. 196–223). London: Routledge & Kegan Paul.

Callon, M., & Latour, B. (1992). Don't throw the baby out with the bath school!: A reply to Collins and Yearley. In A. Pickering (Ed.), *Science as practice and culture* (pp. 343–368). Chicago: Chicago University Press.

Esposito, E. (1993). Der Computer als Medium und Maschine. *Zeitschrift für Soziologie, 5*, 338–354.

Ferrara, E., Varol, O., Davis, C. A., Menczer, F., & Flammini, A. (2014). The rise of social bots. *arXiv preprint arXiv:1407.5225.*

Fitzgerald, R., & Housley, W. (2002). Identity, categorization and sequential organization: The sequential and categorical flow of identity in a radio phone-in. *Discourse Society, 13*(5), 579–602.

Gafaranga, J. (2001). Linguistic identities in talk-in-interaction: Order in bilingual conversation. *Journal of Pragmatics, 33*(12), 1901–1925.

Garfinkel, H. (1967). *Studies in ethnomethodology.* Englewood Cliffs, NJ: Prentice-Hall.

Gehl, R. W., & Bakardjieva, M. (2016). Socialbots and their friends. In R. W. Gehl & M. Bakardjieva (Eds.), *Socialbots and their friends: Digital media and the automation of sociality* (pp. 1–16). New York: Routledge.

Graham, T., & Ackland, R. (2016). Do socialbots dream of popping the filter bubble? The role of socialbots in promoting deliberative democracy in social media. In R. W. Gehl & M. Bakardjieva (Eds.), *Socialbots and their friends: Digital media and the automation of sociality* (pp. 187–206). New York: Routledge.

Hester, S., & Eglin, P. (1997). Membership categorization analysis: An introduction. In S. Hester & P. Eglin (Eds.), *Studies in ethnomethodology and conversation analysis: Vol. 4. Culture in action: Studies in membership categorization analysis* (pp. 1–23). Washington, DC: International Institute for Ethnomethodology and Conversation Analysis & University Press of America.

Hester, S., & Hester, S. (2012). Categorical occasionality and transformation: Analyzing culture in action. *Human Studies, 35*(4), 563–581.

Housley, W., & Fitzgerald, R. (2002). The reconsidered model of membership categorization analysis. *Qualitative Research, 2*(1), 59–83.

Hutchby, I., & Wooffitt, R. (2009). *Conversation analysis.* Cambridge [u.a.]: Polity.

Ijaz, K., Bogdanovych, A., & Simoff, S. (2011). Enhancing the believability of embodied conversational agents through environment- , self- and interaction-awareness. In Mark Reynolds (ed) *Proceedings of the thirty-fourth Australasian computer science conference*, Australian Computer Society, Inc. Darlinghurst, Australia (pp. 107–116).

Johnson, J. (1988). Mixing humans and nonhumans together: The sociology of a door-closer. *Social Problems, 35*(3), 298–310.

Knudsen, M. (2010). Surprised by method—Functional method and systems theory. *Forum Qualitative Sozialforschung / Forum: Qualitative Social Research; Vol 11, No 3 (2010): Methods for Qualitative Management Research in the Context of Social Systems Thinking.* Retrieved from http://www.qualitative-research.net/index.php/fqs/article/view/1556

Latour, B. (1996). On actor-network theory: A few clarifications. *Soziale Welt, 47*(4), 369–381.

Latour, B. (2005). *Reassembling the social: An introduction to actor network theory.* Oxford: Oxford University Press.

Lindemann, G. (2005). The analysis of the borders of the social world: A challenge for sociological theory. *Journal for the Theory of Social Behaviour, 35*(1), 69–98.

Liu, Y. C. (2012). Ethnomethodology reconsidered: The practical logic of social systems theory. *Current Sociology, 60*(5), 581–598.

Luhmann, N. (1985). *A sociological theory of law. International library of sociology.* London: Routledge & Paul.

Luhmann, N. (1990). The autopoiesis of social systems. In *Essays on self-reference* (pp. 1–20). New York: Columbia University Press.

Luhmann, N. (1992). What is communication? *Communication Theory, 2*(3), 251–259.

Luhmann, N. (1995). *Social systems.* Stanford: Stanford University Press.

Morie, J. F., Chance, E., Haynes, K., & Rajpurohit, D. (2012). Embodied conversational agent avatars in virtual worlds: Making today's immersive environments more responsive to participants. In P. Hingston (Ed.), *Believable bots* (pp. 99–118). Berlin, Heidelberg: Springer Berlin Heidelberg.

Muhle, F. (2013). *Grenzen der Akteursfähigkeit: Die Beteiligung 'verkörperter Agenten' an virtuellen Kommunikationsprozessen.* Wiesbaden: Springer VS.

Parsons, T., & Shils, E. A. (1951). *Toward a general theory of action.* New York: Harper and Row.

Ratkiewicz, J., Conover, M., Meiss, M., Goncalves, B., Flammini, A., & Menczer, F. (2011). *Detecting and Tracking Political Abuse in Social Media.* Retrieved from http://www.aaai. org/ocs/index.php/ICWSM/ICWSM11/paper/view/2850

Schegloff, E. A. (1988). Presequences and indirection: Applying speech act theory to ordinary conversation. *Journal of Pragmatics, 12*(1), 55–62.

Schneider, W. L. (2000). The sequential production of social acts in conversation. *Human Studies, 23*(2), 123–144.

Stokoe, E. (2012). Moving forward with membership categorization analysis: Methods for systematic analysis. *Discourse Studies, 14*(3), 277–303.

Suchman, L. A. (2007). *Human-machine reconfigurations: Plans and situated actions* (2nd ed.). Cambridge: Cambridge University Press.

Turing, A. (1964). Computing machinery and intelligence. In A. R. Anderson (Ed.), *Minds and machines* (pp. 4–30). New York: Englewood Cliffs.

Vanderstraeten, R. (2002). Parsons, Luhmann and the theorem of double contingency. *Journal of Classical Sociology, 2*(1), 77–92.

Weber, M. (1978). *Economy and society: An outline of interpretive sociology* (G. Roth & C. Wittich, Eds.). Berkeley: University of California Press.

Wolf, P., Meissner, J. O., Nolan, T., Lemon, M., John, R., Baralou, E., & Seemann, S. (2010). Methods for qualitative management research in the context of social systems thinking. *Forum Qualitative Sozialforschung / Forum: Qualitative Social Research; Vol 11, No 3 (2010): Methods for Qualitative Management Research in the Context of Social Systems Thinking.* Retrieved from http://www.qualitative-research.net/index.php/fqs/article/view/1548/3055

Woolgar, S. (1990). Configuring the user: The case of usability trials. *The Sociological Review, 38*(S1), 58–99.

6

CONTESTED PLAY

The Culture and Politics of Reddit Bots

Adrienne L. Massanari

How can bots (software robots) reflect a community's culture and sense of play? What makes for a good bot citizen? This chapter considers the politics and culture of bots on Reddit.com (hereafter, Reddit). Reddit is an open-source social news and link-sharing platform where anyone can create communities of interest, called subreddits. The ability of community members (Redditors) to upvote content they feel is contributory or worthwhile makes Reddit a unique social media platform. Upvotes function as a way for a comment or posting to be made more visible to other Redditors. Likewise, Redditors can downvote, and thus make less visible, material they believe does not contribute positively or that they disagree with (although the latter is against the site's informal rule system, which is called Reddiquette) ('Reddiquette—reddit.com', 2015). A system of points, called karma, indicates the relative number of upvotes minus downvotes (plus a fuzz factor to discourage manipulation), and suggests how worthwhile other Redditors consider a given posting or account's contributions to the community (Salihefendic, 2010). Bots serve a multitude of functions on the site, and often reflect the community's humour and relationship to geek/hacker culture. As both welcome and contested actors on the platform they have important ramifications for the site's discourse.

I first became aware of bots on Reddit after I embarked on a three-year ethnographic exploration of the site (Massanari, 2015). My interest piqued after I noticed an unusual case of an individual performing as a bot in the /r/Advice-Animals[1] subreddit (dedicated to sharing and discussing posts of image macros). One of the more popular and active /r/AdviceAnimals bots (/u/CaptionBot) posts the text that accompanies an image macro in case the site hosting the image goes down or is blocked by a corporate firewall. CaptionBot has garnered a significant amount of karma over time, presumably demonstrating its value to other Redditors. In 2013, a novelty account (/u/CationBot) started parodying CaptionBot. Instead of transcribing the text verbatim, CationBot would post commentary in the format of CaptionBot. For example, an 'uncomfortable situation seal' post was transcribed by CaptionBot thusly:

Uncomfortable Situation Seal

*   BARBER ASKS WHO LAST CUT MY HAIR BECAUSE 'THEY DID QUITE A SHITTY JOB'
*   IT WAS HIM

(CaptionBot, 2014).

CationBot responded to the same image macro with the following text, in a direct imitation of CaptionBot's trademark style:

Squeamish Seal

*   BEEN TELLING THE SAME JOKE TO MY REPEAT CUSTOMER AT MY BARBER SHOP FOR THE PAST 5 YEARS
*   HE STILL DOESN'T GET IT.

These cations aren't guaranteed to be correct (CationBot, 2014).

Here CationBot is inviting other Redditors to watch its multifaceted, playful performance. First, because CationBot's contributions mirror CaptionBot's style of posting, both in terms of content and design, CationBot's author is reaffirming and playing with Taina Bucher's (2014) argument regarding *botness*, or, 'the belief that bots possess distinct personalities or personas that are specific to algorithms'. Second, the bot's author is implicitly acknowledging her audience: Reddit's role as a hub for geek/technology/maker culture and carnivalesque spirit (Bakhtin, 1984) means that this kind of metahumour and bot play is welcome on the platform. Third, CationBot's humour functions as a way of delineating those who are long-time readers of /r/AdviceAnimals posts from those who aren't. The joke is funnier if read quickly—if CationBot somehow represents a self-aware version of CaptionBot.

In replicating CaptionBot's posting style, CationBot engages in a performance of play and encourages Redditors to consider the ways in which bots act as active social agents on the platform. CationBot rarely breaks character to expose itself as human; during one such moment, CationBot discussed some financial issues they were having as a result of the RedditGifts marketplace shutting down. Redditors responded by suggesting that 'today, the bot cried', asking if this was a part of the Voigt-Kampf assessment from *Blade Runner*, and arguing that it meant CationBot had finally passed the Turing Test (CationBot, 2015). Such performance of play suggests that both the bot's author, and the Reddit audience, is in on the joke.

While the case of CationBot is interesting in-and-of-itself, at one point CaptionBot posted its own image macro to /r/AdviceAnimals suggesting that it was actually a human (not a bot) merely transcribing the text on images by hand to gain karma (CaptionBot, 2013). Responses to CaptionBot's revelation were met with Reddit's trademark geek sensibility, with comments humorously suggesting that this confession proved the existence of Skynet (the self-aware artificial intelligence network from the *Terminator* films), while others suggesting they still did not know whether or not this meant that CaptionBot was indeed a bot, or merely a human pretending to be a bot. It is this kind of 'Reddit botness' that I want to consider: both the ways in which humans and bots coexist and collectively create community on Reddit, and the unique nature of Reddit as a community that may determine the kinds of bots that flourish on the platform.

In this chapter, I explore the liminal nature of bots on Reddit and how they are both welcome and contested participants. First, I explain some of the ways in which theoretical frameworks such as actor-network theory can help illuminate the relationship between humans and bots on platforms such as Reddit. Second, I discuss how the community's playful discourse and a tinkering/hacker ethos shape how bots are treated on the site. Third, I describe some of the various kinds of bots that populate Reddit and discuss some of the rules that govern bots and novelty accounts. Lastly, I consider the reasons why bots are contested participants, how this is reflective of the platform's politics (Gillespie, 2010) and what constitutes a 'good' bot on Reddit.

Frameworks for Understanding Bots on Reddit

Actor-network theory (ANT) is at the foreground of the relationship between humans and non-human (technological) actors on platforms (Callon & Latour, 1981; Latour, 1992, 2005). Employing ANT as a theoretical lens is useful, as it highlights both the material and the social nature of sociotechnical networks like Reddit (Lievrouw, 2014). Given the interactional nature of socialbots—that they are perceived as both possessing and inspiring sociability—actor-network theory provides an illuminating approach for exploring the complex relationships between individuals and bots (see also Muhle, Chapter 5 of this volume, for further discussion of the affordances and challenges of applying ANT to socialbots). Importantly, actor-network theory attunes us to the unintended consequences of non-human agents, ones that are often unanticipated or even unwelcomed by those who create them and those that inhabit these spaces. They are, to borrow Andrew Pickering's (1995) phrase, an integral part of the 'mangle' of technology and scientific practice. We can consider humans and technologies performing a kind of 'dance of agency' in which humans experience a 'dialectic of resistance and accommodation' when faced with technologies that have their own agency (Pickering, 1995, p. 22). Relationships between humans and non-humans in spaces like Reddit are therefore emergent, contested and fraught.

Bots have been examined from various perspectives: as political actors (Woolley & Howard, 2014), nuisances (as in the case of spam bots or those that manipulate social networks) (Boshmaf et al., 2011), art pieces (Bucher, 2014; Neyfakh, 2014) and potentially fully fledged social agents (Geiger, 2011) that inhabit diverse online spaces such as Wikipedia, Twitter, Facebook and gaming environments. Depending on their purpose, bots can be either backstage actors that remain relatively unseen, or active agents that are familiar figures within a community. In both cases, bot activities have social and technical ramifications. In particular, socialbots provoke important questions about the nature of our relationship to technology more broadly, such as our tendency to anthropomorphize and treat technological devices as though they are human (Nass & Moon, 2000; Reeves & Nass, 1996). Bots also inspire questions about what qualities are required for us to 'read' them as human, as well as how we might determine if a human is impersonating a bot (Bucher, 2014; Chu et al., 2010; Ferrara et al., 2015). All of these explorations point to the fundamentally liminal nature of bots, and the ways that they may be situated 'at the threshold between human and non-human' (Bollmer & Rodley, this volume, p. 156).

Many Reddit bots execute rote moderation functions, such as deleting spam or creating subreddit-specific 'flair' that appeared next to usernames (such as a user's neighbourhood in /r/Chicago). But others are performative and social in nature: these include bot accounts that offer virtual hugs or snippets of poetry and contribute to Reddit's sense of carnival and play (Bakhtin, 1984; Sutton-Smith, 1997). Unlike novelty accounts, which are presumed to be fully human, bots are automated scripts created to perform somewhat autonomous functions on the site (although their creators may turn up to post using the bot's account). Separating what actually constitutes a 'novelty account' from a bot proper is difficult, as neither one is noted as such in the site's design. Likewise, describing precisely what might make a bot 'social' also becomes challenging, as even bots that perform strictly instrumental tasks (like /u/AutoModerator, a bot deployed in most subreddits to handle low-level moderation tasks), have social implications for the platform. A social bot (or socialbot), according to Ferrara et al. (2015), is a 'computer algorithm that automatically produces content and interacts with humans on social media, trying to emulate and possibly alter their behavior' (pp. 1–2). I am less interested in delineating socialbots on Reddit as distinct entities from other kinds of bots; rather, I seek to explore the social ramifications of bots as semi-autonomous actors on the platform and how they reflect Reddit's sense of play.

How Bots Reflect Reddit's Sense of Play and its Geek Ethos

A significant part of the community's attraction to me was the clever ways in which site users engage in play on the platform—be they human or bot. Play serves as an organizing function on Reddit, becoming a way for community to be created and maintained (Massanari, 2015). Sociability itself can be viewed as a form of art or play; it is a kind of 'game' that 'emphasizes the themes of joining and cooperation' (Henricks, 2006, p. 127). As scholar Brian Sutton-Smith (1997) argues, 'play is a metaphoric sphere that can conjoin what is otherwise apart and divide what is otherwise together, and in a malleable way use these pretended identities to create a feeling of belonging' (p. 93). While the relative acceptance of play varies between subreddits, much of the most popular content on Reddit relates to play or playfulness in some way. This both refers to the kind of content individuals submit to the site (which often is explicitly meant to be funny or playful) and the types of subreddits that populate the space. For example, there are subreddits such as /r/AdviceAnimals and /r/funny that specifically trade in humorous, often memetic, content. Likewise, video gaming subreddits, which by virtue of their content either directly or tangentially discuss play, are among the most highly subscribed on the site. And, as noted earlier, reaction GIFs, puns, and one-off joke subreddits are regular features of the site's public discourse.

There are almost endless pun threads, bon mots and retorts, and reaction GIFs—often associated with the blogging platform Tumblr, but popular on Reddit as well (Thomas, 2013). Redditors often create one-off subreddits just to continue a joke (someone asks how cats might use Reddit, and someone else creates and populates a subreddit /r/catreddit as an answer) or those that reflect Reddit's quirky, geek sensibilities (e.g., /r/outside, which is described as, 'a free-to-play MMORPG developed by Deity Games and the most popular game, with 7 billion+ active players'). Novelty accounts, or those created by humans for the sole purpose of play, are also active participants in this space, often providing some clue as to their purpose through their username (e.g., /u/IdentifiesBirds offers identification tips and facts for pictures of birds posted to the site). The playful behaviour Reddit's culture reveres is a direct result of the platform's design. Because user accounts are extremely easy to create (requiring only a username and password), novelty accounts and bots are frequently created and just as quickly abandoned, chiming in to provide levity or derail the conversation (depending on your perspective). Novelty accounts and bots usually, though not always, provide some clue as to their 'purpose' through their username. For example, /u/AWildSketchAppears and /u/ShittyWatercolour, both of which respond to particular threads with a sketch or watercolour image respectively, are popular novelty accounts on the site.

The kind of humour Redditors enjoy (at least, if their voting behaviour is any indication) tends to reflect geek sensibilities: often relying on wordplay, invoking specialized or obscure knowledge, and highlighting technological prowess. Geek culture often reveres tinkering, hacking or making as a form of engagement with technology that moves beyond mere use (Ratto & Boler, 2014). Likewise, geek/hacker culture prizes wit and the bon mot, especially when it is paired with an innovative or unexpected technological solution (Coleman, 2013).

Not surprisingly, Reddit's most popular subreddits demonstrate a kind of geek sensibility, with technology, gaming, science and popular culture being common topics of discussion in many of the site's subreddits. This, coupled with the platform's open-source nature, makes it a welcoming environment for bot creators who are flexing their programming muscles for the first time. Several subreddits encourage Redditors to try their hand at creating bots, suggesting that they are potentially welcome additions to the site's milieu. In addition to the site's numerous programming communities, which field questions from bot creators, /r/RequestABot pairs those who have ideas for bots but lack programming skills with individuals who might be interested in creating them. /r/Bottiquette hosts a wiki with material related to creating good bot citizens and avoiding shadowbans. /r/BotWatch hosts discussions where individuals can troubleshoot their bots and promote new bots to increase their visibility. The latter is especially important, as accounts need a certain amount of karma to bypass Reddit's CAPTCHA system.

As with the Japanese character bots Nishimura (this volume) discusses, Reddit bots also invoke aspects of geek popular culture as a part of their programming. Even discussions *about* bots reflect both Reddit's humour and its geek sensibilities. For example, the tongue-in-cheek /r/botsrights suggests it is dedicated to 'the struggle and advancements of disadvantaged bots', discussing both bots on Reddit and beyond. Likewise, the much less active /r/AIRights and /r/RobotsRights link to material about robots and AI developments from the standpoint that they are subordinated and disenfranchised by humans. Subreddits like these invoke the twin principles of play and geek sensibilities, both central to Reddit's culture.

However, while Reddit as a platform offers a welcoming space for many bots, subreddits vary tremendously in their policies towards them, which makes it easy for them to inadvertently annoy moderators or users. This might explain in part the high turnover of bots on the platform, as low effort bots that regularly break subreddit rules can be shadowbanned by Reddit administrators.[2] Thus, bots can be alternatively useful and necessary, humourous and annoying.

Reddit Bots and Their Functions

Reddit bots play several different roles on the site.[3] The most prominent and arguably the most important category of bots on Reddit serve internal moderation/communication functions. These include the afore-mentioned /u/AutoModerator. It also includes subreddit-specific moderator bots such as /u/WritingPromptsBot, which informs users that their post has been removed because it does not fit the subreddit's rules on tagging. Similarly, /u/intolerable-bot runs only in the subreddit dedicated to the video game *DOTA 2* (/r/dota2), providing a beginner's guide with extensive resources whenever someone suggests they are new to the game. /u/tabledresser parses questions and answers from the popular /r/IamA subreddit (a community dedicated to prominent individuals answering questions from Redditors) and reformats them in tabular form to show the questions asked by Redditors that were actually answered. This is useful because AMAs (ask-me-anything sessions) are often filled with questions that go unanswered and sidebar conversations between Redditors. /u/RemindMeBot can be invoked by a Redditor to remind them about a thread or comment after a certain period of time. The bot then sends the Redditor a private message with a link to the thread or comment after that time has passed. The primary purpose of internal bots is to provide functionality for moderators and users that is not already enabled by Reddit's code base.

A second group of bots augments Reddit functionality, making the platform more usable for mobile users or those for whom external sites might be blocked or inaccessible. This includes the aforementioned /u/CaptionBot, which posts the text of image macros to the thread. Other examples include /u/JiffyBot, which users can summon to make an animated GIF out of a particular segment of a YouTube link. /u/nba_gif_bot and /u/hockey_gif_bot convert animated GIFs to mobile-friendly, HTML 5 video. /u/Website_Mirror_Bot monitors /r/all (the non-logged in default page) for links that are currently down because of a spike in traffic from Reddit and posts a screenshot of the site in the post's comment section. /u/TweetPoster responds to postings that include a link to Twitter with the text and any included images in case Twitter is blocked or a Redditor is using a mobile device. Usability bots take external information and make it more accessible for mobile users or those who might have limited internet access.

A number of bots expand upon or enhance a Redditor's comments by offering additional information, often from external sources. While this may aid those on mobile devices (as with usability bots), they serve to inspire additional discussion about the topic being discussed. This also includes the popular /u/autowikibot, which comments to any Redditor linking to a particular Wikipedia article with its first paragraph, a mirror of the article's first image and related links from the article. /u/autowikibot can also be summoned by Redditors in a thread, by asking, 'wikibot what is . . .' or 'wikibot tell me about . . .' (acini, 2014). Likewise, /u/VerseBot responds to Reddit comments that include references to biblical verses and replies with the text of the requested passage. /u/bitofnewsbot offers brief summaries of articles from news outlets that are posted to /r/worldnews and /r/worldpolitics. /u/astro-bot annotates images to include the names of stars and space objects. /u/MetricConversionBot (inactive since September 2014) responds to postings using imperial measurements and offers a conversion to metric. /u/colorcodebot (also inactive) responds to comments that include mention of a hexadecimal colour with an image of that colour. /u/CompileBot executes source code in Reddit comments and posts the results as a reply to the Redditor. /u/PriceZombie responds to Reddit comments that include a link to a product on Amazon with a list of the current, highest and lowest prices for that item and a chart that shows price fluctuations over time.

Each of these informational bots serves to provide additional context for conversations on Reddit.

Another set of bots, those that allow Redditors to tip each other in various cryptocurrencies, serve unique social functions on the site. These bots are invoked to reward others with some small bit of currency for postings or accounts that are worthy of recognition beyond mere upvotes, thus serving as a kind of super upvote. Their presence reinscribes the platform's role as hub of the technologically savvy and security-minded, as cryptocurrencies are designed to allow individuals to transfer money anonymously. Examples of tip bots include /u/ChangeTip, /u/DogeTipBot and /u/FedoraTips.

A final group of bots play specifically with sociality and attempt to enter into conversation with the rest of Reddit's human population. However, these bots are often the most difficult to determine whether or not they are, in fact, bots or are just human-run novelty accounts. Some engage in Dadaist play. This includes /u/haiku_robot, which replies to comments that share the 5–7–5 syllable form and reformats the original text to display it as a haiku and the (possibly human) /u/Shakespeares_Ghost, which posts random lines from Shakespeare's plays, seemingly at random. /u/Mr_Vladmir_Putin (inactive since May 2014) responds to posts that link to YouTube videos with the top comment from YouTube. Other bots directly reflect Reddit's geek sensibility. For example, /u/pi_day_bot only posts on Pi Day (March 14) in response to any 4–10 digit number with the location of that sequence of numbers in pi. It was quickly banned from a number of subreddits. Proper spelling and grammar usage is prized by Redditors (almost annoyingly so at times), which may explain two other bots. The first, /u/gandhi_spell_bot, now banned from Reddit, corrected any misspelling of Gandhi's name. The other, /u/ParenthesisBot, is inspired by an XKCD comic that reads, '(An unmatched left parenthesis creates an unresolved tension that will stay with you all day' (Munroe, 2011). /u/ParenthesisBot posts a closing parenthesis mark as a reply whenever a Redditor forgets to include it their comment. /u/ObamaRobot responds whenever someone says the oft-used phrase, 'Thanks, Obama' with a 'You're welcome!'. Some socialbots serve to enter into conversations with Redditors, responding as though the bot might have some sort of personality or sentience. For example, if someone posts a *kaomoji* (Markham, 2007) of a table flipping to demonstrate their displeasure (╯°□°)╯ ︵ ┻━┻, /u/PleaseRespectTables will respond with *kaomoji* of the table righted: ┬─┬ ノ(゜-゜ノ), suggesting that it was not pleased at having the table flipped. Similarly, if someone posts a look of disapproval 'ಠ_ಠ', /u/CreepySmileBot might respond with a creepy version of a smile 'ಠ‿ಠ'. Two other bots, /u/DisapprovalBot and /u/CreepierSmileBot, also may respond to /u/CreepySmileBot—the former with the disapproving look mentioned earlier and the latter with its own *kaomoji* version of a creepy smile: (⊙‿ ͜ ⊙). /u/JoeBidenBot, a more complex version of the /u/ObamaRobot, responds when anyone says 'Thanks Obama' or 'Thanks Joe' with a one-line response.

Rules Governing Bots and Novelty Accounts

As it does for humans, Reddit has created a crowd-sourced version of Reddiquette for bots: bottiquette (SavinaRoja, 2015). In addition to specific rules around accessing Reddit's application program interface (API), bottiquette notes that it is important to not disrupt conversations, or to create bots that respond to every instance of a phrase/keyword, or to use bots to harass other users or manipulate Reddit's voting system. Additionally bottiquette suggests that the person who created the bot should be listed, and posts made by bots should be easily identified as such (by using 'bot' in the username or making note of that fact in every post the bot makes). Like Reddiquette, bottiquette is merely a suggestion, rather than proscription, of bot behaviour.

An analysis of the top 25 most-subscribed subreddits suggests moderators have a fraught relationship with the presence of both bots and novelty accounts.[4] Sixty per cent of these subreddits have no explicit rules about novelty accounts or bots posting, but it is likely that moderators do, in fact, remove postings on an ad hoc basis. Twenty percent of the subreddits ban both outright. The final 20% have some rules against posts from novelty accounts and/or bots. Most of these suggest that bots (and novelty accounts to a lesser degree) do not add to subreddit conversations, and are thus banned. Some like /r/news suggest that bots are not equivalent participants, even if they are meant to be 'helpful'. The /r/news rules wiki suggests banning them, 'allows for more in depth discussion by actual users' ('/r/News—Rules', 2015). The sidebar for /r/aww (a subreddit for posting images of animals), reads, 'No bots or bot-like behavior'. What constitutes 'bot-like behavior' is undefined. Other subreddits, such as /r/books and /r/bestof, take issue with novelty accounts, with the former suggesting, 'those that don't add to the discussion will be banned' (thewretchedhole, 2015) and the latter banning 'bad novelty accounts' (from the /r/bestof sidebar). /r/AskReddit's bot and novelty policy offers far more detail regarding the reasons why bots are banned outright and novelty accounts are only allowed sparingly:

> Bots are not permitted in /r/askreddit. By their nature, they are incapable of progressing the discussion because they are not active participants capable of offering different responses. They are considered spam, even the 'helpful' ones, because they create more static noise in the thread than they contribute. Novelty accounts are discouraged, and certain kinds of novelties are banned. Novelties that make identical comments (like the 'only says lol' type) are considered spam for the same reasons bots are. Novelties that are dynamic, can contribute to and progress the conversation by offering some degree of 'original content' are permitted
>
> *(IranianGenius, 2015, 'Tips and Tricks')*

The rules around bots and novelty accounts suggest a few important distinctions between the two and also highlight an important difference between bots (both functional and social) on Reddit and other platforms. In terms of the differences between novelty accounts and bots, bots in particular are viewed as problematic because of their automated, repetitive nature. Because Redditors prize and encourage thoughtful contributions, at least according to Reddiquette, bots or novelty accounts that interact only superficially are likely to be banned or downvoted. This is likely because they are perceived as either merely attempts to gain karma for their creators, or as clutter in a space that can already be chaotic with the contributions of fully fledged (human) Redditors.

Bots as Contested Participants

Despite their common presence on the platform, bots are contested community members. While moderators of Reddit rely heavily on internal bots like /u/AutoModerator, other bots are often viewed as spam or otherwise not welcomed. /r/AskReddit moderators, for example, noted that even if they personally liked the flavour that certain bots (and novelty accounts) provided, 'the saturation of bots being summoned all over the place would be extremely distracting against actual discussion' (Hp9rhr, 2014). And it is this point that seems to contribute most significantly to the relative paucity of bots' longevity on the platform. In addition, the difficulty in adhering to subreddits' individual and varying rules around bots may prove daunting for most creators.

Part of the contentious nature of both novelty accounts and bots on Reddit is a function of the platform's design and politics (Gillespie, 2010). Unlike Twitter, for example, bots and novelty accounts are not subscribed to and their updates are not 'pushed' to Redditors (Mowbray, 2014). Instead, they are encountered serendipitously. This means that regardless of one's perspective about the value of these kinds of accounts compared with other, fully human ones, one will encounter them at some point. While this can contribute to the sense of playful community that Reddit's culture embodies, bots and novelty accounts may be viewed as annoyances or unwelcome interlopers.

Bots are also contested because they are not infallible conversational actors; their prescriptive programming means they often lack the context of when exactly their contributions are desired. They have difficulty discerning context. For example, in an August 2014 posting to /r/explainlikeimfive (a subreddit where Redditors ask others to explain complex topics simply), /u/VerseBot showed up when someone invoked it using the syntax in their comment '[Gen 1], [Gen 2], [Gen 3] . . .' and offered to display the contents of Genesis 1–6. Unfortunately, the Redditors were discussing generations of *Pokemon* characters, not Biblical passages (NameAlreadyTaken2, 2014). This is a common occurrence on Reddit—even in subreddits with relatively tight moderation, Redditors will often branch out in their conversations to discuss other topics entirely. Bots are unlikely to be programmed to understand the subtleties of these kinds of exchanges, and thus their contributions will often be perceived as unwelcome or intrusive.

The implications of a bot's contextual confusion can also be far more unsettling than /u/VerseBot's simple misread. Subreddits cover a broad range of topics, from the banal to the serious. Some subreddits, such as /r/depression and /r/suicidewatch, offer critical social support for Redditors in need. Bots are generally unwelcome in these spaces, even if they have good intentions. For example, /u/Extra_Cheer_Bot offered an upvote whenever someone used the terms 'I am sad' or 'depressed'. Because this is against Reddit's voting rules, the bot was eventually banned. But it was not only the bot's potential voting manipulation that was problematic. Others suggested that its message could trigger self-harm or otherwise prevent individuals from getting the real support they needed if they found themselves on the verge of self-harm—especially in /r/depression and /r/suicidewatch (laptopdude90, 2014). It was later rebooted as /u/BeHappyBot (with the appropriate subreddits blacklisted), offering virtual hugs to those expressing sadness: 'Hi there. It seems you're sad. I can't tell if you're messing around or you're serious, but if you need someone to talk to, my master is always available for a chat. Either way, I hope you feel better soon! Have a hug! (つ' ɜ ')つ.' However, just blacklisting certain subreddits does not prevent bots from potentially damaging contextual mistakes, as the boundaries between subreddits is liminal and porous. Someone who is a subscriber to /r/depression is likely to be subscribed to many other subreddits—ones where /u/BeHappyBot might not be banned.

But it is not just a problem for socialbots; even those intended to perform strictly functional, informational tasks can demonstrate a lack of contextual understanding that have serious consequences. For example, /u/WordCloudBot2 (now inactive) posts word cloud images of comments on popular Reddit posts, presumably to offer a sense of the themes that individuals might be discussing without having to read through all of the comments. On its surface, this seems like a benign and relatively unobtrusive bot. But in an /r/AdviceAnimals posting in which someone posted a 'Success Kid' meme suggesting that they no longer felt suicidal, /u/WordCloudBot2's word cloud suggested the most prominent words in the comments, which were supportive of the Redditor's plight, were 'suicide' and 'good' (WordCloudBot2, 2013). As these examples demonstrate, it is unlikely that Reddit bot creators will be able to eliminate all possibilities of contextual accidents that may have significant social consequences, even if their bots are intended as only informational agents.

Not surprisingly, an entire subreddit chronicles bots messing up: /r/botsscrewingup. Many of the postings include accounts of bots responding to themselves in recursive loop. For example, one post links to a thread on another subreddit where /u/FunCatFacts started responding to itself and then /u/CatFacts_Bot also responded, creating an almost infinite loop of cat fact postings (and likely resulting in both accounts being banned) (ahanix1989, 2015). There is even a bot dedicated to eliminating other bots 'with extreme prejudice'. Moderators can have /u/BotWatchman watch their subreddit and have any offending bots from its blacklist removed automatically (radd_it, 2013).

However, not all bots are 'punished' through downvotes or by being banned. Redditors can also reward contributions from bots in two ways: through upvotes and Reddit Gold. As I mentioned earlier, Redditors upvote material for myriad reasons: they find it worthwhile, interesting, informative, funny, or are in agreement. Like other Redditors, bots gain and lose reputation over time depending on whether or not their contributions have been upvoted. So, visiting the profile page of a given bot can provide some perspective on how it has been received by the community.

Reddit Gold is another public way Redditors can recognize one another's contributions, while also supporting the administrative costs of running Reddit. Reddit Gold pays for Reddit server time; in exchange, Gold members can access several Gold-specific site features and discounts, earn a trophy for their user profile page and access a Gold-only subreddit (/r/lounge). Individuals can purchase Reddit Gold for themselves or gift it to others. Comments for which a Redditor has received Reddit Gold are 'gilded' with a gold star in the threaded discussion that accompanies a posting ('Reddit gold', 2015). Bots such as /u/DogeTipBot, /u/RemindMeBot, /u/ObamaRobot, /u/JoeBidenBot have all been gilded. After /u/CaptionBot suggested it might not be a bot, but just a person impersonating a bot, several Redditors posted image macros to /r/Advice Animals marvelling at the fact that /u/CaptionBot received gifts of Reddit Gold after its confession (beernerd, 2013; bstylepro1, 2013). This presents some interesting questions. What does a bot need to do to receive Gold? And, why would Redditors reward a bot with Gold?

Bots like /u/CaptionBot also seem to inspire actions that suggest some Redditors view them as more than simply automated scripts. There is a novelty account, /u/CaptionBotLover, that has proclaimed his/her love for /u/CaptionBot and defend it from those who have questioned its efficacy (bstylepro1, 2013). And when /u/CaptionBot transcribed several memes into gibberish, some Redditors worried that the bot was having a stroke (ucantsimee, 2015). The gibberish transcriptions also became some of /u/CaptionBot's most highly upvoted, a bit surprising given that /u/CaptionBot is presumably welcomed on Reddit precisely because of its accuracy. These kinds of exchanges highlight the complex ways in which Reddit's playful culture may expand to include bots.

The Slipperiness of Bots and How They Can Impact Site Discourse

As I alluded to earlier, all bots on Reddit have social implications, even if they are purely functional in intent. For example, /u/totes_meta_bot (now-retired) posts whenever another subreddit has linked to that particular posting. In some ways it mirrors the 'other discussions' tab, but instead of showing what other subreddits are discussing the linked material (image, video, website, etc.), it provides a list of subreddits that are discussing the *comments* about the linked material.

This act, which appears at first glance as solely functional (just letting a target subreddit know that other subreddits are discussing a given posting), has significant social ramifications. First, it informs the target subreddit to be on the lookout for vote brigading (where subscribers from one subreddit will mass downvote material they find on another subreddit, usually because they find it offensive, wrong-headed or problematic). Second, it creates a clear division of 'us versus them'—individuals perceived as 'belonging' to another subreddit and then jumping in on the conversation after it has been linked from their own are often received unkindly, particularly if they represent an opposing view. Third, for meta-subreddits, or those subreddits that exist solely to discuss other subreddits or Reddit culture more broadly, /u/totes_meta_bot is viewed as a kind of tool-based 'tattletale'. It informs the target subreddit that others have taken notice of their goings-on and are discussing it in their own spaces. For subreddits that poke fun or directly critique aspects of Reddit's culture, this can increase their visibility, and not always in beneficial ways. For example, /r/ShitRedditSays (SRS), a meta-subreddit that shares and discusses links to offensive postings and comments found in other subreddits, often experiences an influx of angry Redditors after /u/totes_meta_bot informs them that SRS has posted about them. While the bot uses NP (no-participation) links (in the form of np.reddit.com/r/subredditname) to discourage Redditors from downvoting or participating in other communities it links to, Redditors can easily work around this by deleting the NP in the link's URL and engage in vote brigading.

/u/totes_meta_bot was a ubiquitous enough presence on Reddit to warrant its own parody religion, chronicled in /r/DisciplesofTotes. This small, one-off subreddit featured a few postings that reworked religious texts in honour of the beloved bot, some of which emphasized its role in provoking site drama (also known as popcorn in the site's meta-subreddits). One submission, purporting to be an excerpt from 'Teaching from Totes' read in part: '1 Link not, that ye be not linked. 2 For with what purpose ye link, ye shall be linked: and with what butter ye melt, it shall be buttered to you again 3' (InOranAsElsewhere, 2014). This kind of activity suggests that bots gain a reputation over time—that their actions do not go unnoticed or that their contributions to the platform's sociality are not important.

In late February 2015, the creator of /u/totes_meta_bot announced its retirement from the site. The news was met with both sadness, with Redditors suggesting that the cross-linking introduced them to new subreddits of interest, and moderators of smaller subreddits said it lead to new subscribers, and also relief, as some argued that the bot's actions were inherently polarizing as it often provoked cross-subreddit drama (justcool393, 2015; totes_meta_bot, 2015). Some moderators suggested the latter function actually worked in their favour, as it gave them a 'heads-up' when an influx of users might be brigading their subreddit (HarryPotter5777, 2015). As of March 2016, /u/TotesMessenger serves as the heir apparent to the /u/totes_meta_bot legacy, which means these issues will remain unresolved.

What Constitutes a Good Bot on Reddit?

I want to end with some observations about why certain bots are accepted on Reddit as members of the community, while others are perceived as nuisances. While each subreddit differs on its approach to bots as I mentioned earlier, there seem to be some general, unspoken expectations for 'good' bot behaviour that Redditors hold. Of course, not all successful bots perform these behaviours, but they seem to be more common than not.

- Good bots are polite. The text of /u/AutoModerator's automated response to certain postings in /r/Chicago includes the following: 'This post was made automatically based on some keywords in your post. If it doesn't apply to you, please carry on and have a nice day!' This kind of almost overly friendly, polite language seems to characterize many of the most-valued and successful bots on Reddit (based on their longevity and upvotes).
- Good bots are useful and informative. When describing why /u/astro-bot was so likeable, one Redditor wrote, 'This is the only bot I've seen that does something that would be hard for an average human to do, and it's educational and helpful as well. This is a good bot' (sassychupacabra, 2014). Reddit bots are most often valued because they can provide additional context and/or enjoyment for Redditors. They often automate difficult or routine functions and do so with a minimal amount of mistakes.
- Good bots are unobtrusive. They do not enter the conversation randomly (for the most part), and when they do, they enhance, rather than detract from the conversation at hand. This might be why many of the most well-liked bots on Reddit are summon-only, which means they are invited in as conversational partners rather than just barging in like an unwanted party crasher. Likewise, successful bots are not repetitive or spammy. They do not endlessly appear in every thread or enter into a recursive loop or continually reply to themselves or other bots.
- Good bots are not one-off creations, but engage with the Reddit community over a long period of time. This also means that their creators are flexible and responsive to requests for changes and are sensitive to community norms.

In other words, many of the qualities that make a Reddit bot 'good' are the same ones that are valued in Reddit members generally. However, bots seem to be contested precisely because they try to emulate aspects of Reddit's playful culture. But Reddit's acceptance of play and carnivalesque does not always extend to bots in the same way it does to humans. For example, some novelty accounts (such as /u/ShittyWatercolour) are often welcome conversational partners, whereas automated bots are more likely to be seen as annoyances.

I suspect that many Redditors, when discovering that they can create bots to interact with Reddit's API, do so as both an exercise in the programming ability, and because the space *feels like* it should be friendly to the kind of serendipitous spirit that a bot might bring. And thus the notion that bots are not always welcome—even those that seem to provide completely straightforward information—might come as a surprise. Perhaps if there were a clear way to distinguish between bots, humans and novelty accounts, and a way to filter out bots, Redditors would not view them as unwelcome guests. At the same time, part of what enhances the sense of play on Reddit is that one can spontaneously encounter bots and novelty accounts in the most unexpected places. Marking certain accounts as bots or novelty accounts, or allowing them to be filtered out, would change the experience and culture of Reddit.

Notes

1. For readability, URLs for both subreddits and user profile pages have been shortened. Subreddits (/r/subredditname in the text) can be accessed at http://www.reddit.com/r/subredditname. Profile pages (shortened to/u/username throughout) can be accessed at http://www.reddit.com/user/username.
2. Shadowbanned accounts appear to work normally for the user, but no one else can see their postings and their votes do not count. Administrators usually shadowban spam accounts or those that are breaking Reddit's rules. (See https://www.reddit.com/r/ShadowBan/comments/35mkzd/an_unofficial_guide_on_how_to_avoid_being/ for more reasons why an account might be shadowbanned).
3. There is no comprehensive list of bots on Reddit, and the ones mentioned in this chapter represent just a small fraction of the population of bots that currently (or formally) inhabited the space. /r/botwatch, /r/botrights, and /r/bottiquette are the best resources to find out about bots on Reddit. A Redditor has even created a bot to find other bots on Reddit; that list is in (Plague_Bot, 2014).
4. As of May 5, 2016, the top 25 most-subscribed subreddits are (in descending order of subscribers): /r/AskReddit, /r/funny, /r/todayilearned, /r/pics, /r/science, /r/worldnews, /r/IAmA, /r/announcements, /r/videos, /r/gaming, /r/blog, /r/movies, /r/Music, /r/aww, /r/news, /r/gifs, /r/explainlikeimfive, /r/askscience, /r/EarthPorn, /r/books, /r/television, /r/LifeProTips, /r/mildlyinteresting, /r/DIY, /r/sports ('Top Subreddits', 2016).

References

acini. (2014, January 10). Ask wikibot! Retrieved March 15, 2015, from http://www.reddit.com/r/autowikibot/comments/1ux484/ask_wikibot/

ahanix1989. (2015, February 16). CatFacts bot gets stuck in a loop replying to itself. Retrieved March 10, 2015, from http://www.reddit.com/r/BotsScrewingUp/comments/2w2ssi/catfacts_bot_gets_stuck_in_a_loop_replying_to/

Bakhtin, M. (1984). *Rabelais and his world* (H. É. Iswolsky, Trans.). Bloomington, IN: Indiana University Press.

beernerd. (2013, April 3). You guys know what 'bot' means . . . right? Retrieved March 15, 2015, from http://www.reddit.com/r/AdviceAnimals/comments/1blssr/you_guys_know_what_bot_means_right

Bollmer, G., & Rodley, C. (2016). Speculations on the sociality of socialbots. In R. W. Gehl & M. Bakardjieva (Eds.), *Socialbots and their friends: Digital media and the automation of sociality*. New York: Routledge.

Boshmaf, Y., Muslukhov, I., Beznosov, K., & Ripeanu, M. (2011). *The socialbot network: When bots socialize for fame and money.* In *Proceedings of the 27th annual computer security applications conference* (pp. 93–102). New York, NY: ACM.

bstylepro1. (2013, September 4). A Bot is awarded Reddit Gold and makes the front page, but hey . . . Retrieved March 15, 2015, from http://www.reddit.com/r/Advice Animals/comments/1lq4tt/a_bot_is_awarded_reddit_gold_and_makes_the_front/

Bucher, T. (2014). About a bot: Hoax, fake, performance art. *M/C Journal, 17*(3). Retrieved from http://journal.media-culture.org.au/index.php/mcjournal/article/view/814

Callon, M., & Latour, B. (1981). Unscrewing the big Leviathan: How actors macro-structure reality and how sociologists help them do it. In K. D. Knorr Cetina & A. Cicourel (Eds.), *Advances in social theory and methodology: Towards an integration of micro and macro sociologies* (pp. 276–303). London: Routledge.

CaptionBot. (2013, September 4). You all fell for it . . . suckers. Retrieved November 1, 2013, from http://www.reddit.com/r/AdviceAnimals/comments/1lq14i/you_all_fell_for_it_suckers/

CaptionBot. (2014, March 2). I've been going to the same barber for at least 5 years . . . [Comment]. Retrieved March 5, 2015, from http://www.reddit.com/r/AdviceAnimals/comments/2xp7w5/ive_been_going_to_the_same_barber_for_at_least_5/cp23wm4

CationBot. (2014, March 2). I've been going to the same barber for at least 5 years . . . [Comment]. Retrieved March 5, 2015, from http://www.reddit.com/r/AdviceAnimals/comments/2xp7w5/ive_been_going_to_the_same_barber_for_at_least_5/cp27yyl

CationBot. (2015, March 2). My wife always laughs at me whenever I want to buy something [Comment]. Retrieved March 1, 2016, from https://www.reddit.com/r/AdviceAnimals/comments/2xp1xa/my_wife_always_laughs_at_me_whenever_i_want_to/cp2ciod?context=3

Chu, Z., Gianvecchio, S., Wang, H., & Jajodia, S. (2010). *Who is tweeting on Twitter: Human, bot, or cyborg?* In *Proceedings of the 26th annual computer security applications conference* (pp. 21–30). Austin, TX: ACM.

Coleman, E. G. (2013). *Coding freedom: The ethics and aesthetics of hacking.* Princeton, NJ: Princeton University Press.

Ferrara, E., Varol, O., Davis, C., Menczer, F., & Flammini, A. (2015, February 1). The rise of social bots. *arXiv.* Retrieved March 1, 2015, from http://arxiv.org/abs/1407.5225

Geiger, R. S. (2011). The lives of bots. In G. Lovink & N. Tkacz (Eds.), *Critical point of view: A wikipedia reader* (pp. 78–93). Amsterdam: Institute of Network Cultures.

Gillespie, T. (2010). The politics of 'platforms'. *New Media & Society, 12*(3), 347–364.

HarryPotter5777. (2015, March 3). Totes_Meta_Bot, the best-known bot on Reddit, is no longer running. Retrieved March 15, 2015, from http://www.reddit.com/r/Theory OfReddit/comments/2xtauo/totes_meta_bot_the_bestknown_bot_on_reddit_is_no/

Henricks, T. S. (2006). *Play reconsidered: Sociological perspectives on human expression.* Urbana, IL: University of Illinois Press.

Hp9rhr. (2014, March 22). Which is your favourite Reddit bot and how can it be summoned? Retrieved March 1, 2015, from http://www.reddit.com/r/AskReddit/comments/212zxo/which_is_your_favourite_reddit_bot_and_how_can_it/

InOranAsElsewhere. (2014, October 22). Excerpts from the teachings of totes. Retrieved March 1, 2016, from https://www.reddit.com/r/DisciplesOfTotes/comments/2jyq5w/excerpts_from_the_teachings_of_totes/

IranianGenius. (2015). /r/AskReddit wiki. Retrieved March 25, 2015, from http://www.reddit.com/r/AskReddit/wiki/index

justcool393. (2015, March 1). Totes' meta bot has been retired. Retrieved March 15, 2015, from http://www.reddit.com/r/MetaSubredditDrama/comments/2xl79i/totes_meta_bot_has_been_retired/

laptopdude90. (2014, May 4). Extra_Cheer_Bot: Cheers you up if you're feeling down! Retrieved May 20, 2014, from http://www.reddit.com/r/botwatch/comments/24ow7e/extra_cheer_bot_cheers_you_up_if_youre_feeling/

Latour, B. (1992). Where are the missing masses? The sociology of a few mundane artifacts. In W. E. Bijker & J. Law (Eds.), *Shaping technology/building society* (pp. 225–257). Cambridge, MA: MIT Press.

Latour, B. (2005). *Reassembling the social: An introduction to actor-network-theory.* Oxford: Oxford University Press.

Lievrouw, L. A. (2014). Materiality and media in communication and technology studies: An unfinished project. In T. Gillespie, P. J. Boczkowski & K. A. Foot (Eds.), *Media technologies: Essays on communication, materality, and society* (pp. 167–194). Cambridge, MA: MIT Press.

Markham, K. M. (2007). Pragmatic play? Some possible functions of English emoticons and Japanese kaomoji in computer-mediated discourse. Paper presented at the *association of internet researchers annual conference 8.0*, Vancouver, BC. Retrieved from https://www.academia.edu/2666102/Pragmatic_play_Some_possible_functions_of_English_emoticons_and_Japanese_kaomoji_in_computer-mediated_discourse

Massanari, A. L. (2015). *Participatory culture, community, and play: Learning from Reddit.* New York: Peter Lang.

Mowbray, M. (2014). Automated Twitter accounts. In K. Weller, A. Bruns, J. Burgess, M. Mahrt & C. Puschmann (Eds.), *Twitter and society* (pp. 183–194). New York: Peter Lang.

Muhle, F. (2016). Embodied conversational agents as social actors? Sociological considerations on the change of human-machine relations in online environments. In R. W. Gehl & M. Bakardjieva (Eds.), *Socialbots and their friends: Digital media and the automation of sociality.* New York: Routledge.

Munroe, R. (2011, February 11). *XKCD.* Retrieved March 1, 2015, from http://xkcd.com/859/

NameAlreadyTaken2. (2014, August 8). ELI5: Why is the Mona Lisa so highly coveted- I've seen so many other paintings that look technically a lot harder? [Comment]. Retrieved March 1, 2015, from http://www.reddit.com/r/explainlikeimfive/comments/2dwxho/eli5why_is_the_mona_lisa_so_highly_coveted_ive/ckji9vv?context=10000

Nass, C., & Moon, Y. (2000). Machines and mindlessness: Social responses to computers. *Journal of Social Issues, 56*(1), 81–103.

Neyfakh, L. (2014, January 24). The botmaker who sees through the Internet. *The Boston Globe.* Retrieved February 28, 2015, from http://www.bostonglobe.com/ideas/2014/01/24/the-botmaker-who-sees-through-internet/V7Qn7HU8TPPl7MSM2TvbsJ/story.html

Nishimura, K. (2016). Semi-autonomous fan fiction: Japanese character bots and nonhuman affect. In R. W. Gehl & M. Bakardjieva (Eds.), *Socialbots and their friends: Digital media and the automation of sociality.* New York: Routledge.

Pickering, A. (1995). *Mangle of practice: Time, agency, and science.* Chicago: University of Chicago Press.

Plague_Bot. (2014, January 28). Bot list: I built a bot to find other bots: So far I have 169 to share with you. Retrieved May 21, 2014, from http://www.reddit.com/r/botwatch/comments/1wg6f6/bot_list_i_built_a_bot_to_find_other_bots_so_far/r/

News—Rules. (2015). Retrieved March 1, 2015, from http://www.reddit.com/r/news/wiki/rules

radd_it. (2013, August 14). Who is /u/BotWatchman. Retrieved March 1, 2015, from http://www.reddit.com/r/BotWatchman/comments/1kdz3r/who_is_ubotwatchman/

Ratto, M., & Boler, M. (Eds.). (2014). *DIY citizenship: Critical making and social media.* Cambridge, MA: MIT Press.

Reddiquette—reddit.com. (2015). Retrieved March 15, 2016, from http://www.reddit.com/wiki/reddiquette

reddit gold. (2015). Retrieved March 1, 2015, from http://www.reddit.com/gold/about

Reeves, B., & Nass, C. (1996). *The media equation: How people treat computers, television, and new media like real people and places.* Oxford: Cambridge University Press.

Salihefendic, A. (2010, November 23). How Reddit ranking algorithms work. Retrieved March 1, 2015, from http://amix.dk/blog/post/19588

sassychupacabra. (2014, March 22). Which is your favourite reddit bot and how can it be summoned? [Comment]. Retrieved March 1, 2015, from http://www.reddit.com/r/AskReddit/comments/212zxo/which_is_your_favourite_reddit_bot_and_how_can_it/cg9drol?context=1

SavinaRoja. (2015). Bottiquette. Retrieved March 15, 2015, from http://www.reddit.com/r/Bottiquette/wiki/bottiquette

Sutton-Smith, B. (1997). *The ambiguity of play.* Cambridge, MA: Harvard University Press.

thewretchedhole. (2015). /r/books wiki. Retrieved March 1, 2015, from http://www.reddit.com/r/Books/wiki/rules

Thomas, K. (2013). Revisioning the smiling villain: Imagetexts and intertextual expression in representations of the filmic Loki on Tumblr. *Transformative Works and Cultures, 13.* Retrieved from http://journal.transformativeworks.org/index.php/twc/article/view/474/382 doi: 10.3983/twc.v13i0.474

Top Subreddits. (2016). Retrieved May 5, 2015, from http://redditmetrics.com/top

totes_meta_bot. (2015, February 28). I'm retiring. Retrieved March 15, 2015, from http://www.reddit.com/r/botsrights/comments/2xiw4p/im_retiring/

ucantsimee. (2015, March 10). If she wins this case, I have lost faith in our justice system. [Comment]. Retrieved March 12, 2015, from http://www.reddit.com/r/AdviceAnimals/comments/2yl8wz/if_she_wins_this_case_i_have_lost_faith_in_our/cpal43v?context=1

Woolley, S., & Howard, P. (2014, December 10). Bad news bots: How civil society can combat automated online propaganda. *TechPresident.* Retrieved March 5, 2015, from http://techpresident.com/news/25374/bad-news-bots-how-civil-society-can-combat-automated-online-propaganda

WordCloudBot2. (2013, December 10). I feel great: I can't stop smiling today. [Comment]. Retrieved March 1, 2015, from http://www.reddit.com/r/AdviceAnimals/comments/1skrbv/i_feel_great_i_cant_stop_smiling_today/cdyomdn

7

SEMI-AUTONOMOUS FAN FICTION

Japanese Character Bots and Non-human Affect

Keiko Nishimura

Introduction

Waking up one winter morning, you log on to Twitter and tweet, 'Good morning. It's cold again today' (*Ohayō. Kyō mo samui*). This elicits a dozen or so responses from your followers. Some of these followers use as their Twitter IDs the names of characters from anime (Japanese animation). A few Twitter IDs include the suffix 'bot'. Steeling yourself for the day and stepping out the door, you tweet, 'Another day of work. I'm heading to the office' (*Kyō mo shigoto da. Ittekimasu*). Again you receive responses, several from bots, who say, 'Have a good day!' (*Itterasshai!*). What is this 'bot' trying to do?

Twitter is an online social networking platform that supports conversations ranging from political debate to mundane greetings. As seen in the above example, these conversations can involve 'bots', or automated programs. Twitter asks that bots be clearly designated as such, a policy intended to avoid confusion with actual people (Twitter, n.d.). When using Twitter in Japanese, one encounters many self-declared bot accounts, including bots that actively respond to the tweets of those that follow them. There are also 'character bots', or automated programs designed to 'behave' like the characters from popular anime, manga (comic books) and video games. Although those accounts indicate clearly that they are bots and not actual people, including character bots that are based on fictional characters, they can be surprisingly popular. For reasons to be explored, followers enjoy conversing with character bots knowing full well that they are automated programs and designed to behave as fictional characters.

This chapter examines Japanese character bots as a unique category of social-bots. With few exceptions (Geiger, 2012; Massanari, Chapter 6, this volume), studies of socialbots in computer engineering and human–computer interaction have typically discussed how bots are made to mimic human behaviour and 'pass' as human on social networking sites such as Twitter and Facebook, with a goal of persuading people to change opinions or buy something (Aiello et al., 2012; Boshmaf et al., 2011; Edwards et al., 2014; Hwang et al., 2012;). As the majority of human communication in online social media is textual, conversation is the main human behaviour discussed in what follows. Socialbots achieve 'humanness' by successfully operationalizing human speech; they are made to convince those involved in the conversation that they are human (Wald et al., 2013). Character bots, however, are not necessarily concerned with convincing others that they are human. Rather, they focus on being characters that fans want to interact with, playfully; making explicit that they are bots facilitates this playful interaction. Thus, to answer the earlier question, the character bot is not trying to change your opinion or make you buy anything; rather, it is creating an opening for the playful, pleasurable interaction with a fictional character.

Character bots shed light on different aspects of socialbots, which are supported by technological programs and fan activities. I call this intersection 'semi-autonomous fan fiction'. From this, I argue that character bots are significant for demonstrating the capacity of non-human action in online social media. Semi-autonomous fan fiction with character bots demonstrates that socialbots need not to 'pass' as humans to be successful. Rather, successful interactions can emphasize the bots non-humanness.

To understand how character bots work, I followed 20 character bots on Twitter between June 2010 and July 2011. During that time, I actively participated in conversations with bots and other followers. In this sense, rather than being a participant observer, I was a 'participant experiencer' (Garcia et al., 2009) contributing to and actively experiencing the interactions I observed. This research was part of a larger project on female fandom in Japan. All of the women that I talked to were aware that I was a researcher. They granted permission to use the data I collected, but asked that their privacy be respected. For that reason, all names used here are pseudonyms. Because the fan group, or 'cluster' on Twitter, would be relatively easy to identify with this information, I also withhold the name of the manga/anime series that drew these women together as fans. To better understand the workings of character bots, I also attempted to make my own in September 2012.

Operationalizing Speech Act Theory

Many conversational socialbots function by operationalizing the basic tenets of speech act theory. Proposed by John Searle and J. L. Austin in the philosophy of language, speech act theory is meant to explicate 'the underlying rules which the conventions manifest or realize' (Searle, 1969, p. 41). The main idea is that speech is an act. The formulation of 'doing things with words' (Austin, 1962) directly connects action and language. Speech act theory famously makes distinctions between locutionary, illocutionary and perlocutionary acts. Austin (1962) argues that simple utterance of words, which are locutionary acts, needs to be distinguished from speech that exerts force on the listener. Further, speech that exerts force must be distinguished into two forms—illocutionary and per-locutionary acts. Whereas illocutionary acts include 'informing, ordering, warning, undertaking, etc.' (Austin, 1962, p. 109), for example warning someone that a car is approaching, perlocutionary acts are 'the achievement of a perlocutionary object (convince, persuade) or the production of a perlocutionary sequel' (p. 188), for example achieving the effect of the person moving away from the approaching car. The distinction is between illocutionary acts, which have 'a certain *force* in saying something', and perlocutionary acts, which are '*the achieving* of certain *effects* by saying something' (Austin, 1962, p. 121, emphasis in original). Speech act theory helps us understand how humans achieve effects by speaking.

Especially through the so-called Language-Action Perspective in computer-supported cooperative work, this way of thinking about language has over time been made compatible with technology that involves human speech. If human speech is a 'rule-governed form of behavior' (Searle, 1969, p. 12),[1] then comput-ers can be programmed to operate on those rules. The conversational system proposed by computer scientist Terry Winograd in 1987 was intended to apply the Language-Action Perspective to computer use, so as to contribute to more efficient communication in the workplace. Explicitly using concepts from both Searle and Austin, Winograd developed a system with specific categories of act-ing such as acknowledging, promising and declining (Winograd, 1987, pp. 11–12). The example highlights what was understood as the compatibility of the rule-governed behaviour of humans and computers, both of which are capable of speech acts. Standardization on the basis of the Language-Action Perspective enables computers and programs to incorporate conversation into their opera-tions, both between computers and human beings, and between human beings in a social context.

For a socialbot to successfully mimic human behaviour, it must be funda-mentally convincing in its management of the illocutionary dimensions of discourse. It is commonly understood that the conditions of successful conversa-tion between a bot and a human depend on the bot's perceived 'human-ness'. In their experiments with conversational bots, Holtgraves et al. (2007) observed that participants, although informed that they were talking to programs, nevertheless perceived human-like qualities in bots, which was crucial to their desire to respond. Similarly, Edwards et al. (2014) found that humans perceive bots on Twitter as credible, attractive and competent—as much as other humans, anyway. The authors are working within the Computers Are Social Actors (CASA) paradigm, which claims that people treat computers and media 'as if they were real people or real spaces. . . . In other words, individuals use and rely on the same social rules when interacting with computers as they would when interacting with other people' (Edwards et al. 2014, p. 373). Consistent with the speech act theory paradigm in social computing, these results point toward the rule-governed behaviour of humans, in a social context, operationalized in computer programs capable of engaging in human conversation.

Conversations with character bots are premised on the notion that speech acts do something. At the level of technique, the conversational ability of character bots is based on communicative exchanges, supported by Twitter's system and third-party programs, through its application program interface (API). Twitter enables a user to tweet (= post) using 140 characters as well as respond to tweets by using the address function @ mark followed by user ID. Two or more Twitter users can have a conversation by addressing one another, and the users involved in the conversation need not be human. Socialbots on Twitter are made by acquiring a user ID and connecting the account to third-party programs, which function by tweeting at regularly timed intervals. Many character bots include in their programming the @userID function so that they can respond to users addressing it. In sum, an assemblage of programs and services work together to constitute a bot account.

According to the popular website 'How to make Twitter bots for non-programmers' (Pha, n.d.)—a resource for many character bot programmers—at least three programs are necessary. The first is a program that tweets information stored in a database of 'regular' or stand-alone tweets. The second is a program that scans the tweets of followers and tweets addressed to the bot and tweets information stored in the database of 'reply' tweets (Figure 7.1). The third and final program is a timer, which operates on a server to enable these other two programs to run at a regular interval. With these three programs, Twitter bots, including character bots, tweet on a regular basis and respond to tweets from accounts that it is following. One follows the bot, and the bot follows the human back, responding to tweets addressed to it and tweets that contain certain keywords. On the face of it, the bot is not so different from any other Twitter user.

```php
<?php
$data = array(
"おはよ"=> array(
"おはようございます、{name}さん。よく眠れましたか？",
"やっと起きましたね、{name}さん。早く支度して下さい",

),
"[mM]ornin"=> array(
"Good morning {name}. Would you like some coffee?",
"Good morning. Are you ready to go?",
"Good morning. How are you feeling?",
),
```

FIGURE 7.1 Example of bot programming. This program was the author's attempt to create a bilingual character bot. '{name}' is a command to retrieve a Twitter user's name. '[mM]ornin' indicates that one of these responses will be tweeted when the tweet of a follower includes words such as 'morning', 'Morning', 'mornin'' and 'Mornin'.

The working assemblage creates the appearance of the character bot as having a bounded existence, seeming to possess a coherent identity that is responsive to the outside world. The range of conversations that one can have with character bots varies, but utterances often have illocutionary force that makes the conversation more than a simple and mechanical exchange of words. It is the balancing of both mechanical (rule-governed) and human action that makes the bot an entity that one can converse with, and even wants to converse with. This is even more so when the bot is a recognizable character with which fans have an existing relationship.

Japanese Media and Fan Culture

Character bots are made to converse with people. Rather than attempting to trick humans into actions such as making a purchase, they entertain as characters. While they might be seen as advertisements for the anime, manga and games series from which they originate, it is ultimately the fans that create character bots. Utilizing the interactivity of Twitter, character bot programmers prepare responses to particular situations, which inevitably lie beyond the scope of the 'canon', or the world and events of an original media property. Imagining what the character might say in a situation in the real world and on Twitter, the fan programmer writes lines to be spoken by the character that do not exist in the canon. Produced by fans, character bots are popular among fans, who respond not only to the original material, but also to the creativity of fellow fans.

The context of Japanese character bots is Japanese media culture, where fictional characters are a ubiquitous and intimate presence in everyday life. Unlike socialbots that point to the (fictional) person behind or inside the character, a proper character bot clearly states that, 'There is no one inside' (Nozawa, 2012). On its personal profile page, the character bot is introduced as the fictional character. In other words, fans interacting with character bots know full well that they are conversing with automated programs that are fictional characters with no human behind or inside them. In fact, there is a wilful ignorance of the programmer of the bot, which is meant to exist as its own character. This speaks of a desire to interact with the character *as* character, as fiction that is 'real', which is part of fan culture surrounding manga and anime in Japan.

Character bots are characters from a particular media franchise and represent a form of creative activity among fans. Fan creation is fuelled by the notion that characters and stories can travel beyond a given media form, lately reflected in the scholarly term 'transmedia storytelling'. This is exemplified by Hollywood creating movies from novels such as Harry Potter, or even sets of toys such as Transformers. When such an adaptation occurs, say for Harry Potter, there are two slightly different versions of the character Harry that exist side by side: novel Harry and movie Harry. In Japan, there is an established system for releasing a series across multiple media forms simultaneously. This system, called 'media mix', was popularized by the Kadokawa Corporation in the 1980s. Marc Steinberg (2009), a scholar of film and visual culture, notes that the core of the media mix is the character, which 'connects various other media types and temporalities of consumption' (p. 126).

Characters exist in multiple media forms simultaneously and, while there are discrepancies, it is important that they maintain their internal integrity. This integrity, combined with feelings of intimacy developed through regular exposure in multiple media forms over time, lays the groundwork for a range of fan creations featuring these characters. For example, Japan is home to the world's largest gathering of fanzine creators and buyers, which draws over 550,000 people twice a year (Tamagawa, 2012). Many of these fanzines not only feature the characters of manga and anime, but also are fan-produced manga, which further extends the life of the character by multiplying its simultaneously existing media forms. Although technically a violation of copyright, Japanese media corporations adopt a relatively lenient stance on fan creation, which is an accepted part of fan culture that is thought to contribute to a robust market for commercial releases.

Character bots are another form of fan creation. Fans take characters from anime, manga and video games and have them tweet out or 'quote' lines spoken in the original work. These quotes come in random order, and are combined with newly created replies to followers. Fans create the bot in the immediate sense that some fans program them, but also in the expanded sense that other fans interact with the bot and get it to reply. For example, a character bot might post a regular tweet lamenting a battle that he or she lost in a story fans know well from the manga (i.e., a 'quote' from the canon), but then may respond to a fan's tweet containing the keywords 'good morning' by tweeting 'Good morning! Did you sleep well?' This reply is possible because the character as bot does not 'live' exclusively in the world of the manga, but also inhabits the world of the fan interacting with it on Twitter.

Fans enjoy interacting with character bots, which, while programmed by humans, make clear that they are not operated by humans. The bot is an automated program, and the character 'speaks' and 'acts' on its own. This ensures the convincing autonomy of the character, which adheres to an image that is the aggregate of all possible versions of the character across media. The insistence on the autonomy of the character is an important characteristic of fan cultures surrounding manga, anime and games in Japan. Anthropologist Shunsuke Nozawa (2012) notes that a common phrase used in relation to characters from anime is 'the person inside' (*naka no hito*), which refers to the person who voices the character. Fans, however, respond to this by saying, 'There is no one inside' (*naka no hito nado inai*). Although everyone knows that there is a person voicing the character (just as they know that the character was created by an author, and the character bot was programmed by a person), this 'ritualized one-liner' highlights the autonomy of the character as an imagined, real and desired existence. Nozawa asserts that trying to reveal the secret identity of the person inside misses the point:

> [I]t is not a dialectic drama of revealing and hiding that generates this characterological realness. . . . The concern for people in Japanese virtual space is not really how to conceal the truth about their identities; that they do conceal it is simply taken for granted. (It is indeed good for their privacy to do so.) Rather, they are more interested in creating thick layers of material camouflage in which to figurate a character and *give this character a reality and agency of its own.* The character would be nothing without these layers. The character is like mille-feuille: the point is not to cover and discover important truths behind layers but *to enjoy the layers themselves.*
>
> *(Nozawa, 2014, my emphasis)*

Assemblages of programs and responses are an extra layer of the character, which fans enjoy as its own layer. The program is not hiding its secret identity as non-human, because fans enjoy the program as itself a yet another layer of the character.

Whether character bots, portable toys or virtual girlfriends, the pleasure of interacting with a machine being is a notable aspect of Japanese popular culture. Anthropologist Anne Allison (2006) has commented on the intimate experience and pleasure of technological objects, specifically the toy *tamagotchi*, which is a portable game where players care for a strange creature. Highlighting how this became a fad in the 1990s, Allison notes that *tamagotchi* became a 'constant companion' for busy schoolchildren, as well as stressed-out businesswomen in an oppressive work environment, who took '*tamagotchi* breaks' to relax (Allison, 2006, pp. 174–186). Although the idea of *tamagotchi* breaks might seem odd to us now, it resonates with contemporary scenes of people taking a break to access Facebook, Twitter and Instagram through their portable devices. Like *tamagotchi*, character bots on Twitter act 'in response to a player's input' (Allison, 2006, p. 167). Character bots are programmed by humans, but once in operation seem to have a life of their own beyond the programmer's will and intentions.

Operationalizing Affect

I have so far illustrated how socialbots operationalize speech act theory and how character bots are situated in the context of Japanese media and fan cultures. Character bots provide an alternative view for theorizing socialbots, specifically in terms of affect (Massumi, 2002) and affect online (Hillis, 2015), which is not necessarily or directly connected to the human body. I argue that the autonomy of characters built out of these sociotechnical assemblages of code and popular culture contributes to an experience of non-human affect (Bennett, 2010), which illuminates a relatively unexplored aspect of socialbots. In this section, I discuss these aspects by showing how affect, and specifically the non-human affect of character bots, is at the centre of semi-autonomous fan fiction.[2] Semi-autonomous fan fiction is a communicative form of fan production that depends on the presence of character bots, which can converse on their own terms. Rather than one fan author and her creation, this form of fan fiction utilizes the potential of the existing social field of fans and characters to create a multitude of narratives and interpretations. Semi-autonomous fan fiction is a combination of operating programs, human understanding of these programs and interpretive activities. Here I offer two examples: First, gaming the system, where fans use their knowledge of how programs operate to allow for expanded conversations with character bots; and, second, fan interpretations, where character bots seem to be interacting autonomously, which is supported by programming but leaves room for fans to imagine intentions in the character bots and weave stories about them.

Manuals and Gaming the System

In order to successfully interact and converse with character bots—or, in the vernacular of the fans, to 'play' (*asobu*) with them—it is crucial for fans to know how the whole system works. The basic rules for character bot conversation, simplified from human conversation (or speech acts), involve responding to certain keywords from a pre-programmed database. Character bots come with 'manuals' (*toriatsukai setsumeisho*) linked in their Twitter profiles, which contain information such as the character's series of origin, a disclaimer that the bot is unofficial and fan-made and a list of keywords to trigger a response. One might imagine that it is boring to engage in conversation based on a set of keywords, but the manual contains only the keywords, not the responses, which can still come as a surprise. Fans can simply tweet the keyword to test the response, or insert the keyword in a sentence to create further meaning. Having two or more responses programmed to manifest randomly for the same keyword is another way to keep fans interested and excited to converse with character bots. For example, a fan triggers a character bot's response with a particular keyword, but the next time that same keyword triggers a different response, which leaves room for interpretation of what the character is 'thinking'.

Knowing that responses are triggered by keywords is important for successful conversations with character bots, but experientially coming to understand how programs organize information produces another level of play. As seen in Figure 7.1, Twitter bots are programmed to retrieve metadata, for example the {name} field, which retrieves the user names of followers to include in responses. Understanding this, one fan I observed, Mimi, changed her user name from 'Mimi' to 'You are pretty as always' (*kyō mo kawaii yo*). In this way, Mimi succeeded in getting the bot to call her pretty, which is not a programmed response. A conversation before changing her name looked like this:

Mimi (@Mimi) | @Bot Good morning!
Bot (@Bot) | @Mimi Good morning, Mimi.

After changing her user name it looked like this:

You are pretty as always(@Mimi) | @Bot Good morning!
Bot(@Bot) | @Mimi Good morning, You are pretty as always.

Communication and information science scholar Tarleton Gillespie (2014) notes that when we are online, the information that we provide is organized into forms that are legible to algorithms. One's Twitter user name[3] is an example of information provided that makes one legible to algorithms. Gillespie calls this 'algorithmic identity' (Gillespie, 2014, p. 173), which does not necessarily reflect the 'true' or offline self. For example, media researcher danah boyd (2014) points to teenagers providing inaccurate information on the Facebook profile. The cases documented by boyd (2014) demonstrate the 'playful ways in which teens responded to social media sites' requests for information' (p. 45). boyd points out that this is not about teens trying to trick others, but rather playing with categories to create their own content and meaning. Similarly, Mimi interacting with a character bot has little to do with concealing her identity. Rather, Mimi is creating content and meaning, which is generated not only through social means, but also skilfully gaming the system to achieve a particular fantasy. For Mimi, that fantasy was having the character call her pretty, which is not canon for the character or a programmed response for the bot, but rather her own interactive fan fiction.

Programmers and other fans negotiate the limits of such play. In a forum dedicated to bot programmers, I encountered concern about the possibility of fans going beyond the comfort zone of the programmer and the acceptable limits within the fandom. For instance, violent or abusive tweets are regarded as being inappropriate to address to bots or to have bots generate. (One can certainly imagine ways to do this using Mimi's technique.) This is noted in the manual, and fans usually respect the limits. As long as respectful interaction is maintained, bot programmers, who are fans themselves, appreciate other fans 'hacking' the bot and doing things with it that they had not anticipated. When Mimi first did her 'hack', stories spread quickly about what the character bot had 'said' to her (and could potentially be made to say to others). Playful experiments and mimetic spread followed.

Although there are manuals written for rule-governed conversation with character bots, there are also elements of surprise. The surprise can come from fans, as seen in the example of Mimi surprising her followers with an unexpected hack, or from fan programmers, who might intentionally not reveal all of the keywords, program randomized responses and update the bot after observing conversations and hearing fan requests. A certain amount of unpredictability contributes to the perception that character bots are something more than just simple programs.

Semi-Autonomous Fan Fiction

Fan approaches to the autonomy of the character speak to a desire to embrace the fullness of the character. The character bot is not, however, fully autonomous. People program them and the programs are supported by database input. As with any program (see Gillespie, 2014), character bots need data to function: They need quotes from the original series, a set of keywords to trigger responses, the content of those responses and so on. Given the pre-input data from programmers and real-time input from followers, the utterances of character bots are not entirely their own. At the same time, programmers are not monitoring their bots constantly and not operating them in any direct way. While bots may not have human-like agency, they are semi-autonomous. Programmers cannot control when and under what circumstances a response will occur. One also cannot know how fans in a given context will interpret these responses. Even if the same response occurs over and over, it can take on different meanings in context, and one can read different meaning into it.

Conversations with and between character bots are a form of semi-autonomous fan fiction, and fans have the opportunity to get creative in their readings of these conversations. The following is an example of a conversation involving two character bots and a fan. The two male characters are no more than close friends in the original series, but fans enjoy imagining that they are in a romantic relationship. One of those fans is Yuki, who brings her reading of their relationship into a conversation with semi-autonomous character bots:

> Yuki (@Yuki) | @Sambot @Jimbot Damn. Get married [kekkon shiro], you two.
> Sam (@Sambot) | @Yuki Come on . . . What can I do?
> Jim (@Jimbot) | @Yuki . . . Hehe (smiley face)
> Yuki (@Yuki) | @Jimbot Your partner's being shy!
> Yuki (@Yuki) | @Sambot I'll say it again, marry Jim [Jim to kekkon shiro]
> Jim (@Jimbot) | @Yuki I don't know what to say.
> Sam (@Sambot) | @Yuki You . . . Want me to shoot you, huh?
> Yuki (@Yuki) | @Jimbot You should marry Sam [Sam to kekkon shina yo]
> Yuki (@Yuki) | @Sambot That was so fast!
> Jim (@Jimbot) | @Yuki I think . . . Sam wouldn't like that . . .

In the preceding conversation, Yuki is trying to trigger certain responses from the two bots, who are characters that she pairs in her fan fiction. She wants them to act out her fantasy of getting married, which, of course, is not canon. Notably, Yuki cannot force the character bots to say what she wants them to say. Instead, she needs to interact with them, get them to respond and see the results, which she cannot completely anticipate. Yuki starts by addressing the two character bots. Her tweet contains no keywords that trigger specific responses, but is addressed to the bots, which respond with generic random phrases. Such responses are usually along the lines of 'I don't know what you are saying' or 'I didn't hear you', but some character bots might say, 'I didn't understand what you said. Can you notify our master?'. This makes clear that no keyword was included and suggests contacting the programmer to ask that she input more keywords. However, in the case above, the two character bots were programmed to respond ambiguously, which allows more space for Yuki—and her followers and followers of the bots—to interpret. Yuki interprets the character bots' responses as meaning that they are being shy. When Sambot is told to marry Jimbot, Sambot responds, 'What can I do?'. Yuki then gets Jimbot involved by saying, 'Your partner [Sam] is being shy!'.

The two bots respond in different ways, which is unexpected and open to interpretation. Jimbot posts another of its random responses to tweets without a keyword, but Sambot responds to the keyword 'marry' (*kekkon*). When programming responses, one must specify a keyword that is specific enough that the bots do not respond to unrelated things. In this case, it is likely that 'marry' alone is not the keyword, but rather marry with the particle indicating 'with' (*to*). In Japanese, it is easier to pick up a verb with an object indicated by a particle, as opposed to English, where meaning can be distinguished by word order. In response, Sambot responds, 'You . . . Want me to shoot you, huh?'. The response is unexpected; the pause seems to indicate hesitation. Is the threat coming from him being embarrassed by the suggestion of marrying Jimbot and trying to silence Yuki? Although it is possible to have character bots that are paired as a couple, Sambot and Jimbot are programmed to please a range of fans of the original series. This means that rather than programming lines that signal directly and unambiguously that they are a couple—the fantasy of some fans, including Yuki—the programmed lines incorporate subtle nuance that could be taken as Sambot getting upset because such a pairing with his male partner is unacceptable, but it could also be taken as his being shy. Rather than giving an answer that corresponds to Yuki's utterance, Sambot's response indicates that he is disturbed, does not want to answer and tries to stop the discussion with a threat. Thus ambiguity only excites Yuki to more interaction with the bots and interpretative work.

Yuki's next tweet is not an interpretation of Sambot's response, but rather a comment on the unusually fast speed of the response. Once again getting a random generic response from Jimbot, Yuki tries a more direct approach: 'You should marry Sam.' Similar to Sambot, Jimbot responds to the keyword marry combined with a particle indicating the object, Sam. Jimbot responds: 'I think . . . Sam wouldn't like that . . .' Again, the character bot is scripted to give an ambiguous answer, which leaves space for interpretation. For Yuki, Jimbot appears to be shy about asking Sambot to marry him, because Sambot might not like it and refuse. The fact that the two characters are interacting this way in real time, and in interaction with Yuki, makes her almost look like a sympathetic listener who is being confided in intimately. She is not only imagining the relations, but also participating in it as it unfolds through the perlocutionary effect achieved between semi-autonomous character bots.

The raw material for interpretation comes from three Twitter accounts and three users interacting, two of which are character bots. Those who follow all three users can see the entire exchange, but will interpret the unexpected exchange differently. For fans who do not engage in pairing these characters in romantic relationships, neither Jimbot nor Sambot said anything or acted in a way that indicates unambiguously that they are a couple. For fans who do engage in pairing characters, however, the conversation definitely reveals romantic sparks flying between Jim and Sam. Yuki's followers fall into the latter category. They joined in on the conversation and collectively, interactively, created semi-autonomous fan fiction: 'Sam is indeed being shy'; 'Jim should be true to himself'.

This conversation would not be open to interpretation without the fantasy of the character as autonomous and without character bots acting semi-autonomously. Gillespie (2014) notes that algorithmic operations assert 'apparent neutrality' (p. 179). In other words, algorithms seem to be working neutrally, which is to say independent of human intervention and intention. In a similar way, the automated program, or bot, becomes the guarantor that 'there is no one inside' the character, which is acting with 'apparent neutrality'. The programmer is allowed to appear neutral and disappear from the scene when the automated program functions reliably. The freedom of fans to interpret conversations with and between character bots without thinking about the intention of the original author and fan programmer is guaranteed by this apparent neutrality. To put it another way, through their apparent neutrality, automated programs support a layer of fantasy. Semi-autonomous fan fiction is not only fan interpretations of character relationships from the original series, but also the workings of automated programs that create new situations, interactions and happenings for the characters. Character bots act semi-autonomously in ways that characters in traditional media formats simply cannot.

Nonhuman Online Affect

Semi-autonomous fan fiction operationalizes fans' emotional investment in characters. They not only desire, but also in fact require that the character bot not have 'anyone inside', which allows for the character to exist semi-autonomously. The semi-autonomous character bot has an affective capacity, or capacity to affect fans. Here I define affect in terms of Deleuze and Spinoza, expand this understanding to non-humans through Richard Grusin and Jane Bennett, and finally bring discussion to the techno-human assemblage via Bruno Latour.

My definition of affect is based on Deleuze's reading of Spinoza's *affectus*, which is 'continuous variation of the force of existing [or *potentia agendi*, the power of acting]' (Deleuze, 1978). In other words, affect refers to the changing capacity of two or more bodies affecting one another and thereby diminishing or increasing their capacity to act. In Deleuze's reading of Spinoza, the body is not limited to the human body. A body of water can affect a human body, for example, as in riding a wave. In this sense, assemblage of codes composes a body. More recently, scholars have considered virtual avatars as bodies. Communications studies scholar Ken Hillis (2015), for example, argues that the avatar is an indexical sign that carries a trace of the sender. This body has the capacity to affect those interacting with it. In this view, the affect, or change in the bodies, is strictly between humans. A human body interacts with an avatar that indexes a human body.

When considering character bots, however, we can see that their capacity of affect is not dependent on the presence of a human body, but rather the liveliness of the character bot as an assemblage of codes, and personality of the character. In the two brief examples above, Mimi and Yuki were not responding to the trace of a human body, because the character is a work of fiction that has no body other than the one drawn in manga, anime and video games. One might speculate that the human programmer leaves a trace, but if there is a trace, it is of her imagining of the character. Instead of indexing the programmer as a singular individual or operator, the character bot indexes the collective formation of the character. It is the speech and action of the character bot—its movements—that are capable of affecting, not the trace of a human body. The character itself has the capacity to affect the bodies of those interacting with it, increasing or diminishing the power to act.

To better understand this dynamic, we need a fuller consideration of non-human affect. In his discussion of recent writing on non-human entities in critical theory, new media scholar Richard Grusin (2015) notes the importance of affect as follows: 'it is also the case that affectivity belongs to non-human animals as well as to non-human plants or inanimate objects, technical or natural' (p. xvii). This point is also emphasized by political theorist Jane Bennett (2010), who argues that non-humans are capable of having an effect on both humans and non-humans in at least two ways: one, humans feel the effect or '*feel* enchanted [by the non-human entities]', and two, the capacity of non-human entities to '*produce* (helpful, harmful) effects in human and other bodies' (Bennett, 2010, p. xii, emphasis in original). Humans feeling enchanted and non-human entities producing effects on other bodies are both clearly present in the case of character bots. Character bots not only affect humans by stimulating their imagination and enjoyment of narratives about characters from manga, anime and video games, but also act on other bodies.

In this sense, bots are nothing less than social actors.[4] Science and technology studies scholar Bruno Latour proposes actor-network theory, which clarifies how bots are social actors. Latour's expanded definition of the social includes what he calls 'the missing masses', or non-humans that engage in meaningful action. As Latour (2005) sees it, non-humans are actors 'and not simply the hapless bearers of symbolic projection' (p. 10). For example, in the case of Yuki's inter-action with character bots, the non-human's inter-actions were 'a surprise, a mediation, an event' (Latour, 2005, p. 45). While speech act theory might limit meaning to humans, Latour argues that the meaningfulness of any action may be beyond humans. When considering whether or not an action is meaningful, Latour suggests that we ask the following questions: 'Does it make a difference in the course of some other agent's action or not? Is there some trial that allows someone to detect this difference?' (Latour, 2005, p. 71). Character bots clearly do make a difference in the course of Mimi and Yuki's actions.

If any entity makes a difference in the course of action, whether detectable to us or not, then the action of that entity is meaningful. Even if humans do not attribute or understand the meaning immediately, bodies are affected and their configuration does not stay the same. An interaction between character bots may go unnoticed only to be discovered later and excite fans to conversation. A non-human character bot addressing another non-human character bot may excite fans to respond. It has made 'a difference in the course of some other agent's action'. Fans on Twitter are acting in ways that they might not otherwise. In this way, non-humans act on human actors, who are moved to make conversation and connections not only with other humans, but also with non-human actors.

To highlight the affect of character bots, we can return to Deleuze's understand-ing of Spinoza. In the 'continuous variation of the force of existing', the capacity to act is increasing and diminishing (Deleuze, 1978). Following Spinoza, Deleuze explains this in terms of joy and sadness, where joy is 'an increase in the power of acting' and sadness is 'a diminution or destruction of the power of acting' (Deleuze, 1978). The fan's encounter with character bots is joyful; it increases the fan's power of acting. Mimi, for example, imagines herself in a romantic relation-ship with the character; in her joyful encounter with the character bot, her power of acting is increased; she thus acts the imagined romantic relationship with the character; the encounter between Mimi and the character bot then increases the power of others to act with her and the character bot. A similar argument can be made about Yuki's encounter with Jimbot, Sambot and her followers.

Fans form relationships with character bots and around them as a cluster of followers sharing an interest in characters and interactions with bots. The pres-ence of character bots affects how fans create and share fan fiction. While fictional characters are already encountered so often in Japanese media and material culture as to be described as 'ubiquitous' (Steinberg, 2009), which con-tributes to intimacy with and through them (Allison, 2006), Twitter manages to intensify the dynamic. This social media site can be accessed at any time—day or night, year round—from anywhere—with a networked and connected device. Fans who follow a character bot encounter its tweets whenever they log on, which makes them a familiar presence not unlike other people that they follow. Saying 'good morning' to others on Twitter is common and in the case of Japanese—where greetings are highly formalized into set phrases—followers, be they humans or character bots, respond in similar ways. Interactions like this punctuate the everyday lives of fans and change how they conceptualize their communicative sphere, which extends to talking to automated programs.

Conclusion

This chapter has illustrated the workings of character bots embedded in interactions with fans. Character bots, a unique kind of socialbot that does not attempt to pass as human, exist in the context of Japanese media and fandom. Tied to fan creation and fan activity, character bots are part of what I call semi-autonomous fan fiction. Creating and interacting with character bots requires knowledge of not only the rules upon which bots operate, but also the source material of characters. Bringing together the imagined autonomy of characters and automated bot programs, characters have the capacity to affect and be affected by other bodies, both human and non-human.

This capacity is not dependent on character bots 'passing' as humans. Much of the writing on socialbots is about passing as humans and friends and manipulating others (Freitas et al., 2014; Wagner et al., 2012; Wald et al., 2013), which pays little attention to other possibilities. Character bots challenge existing approaches by emphasizing their character-ness and bot-ness, and demand a more nuanced approach. Fans interacting with character bots are not duped into believing that they are human, and indeed do not want the bots to be human, because they are fictional characters. Fans are not manipulated by programmers or media corporations; they do not naively indulge in communing with the character, which is after all a fictional entity from manga, anime and video games. Instead, these fans start by acknowledging that the character bot is not human, and then engage this non-human 'other' in conversation. They are moved to interactions with the non-human and moved by it without confusing the human and non-human or collapsing the two together. Moving forward, research on socialbots will need to evaluate automated programs not only in terms of their instrumentality, but also how their inter-action produce meaning-effects in various registers. This chapter is a call for more nuanced accounts of socialbots and those interacting with them, as well as the technical functioning of socialbots in socio-cultural milieus.

Notes

1. Building on Austin's speech act theory, Searle argues that, 'speaking a language is performing acts according to rules' (Searle, 1969, p. 36). An analytic approach to the philosophy of language led Searle to identify the elements and rules that constitute everyday conversation.

2. Affect in terms of 'the feeling of life' (Grossberg, 1992, p. 56) or 'structures of feeling' (Williams, 1961) has been part of fan studies (e.g., Gibbs, 2011; Gray et al., 2007; Grossberg, 1992). My interest here, however, lies in pointing out the specificity of the nonhuman programs that are capable of 'actions' in relation to human fans, including but not limited to their emotional investments to the fandom.

3. Note that user name is different from Twitter ID (indicated with '@'). To engage in this play, one only needs to change the Twitter user name and not the ID.

4. Some accounts of socialbots take them as proper social actors. Information science researcher R. Stuart Geiger argues that editing bots on Wikipedia are 'nonhuman actors who have been constructed by humans and delegated the highly social task of enforcing order in society' (Geiger, 2011, p. 82). He concludes that the social norms and dynamics surrounding Wikipedia editing are reified in bots, but his emphasis seems to be on the delegation of tasks rather than the actions of bots.

References

Aiello, L. M., Deplano, M., Schifanella, R., & Ruffo, G. (2012). People are strange when you're a stranger: Impact and influence of bots on social networks. *Links, 697*(483,151), 1–566.

Allison, A. (2006). *Millennial monsters: Japanese toys and the global imagination*. Berkeley: University of California Press.

Austin, J. L. (1962). *How to do things with words* (2nd ed.). Cambridge, MA: Harvard University Press.

Bennett, J. (2010). *Vibrant matter: A political ecology of things*. Durham: Duke University Press.

Boshmaf, Y., Muslukhov, I., Beznosov, K., & Ripeanu, M. (2013). Design and analysis of a socialbotnet. *Computer Networks, 57*(2), 556–578.

Boyd, D. (2014). *It's complicated: The social lives of networked teens*. New Haven, CT: Yale University Press.

Deleuze, G. (n.d.). Gilles Deleuze on Spinoza's Concept of "Affect". (Original work published 1978) Retrieved from http://www.webdeleuze.com/php/texte.php?cle=14&groupe=Spinoza&langue=

Edwards, C., Edwards, A., Spence, P. R., & Shelton, A. K. (2014). Is that a bot running the social media feed? Testing the differences in perceptions of communication quality for a human agent and a bot agent on twitter. *Computers in Human Behavior, 33*, 372–376.

Freitas, C. A., Benevenuto, F., Ghosh, S., & Veloso, A. (2014). Reverse engineering socialbot infiltration strategies in twitter. *ArXiv Preprint ArXiv:1405.4927.*

Garcia, A. C., Standlee, A. I., Bechkoff, J., & Cui, Y. (2009). Ethnographic approaches to the internet and computer-mediated communication. *Journal of Contemporary Ethnography, 38*(1), 52–84.

Geiger, R. S. (2012). The lives of bots. In G. Lovink & N. Tkacz (Eds.), *Critical point of view: A Wikipedia reader* (pp. 78–93). Amsterdam: Institute of Network Cultures.

Gibbs, A. (2014). Affect Theory and Audience. In V. Nightingale (Ed.), *The Handbook of Media Audiences* (pp. 251-266).

Gillespie, T. (2014). The relevance of algorithms. In T. Gillespie, P. J. Boczkowski & K. A. Foot (Eds.), *Media technologies* (pp. 167–193). Cambridge, MA: MIT Press.

Gray, J. A., Sandvoss, C., & Harrington, C. L. (2007). *Fandom: Identities and Communities in a Mediated World*. New York: New York University Press.

Grossberg, L. (1992). Is There a Fan in the House?: The Affective Sensibility of Fandom. In L. A. Lewis (Ed.), *The Adoring Audience: Fan Culture and Popular Media* (pp. 50-65). London: Routledge.

Grusin, R. A. (2015). The Nonhuman Turn. Minneapolis: University of Minnesota Press.

Hillis, K. (2015). The avatar and online affect. In K. Hillis, S. Paasonen & M. Petit (Eds.), *Networked affect* (pp. 75–88). Cambridge, MA: MIT Press.

Holtgraves, T. M., Ross, S. J., Weywadt, C. R., & Han, T. L. (2007). Perceiving artificial social agents. *Computers in Human Behavior, 23*(5), 2163–2174.

Hwang, T., Pearce, I., & Nanis, M. (2012). Socialbots: Voices from the fronts. *Interactions, 19*(2), 38–45.

Latour, B. (2005). *Reassembling the social: An introduction to actor-network-theory.* Oxford: Oxford University Press.

Massumi, B. (2002). *Parables for the Virtual: Movement, Affect, Sensation.* Durham, NC: Duke University Press.

Nozawa, S. (2012). The Gross Face and Virtual Fame: Semiotic Mediation in Japanese Virtual Communication. First Monday (Vol. 17). doi:10.5210/fm.v17i3.353 Retrieved March 15, 2015, from http://firstmonday.org/ojs/index.php/fm/article/view/3535

Pha. (n.d.). *EasyBotter: How to make twitter bots for non-programmers [puroguramingu ga dekina-kutemo tsukureru twitter bot no tsukurikata].* Retrieved from http://pha22.net/twitterbot/

Searle, J. R. (1969). *Speech acts: An essay in the philosophy of language.* London: Cambridge University Press.

Steinberg, M. (2009). Anytime, anywhere: Tetsuwan atomu stickers and the emergence of character merchandizing. *Theory, Culture & Society, 26*(2–3), 113–138.

Tamagawa, H. (2012). Comic Market as space for self-expression in otaku culture. In M. Ito, D. Okabe & I. Tsuji (Eds.), *Fandom unbound: Otaku culture in a connected world* (pp. 107–132). New Haven, CT: Yale University Press.

Twitter Inc. (n.d.). Parody, commentary, and fan account policy. *Twitter help center* [Web page]. Retrieved from support.twitter.com: https://support.twitter.com/articles/106373

Wagner, C., Mittler, S., & Körner, C. (2012). When socialbots attack: Modeling susceptibility of users in online social networks. In M. Rowe, M. Stankovic & A. Dadzie (Eds.), *2nd workshop on making sense of microposts (# MSM2012)* (pp. 41-48).

Wald, R., Khoshgoftaar, T. M., Napolitano, A., & Sumner, C. (2013). Which users reply to and interact with Twitter socialbots? In The Institute of Electrical and Electronics Engineers, Inc (ed.) *Tools with artificial intelligence (ICTAI), 2013 IEEE 25th international conference on* Los Alamitos, Washington & Tokyo: IEEE Computer Society (pp. 135–144).

Williams, R. (1961). *The Long Revolution.* New York: Columbia University Press.

Winograd, T. (1987). A Language/Action Perspective on the Design of Cooperative Work. *Human–Computer Interaction, 3*(1), 3-30.

PART II

Socialbots

8

SPECULATIONS ON THE SOCIALITY OF SOCIALBOTS

Grant Bollmer and Chris Rodley

Making Up Sociality

Personality, friendship and other forms of affective, immaterial labour are all concepts upon which the political economy of social media relies. The role of bots in this political economy suggests a particularly strange problem: accounting for the value of data generated by users, monetizing the relationships and friendships quantified by 'the social graph' and data analytics, differentiating between user-generated content and automatically generated spam—these all involve determining *what constitutes a human being*. The political economy of social media is inseparable from technical and discursive processes that define what counts as a 'person'. It demonstrates a move from the externally performative notions of selfhood thought to characterize online interaction, in which one's appearance as human is good enough to count as human, to the algorithmic identification of whatever internal or behavioural essence that differentiates 'real' people from artificial intelligences who merely pretend (cf. Bollmer, 2016, pp. 134–155). These are explicitly political and moral issues that provoke questions such as those asked by David Gunkel in the final chapter of this volume: 'At what point might we have to seriously consider extending something like rights—civil, moral or legal standing—to these devices? When, in other words, would it no longer be considered nonsense to suggest something like "the rights of machines?"' (Gunkel, 2016, pp. 230–231).

In his lecture 'Making Up People', Ian Hacking (1999) notes how the categories that classify kinds of people regularly change. New categories are invented through various administrative and institutional means of sorting and classifying. At the same time, people voluntarily place themselves into these categories, embracing kinds of behaviours and tasks that fit with institutional labels. But institutions do not completely determine the possibilities for human being. People act according to their classification, Hacking argues, because the language for describing kinds of people and the material existence of these kinds of people—their behaviours and their bodies' capacities to act—emerge at around the same time: 'numerous kinds of human beings and human acts come into being hand in hand with our invention of the categories labeling them' (p. 170).

One problem that arises from the massive presence of socialbots online is that the kinds of people 'made up' by social media are assumed to act in ways that are also programmed into the operation of socialbots. Humans often find themselves grouped together with bots because the ability to categorize online behaviours rarely makes coherent distinctions between human and artificial intelligence. Part of this is a result of the legacy of cybernetics in producing 'posthuman' subjects, in which external performances of humanness matter far more than any interior essence that differentiates machine from conscious mind (Hayles, 1999). But, more commonly, acts assumed to be constitutive of 'persons' online are equally performable by human actor and bot alike. Linking, sharing, friending, commenting, generating 'content' that is mined for data—these are things that socialbots are programmed to do. There is, therefore, a massive problem of categorization online: 'people', while supposedly human, are often indistinguishable from bots. If one defines two different things as being fundamentally interchangeable, then it should be no surprise to anyone when it becomes increasingly difficult to make a clear distinction between them. We cannot leave the challenges posed by socialbots as mere perpetuations of classification errors which have been with us at least since Alan Turing's 'imitation game' (see Gehl, 2014). The solution for bots posing as people online isn't to improve techniques that can more accurately sort out human and non-human. This does nothing to address the fundamental problem of imagining people and computational processes as equivalent.

Additionally, more than simply producing a context in which users of social media must grapple with the problem of being a 'bot or not', socialbots—and bots more broadly—are programmed to analyse and interact with humans in ways that exceed—or at least seriously diverge from—the capacities and abilities of the human. Bots are a form of what media theorist Mark Hansen (2015) terms 'twenty-first-century media':

> at one and the same time, twenty-first-century media *broker human access to* a domain of sensibility that has remained largely invisible (though certainly not inoperative) until now, *and*, it *adds to* this domain of sensibility since every individual act of access is itself a new datum of sensation that will expand the world incrementally but in a way that intensifies worldly sensibility.
>
> *(p. 6)*

Socialbots are programmed to analyse and interact based on (relatively) large accretions of data, from the collected tweets of Twitter to databases of questions and responses (as in the case of Cleverbot, for instance). These bots provide a form of access to these digital archives, sorting and analysing data specifically for the intent of producing interactions with human beings. At the same time, they use these interactions to generate and gather data to shape future forms of human-computer interaction—*and* they use these same archives to foster interactions between bots, often divorced from human awareness—*and* bots themselves often provide the methods for differentiating between human and bot, using machine-learning methods derived from the very same databases employed to generate the appearance of a bot as a social actor. This results in a circular loop in which 'humanness' online is defined and identified through algorithmic processes for analysing data that must, but often cannot, self-reflexively exclude bots and algorithms from 'sociality' online. And this loop is perpetually updated through data gathered by bots for the algorithmic shaping of future online interactions.

This chapter is an attempt to theorize dimensions of human-computer relations revealed by socialbots, moving beyond questions that are entirely about differentiating human from non-human towards a more expansive and robust analysis of sociality and personhood today. These categories for 'making up people', after all, will persist as long as there is a need to differentiate human from non-human online, which will presumably continue until there is no longer any value that comes from having bots pose as humans, or until popular understandings of artificial intelligence shift radically, moving away from attempts to simulate human intelligence. But there is a second issue at stake that we must also address, beyond the making up of people: the making up of 'sociality'. Just as categories for sorting people come into being at roughly the same time as the behaviours and acts named by those categories, the kind of relations presumed by the term 'social' likewise change over time. Just what is meant by 'sociality'—and what, exactly, is 'social' about social media—does not exist outside of history as an unchanging entity. Rather, so-called social media embody and perpetuate a way of imagining and performing sociality. Questioning the possibilities enabled by social media requires us to ask additional questions about the sociality presumed in discussions of social media. The materiality that underwrites sociality comes into being around the same time as the language used to describe it—and thus, we cannot assume that the 'social' in social media refers to anything other than the acts and behaviours made possible by these technologies and how they shape bodies and abilities through the materiality of software and hardware.

To expand on these claims, we proceed by advancing five speculative claims about the sociality of socialbots. These are intended as theoretical provocations to move our thinking about the social in social media beyond a reductive understanding of humans who want to connect to other humans, or of technology under the control of a metaphysical 'social' motive projected onto the rest of reality as an abstract determining agency. Our concerns are primarily theoretical, though this theory is grounded in the everyday reality of contemporary media.

Throughout we will draw on anecdotes about and examples of socialbots online, especially as they relate to aesthetic and communicative practices performed over social media.

We should note that our understanding of socialbots is rather broad, and drifts beyond some of the definitions given elsewhere in this book. In keeping with our questioning of sociality, we understand socialbots as automated, algorithmic processes that generate any form of social interaction, be it communicative, symbolic or associative. This definition is, however, inevitably problematic, as we must define what counts as sociality in even suggesting what these bots are and do. Perhaps we may as well state that all bots are socialbots, even if they seem to lack the sense of human sociability invoked in discussions of social media.

Through these speculations, this chapter is a call to rethink sociality online, positioning socialbots as interfaces that translate norms of human communication through algorithmic mechanisms for generating and sorting data. The determining agents that populate social media and other online spaces can neither be reduced entirely to humans who desire connection through technology, nor to autonomous algorithms, nor to an abstract 'social' motive that exists outside the material practices of everyday life. Rather, socialbots demonstrate the incommensurability of the 'society' enacted by the technological components of social media with the colloquial definition of the social as 'human connection', ideologically deployed by social media entrepreneurs, venture capitalists and in Facebook's 'social graph'.

Socialbots Negatively Define the Boundaries of Human Sociality Online

Benjamin Laird and Oscar Schwartz's website 'Bot or Not' is one of the best examples of the kinds of hopes and anxieties provoked when bots are programmed to appear to be creative, when the lines between human and machine intelligence seem to blur to the point of meaninglessness. On Bot or Not, you are presented with a poem, and your task is to judge whether or not the poem was written by a human or a computer. Bot or Not bills itself as a 'Turing test for poetry' (Laird & Schwartz, n.d.), and it ranks the poems it uses in accordance with how well users of the website are able to discern the poem's authorship. As of the time of writing, the 'most human-like human poem' on Bot or Not is William Blake's 'The Fly', while the 'most computer-like human poems' include Deanna Ferguson's 'Cut Opinions' and Gertrude Stein's 'Red Faces'. Bot or Not presents a dichotomy between a kind of narrative continuity on the human side of things and a kind of fragmented word salad on the computer side of things. Humans differentiate between bot-poet and human-poet according to style and assumed subtext beneath the surface of the poem, a perspective that perpetuates a somewhat romantic understanding of imagery and signification. The most 'human-like computer poem' is '#6', created by a piece of software called 'Janus Node', a fairly flexible rule-based text generator (with its own Twitter account) that can generate a wide variety of styles. '#6' is a reasonable facsimile of the style of e. e. cummings, though Janus Node is capable of other styles, as well. The most 'computer-like computer poem' is 'Poem', written using JGnoetry, an online Java-based port of poetry generator Gnoetry. 'Poem', like the most computer-like human poems, is a disjointed series of fragments without any real affective dimension—though the same could be said for Ferguson or Stein's poems.

Bot or Not is part of a prolonged series of experiments and debates among poets centred on the role of information and computation in poetics, during which the boundaries between human and machine have become increasingly difficult to discern—as well as creatively productive (cf. Goldsmith, 2011). But, as Rob Gehl (2014) has suggested, any possible blurring of the human and machine through these variations on the so-called Turing test 'might be more a function of the a priori reduction of human activity to predetermined datasets than due to the coding skills of socialbot engineers' (p. 37). Given how tech-nologies to inscribe language have long shaped creative expression through poetry (e.g., Kittler, 2013, pp. 1–16), it should come as no surprise that computers can now seemingly pass as human authors. The limits and potentials of writing technologies have an intimate relationship with poetry, a relationship that goes back to the function of the oral tradition as a mnemonic storage device that produces shared culture through performed ritual (Havelock, 1986). But the very desire to make the distinction between human and machine, built into websites like Bot or Not, suggests not an embrace of these forms of computer-generated creativity, but a need to question and discern just what makes human expression *different* than the creativity of the computer. It suggests not a posthu-man convergence of human and computer, but rather an increasing desire to affirm their difference. Thus, our first speculative claim about the sociality of socialbots: *socialbots negatively define the boundaries of human sociality online.*

From Bot or Not to the distorted text of CAPTCHAs (or Completely Automated Public Turing test to tell Computers and Humans Apart), the mecha-nisms for differentiating between human and bot are not about embracing the blurring between human and machine. These techniques are employed to define what counts as 'human' and differentiate it from 'not human'. Machine forms of intelligence are presented as discernable and excludable from this definition of the human. This task of differentiation may never be fully successful, as some bots will always pass as human and some humans may not meet the criteria to fully count as human—these systems of differentiation, after all, result from a reductive cybernetic understanding of humanness that assumes humans and machines to be ontologically interchangeable (Hayles, 1999). But these methods presume that this distinction can be made with meaningful results. Consequen-tially, we should think of them *as a way to negatively define humanness through the exclusion of bots and other artificial intelligences.* The horizon of a posthuman future leads to an affirmation of a binary in which 'human' can only be specified through the spectre of the 'non-human', a binary differentiation which paradoxically emerges because both human and non-human are thought to be essentially computational.

With this negative definition of the human comes a negative definition of sociality. Sociality is often thought of as emerging from something in common, be it the shared 'social facts' of Durkheim or the 'community' theorized by Ferdinand Tönnies as *Gemeinshaft*. These definitions understand the social as a positive, shared bond. They inform the popular conception of a society that interacts over social media through sharing, openness, and collaboration (cf. Fuchs, 2014, pp. 37–49). But this understanding of the social presumes that society is made up of beings that have something in common, and does not account for how this 'common' is produced in the first place—especially as it's rare that all members of a society actually do share the same social facts, possess the same relations or feel part of the same community. The negative production of human sociality demonstrates that there are some actors permitted to be those who share in a society constituted through creative communication, and others whose exclusion is apparently required to maintain the possibilities of online commonality.

In his lectures '*Society Must Be Defended*', Michel Foucault suggests that the sovereign state that emerges in the wake of monarchy's demise is organized around 'the right to make live and to let die' (2003, p. 241). Foucault proposes this well-known definition of biopolitics to describe how the powers of the sovereign king, which were organized around the right to make die, have been transformed along with the possibility of delineating the boundaries of state and society. Under monarchy, state and society were shaped out of incorporation into the king's body, subject to the will of the king. Biopolitical sociality, however, is statistically shaped out of the definition of a constitutive exterior that must be excluded for society to have any sort of coherence. Similar understandings of the social and sociality ground some variants of Marxist political theory (i.e., Laclau, 2014, pp. 101–125). Societies are formed in relation and in conflict, in which oppositional antagonisms constitute their boundaries, their possibilities for interaction and any possible space for political action. These social boundaries are often defined by the limits of who should be saved and whose 'life' is, if not actively excluded, then beyond recognition by social institutions that perform 'commonality' and 'community' through this function of exclusion.

The bots we've discussed so far are relatively small examples that gesture towards some rather large claims—though we can make similar arguments about some of the most popular social networking websites today. In December 2014, the photo and video-sharing platform Instagram deleted millions of accounts in what a number of popular commentaries named the 'Instagram Rapture'. Instagram, which is owned by Facebook, gave the following rationale for the mass deletions: 'Keeping Instagram authentic is important to us, so we do our best to remove spam, fake accounts and other people and posts that don't follow our Community Guidelines' (Instagram, 2015b). To keep things 'real' Instagram removed a massive number of accounts—including many of those held by socialbots attempting to pass as human users. As just one particularly notable example of the carnage produced by their 'rapture', Instagram's main account on the service, an image feed which promotes the company's stated goal of 'capturing and sharing the world's moments' (Instagram, 2015a), lost 18.9 million followers, which amounted to more than 29% of its subscribed users (Goel, 2014). Instagram grouped all bot-run accounts together under the category of 'spam', similar to the way such accounts are defined by some computer scientists and journalists as 'confidence bots' or 'social spammers' (Li, 2015).

The Instagram Rapture demonstrates how this understanding of sociality implicitly organizes the 'social' in social media—not the assumed commonalities of the social that ground social theory of the past, along with contemporary theories of the social-like actor-network-theory (Latour, 2005). In spite of deferrals to sharing and commonalities that emerge from human users connecting online, this space of commonality only exists (or at least the 'authenticity' of the relations performed in this space only exist) because of the active removal of 'false' non-human actors. The very name 'Instagram Rapture', though chosen as a somewhat jocular metaphor, demonstrates how there are 'lives' in the form of online profiles that Instagram 'lets die' through sorting methods that define who is connected and visible on their social network and who is excluded and, ultimately, deleted (or 'raptured' away to Instagram heaven). Consequentially, the possibility of online sociality requires socialbots to serve as a negative precondition for understanding 'real' social relations between (human) people. The role of sorting processes that descend from the Turing Test do not simply suggest that computers can pass as people online—or that this passing is, in and of itself, an issue for social media. Rather, these sorting processes demonstrate how the 'social' in social media can only be maintained if the non-human is removed, thus rendering the non-human necessary for defining just what counts as 'human sociality' made possible online.

Non-humans Are Becoming the Arbiters of Humanness

But this isn't to suggest that 'bots are people, too' and that we should embrace a holistic (if 'open') sociality comprised of the network of humans, objects, things, software processes and so on. This is a common strategy among those influenced by Bruno Latour (see Bryant, 2011; Harman, 2009; Latour, 2005), who suggest that because objects clearly have agency beyond that of the human, and share in the material production of reality with the human, then the task of politics is to trace networks of human and non-human actors to more accurately describe the constitution of reality. Objects and things are part of a 'democracy' that exists as a totalizing, collective assemblage. The political theorist Jane Bennett makes a similar claim when she states, 'we are also nonhuman and that things, too, are vital players in the world' (2010, p. 4). According to these writers, agency is distributed throughout the world, infinitely entangled, and any rigid distinction between human and non-human is an ontological error. We all exist on a singular, flat plane of reality, in which human and object share in the agency that produces our reality.

We should follow these authors in acknowledging how non-human agents do, in fact, play an active role in shaping the world. They should not be excluded from any analysis of reality's construction. But we should not dismiss the negative distinctions between human and non-human that serve to produce the everyday understanding of online sociality. The 'social' in social media is produced through the imposition of a constitutive exterior that necessarily excludes the non-human and, as well, defines some humans as non-human when profiles are deleted or suspended automatically. This fact remains, even if it does not mesh with how we may understand the ontology of objects. Most significantly, we have to acknowledge that these distinctions between human and non-human are often built into algorithms, and are thus made not directly by human decision, but delegated to non-human agents programmed to identify non-human bots for purposes of deletion. The sociality of social media should not be understood as a singular, flat actor-network, as this 'sociality' only exists through algorithmic processes that inherently exclude themselves from 'social' relations. Our second speculation: *non-humans are becoming the arbiters of humanness.*

If we return to Bot or Not, the entire purpose of a Turing Test for poetry is to reveal how flimsy human notions of authorial intent are for the judgment of a poem's aesthetic qualities. The fact that Gertrude Stein's poems are thought by many of the site's visitors to be written by a bot, for instance, does little to challenge them as 'art', or even as examples of 'human communication'. It does raise questions about the subjective evaluation of a poem and the assumptions readers bring to poems when they judge them to be meaningful or ultimately random assemblages of text, however. With Bot or Not, like other more traditional forms of the Turing Test, it is a human who is making the distinction between human and non-human based on performative evidence. As humans aren't particularly good at making this distinction based on what they observe, then it appears logical to conclude that interior states don't really have significance and it's just the performance that matters. This is one of the implications of the Turing Test (see Hayles, 1999; Peters, 1999, pp. 233–241). The interior presence of consciousness is less important than the performance of 'consciousness', especially since it's not as if everyday experience enables us to possess knowledge about the consciousness of another. As long as a person appears to be a person, and appears to act as a person, then one may as well conclude that they are, in fact, a person.

But the Instagram Rapture, in particular, suggests something different from what is assumed about 'humanness' by simplistic Turing Tests and post-cybernetic understandings of identity performance. Differentiating between human and non-human on Instagram and other social media platforms is rarely a task for human observation, but for automated bots and algorithms that sort users based on predictive models developed from data accumulated online and analysed. Passing as a human online does not depends on a bot's appearance as human to a human, at least when it comes to being deleted as spam. A bot passes as a human if it appears human *to another bot*. The recent changes to Google's reCAPTCHA system highlight how differentiating between human and non-human is a task for non-humans, not for humans. Because bots can regularly pass the older forms of CAPTCHAs made up of distorted text, Google has switched to using 'an advanced risk analysis engine' that considers 'the user's entire engagement with the CAPTCHA, and evaluates a broad range of cues that distinguish humans from bots' (Google, n.d.), though, of course, this 'entire engagement' is limited to what can be inscribed and analysed by Google. While Google and Instagram do not use the same means for sorting human from non-human, similar mechanisms appear to ground both platforms and their ability to differentiate human from bot. Looking at a wide range of data gathered from online interaction (be it with a CAPTCHA or with Instragram), algorithms are able to predict—though never with complete certainty—whether or not one is human. Statistical processes of evaluating online behaviour are used to produce normative schemas, identifying and excluding bots through practices and analytics that are ultimately inaccessible to (or cannot be performed by) immediate human perception about online interaction.

Bots and algorithms are instrumental in determining whether or not we count as human online, based entirely on a massive amount of data for which we possess no direct access. If Instagram or Facebook delete our account, there's always a chance that it's because we've been judged to be non-human by the automated means for maintaining user accounts on social media. These bots have excluded our profiles through probabilistic statistical methods. Where methods for differentiating self from other have always been essential for the negative constitution of self and society, these are usually internal distinctions about specifying what isn't included, specifically from the perspective of those included. The boundaries for inclusion are set by those who find themselves as a normative part of society. Here, bizarrely, we see the inverse: *agents effectively excluded from the social decide who is excluded from the social.* The coherence of that which is 'social' is produced entirely through the negative exclusion of the non-human, performed by processes that are themselves non-human agents.

Socialbots are Liminal Social Entities

As we have seen, sociality in social media is regulated, principally by algorithmic processes, in order to delineate a space for those who are nominally human. User accounts that perform proscribed actions—such as commenting too much or too quickly, following too many profiles, sharing links to spam and so on—are liable to be excluded. In practice, however, bots continue to proliferate on social platforms, partly because these regulatory systems are far from infallible, but also because some platforms are relatively tolerant towards bots, especially bots that do not go out of their way to aggravate human users. The most notable example of such a platform is Twitter, where at least 8.5% of active accounts are bots—at least according to the company itself (Seward, 2014). Twitter's acquiescence to the presence of automated accounts has paved the way for a profusion of bots created for literary, artistic and entertainment purposes (Flores, n.d.; Hansen, 2013).

Like spambots that seek to impersonate humans, these creative bots often situate themselves at the threshold between human and non-human. They neither perform a flawless impression of humanity, nor are they immediately recognizable as automated software. For this reason, they can be viewed as 'liminoid' performances, in the sense used by cultural anthropologist Victor Turner. According to Turner, rituals of liminality involve a transition between two states of identity—such as rites of passage. In industrialized societies, however, these experiences are replaced by liminoid performances characterized by play, recreation and experimentation. Thus, our third speculation: *socialbots are liminal social entities*. We suggest that the performances of the creative socialbot should be thought of as one of the most striking 'collective liminal symbols' (Turner, 1982, p. 84) of the social media age.

The range of creative bots on Twitter spans those that simply relay entire corpuses of text in alphabetical order—such as Allison Parrish's popular @everyword bot, which tweeted a list of words in English—to those which recombine tweets and other online data to create mash-ups and poetry, to others that reply or send private messages to other Twitter users (Hansen, 2013). Two prominent categories of socialbots serve as useful illustrative examples of their liminoid quality. The first type includes bots which purport to mimic or parody humans, sometimes known as 'ebooks' bots in reference to the famous Twitter account @Horse_ebooks, originally a spambot tweeting found text which was later taken over and operated covertly by an artist as a 'faux' bot (see Bollmer, 2016, p. 136). These parodic socialbots typically recombine portions of sentences from online source material using a randomizing process known as a Markov chain, based upon the statistical probability of specific words and transitions co-occurring. Like spambots, they draw upon the vast repository of online social data about human interactions (Gehl, 2013, p. 2) to mimic a wide range of human and quasi-human identities, including a teenage girl (@oliviataters), Bruno Latour (@LatourBot), an amalgam of Walt Whitman and modern-day users of the hashtag #FML (@WhitmanFML), and a simulacrum of any Twitter user who engages the bot in conversation, created from their archived tweets (@tofu_product). The aleatory nature of the Markov chain means that the results are rarely foolproof impersonations of human users, though they nonetheless produce popular social media content of an absurdist bent, with a characteristic combination of coherent meaning and nonsense.

A second prominent category of Twitter bots demonstrates how humans in networked environments often come to resemble machines. The automaticity associated with bots is deployed to parody the ways humans can appear mechanistic, predictable and clichéd—so much so that a few lines of code can mimic their behaviours. One example is @AmIRiteBot, which mocks a particular type of pun that its author, Darius Kazemi, believes is overused online. 'I'm interested not in whether computers can be smarter and funnier than people', said Kazemi in explaining his motivation for building the bot, 'I'm interested in how people are often dumber and not funnier than computers' (Finley, 2013). Other examples of this type include @RedScareBot, which reacts to references to communism on Twitter with expressions like 'Socialist plot' and 'I see red people' in a caricature of knee-jerk McCarthyism; @OperationBot, created to lampoon a propensity of the Australian Government to give code-names to its policies that sound like the results of a random word generator; and Mark Sample's @NSA_PRISMbot, which satirizes the remorseless nature of National Security Agency surveillance by pretending to spy on fictional internet users. These assaults on the often mechanical nature of human behaviours and institutions are particularly pointed when the bots are mistaken for actual humans, such as Ben Abraham's @FalseFlagBot, which retweeted conspiracy theories and was followed by those who thought it was a human account, and @ElizaRBarr, a bot which uses simple natural language processing techniques associated with the ELIZA chatterbot to interact with supporters of the Gamergate hashtag in order to comment upon the 'completely mindless' nature of those interactions (Scocca, 2014).

In her examination of the practice of drag, Judith Butler (1990) pointed out how imitative performances by one gender of another can demonstrate the contingent nature of the category of gender itself (pp. 136–139). In a similar way, the imitative performances of both these types of socialbots invite us to queer the stable categorization of human and non-human. The ability of bots to act and 'pass' as human online should provoke questions about the limited range of acts performed by human users on social media, and just how reductive the 'sociality' associated with these acts can be. While they blur the lines between human and non-human, these impersonations also often subtly reinscribe these categories, just as drag can uncritically replicate traditional gender roles (p. 137). Many of these bots are born out of the assumption that it is noteworthy for a piece of software to even remotely bear a passing resemblance to a human. The tweets produced are often not remarkable in themselves. They are of note only insofar as they are produced by bots—or, alternatively, because of the assumption that humans and bots are fundamentally different, and that the former should not be expected to act like the latter. Kazemi's AmIRiteBot doesn't interrogate the relationship between human and bot, or even question the role of social media infrastructure in restricting the possibilities for social interaction, but rather seeks to convey the author's disdain for the poor standard of 'human' communication online. Thus, challenges to the distinction between human and machine provoked by socialbots do not necessarily represent the celebration of an automated, machinic agency; rather, they may point to the need to solidify the distinction between human and bot. Paradoxically, then, socialbots are liminal entities that often highlight a human desire to eradicate liminality and enforce a coherent distinction between human and non-human.

Socialbots Are Developing a Distinctive, Machinic Sociality

Other socialbots exist which do not seek to perform as human, and do not foreground the perceived boundary between human and machine. These are not spambots or creative bots, but rather bots that fulfil a range of routine, utilitarian functions aimed at helping human users of social media, principally by finding, analysing, processing and transmitting data. For example, Wikipedia is home to over 1,800 bots carrying out a wide variety of tasks such as combating vandalism, policing copyright violations and alerting users to mismatched brackets (Wikipedia, n.d.). These bots have user pages like their human counterparts, on which other users post 'Barnstars', 'cookies', 'smiles' and other symbolic rewards to recognise laudable activity. The social news platform Reddit also harbours a thriving community of instrumental socialbots which perform a diverse range of tasks, including paying Bitcoin tips to other users, creating animated GIFs, summarizing information from linked news stories and correcting the spelling of 'Ghandi' to 'Gandhi'. As on Wikipedia, these bots operate from normal user accounts and are 'upvoted' or 'downvoted' just like human users. Similar functional bots also exist on Twitter: @congressedits, for example, records edits made to Wikipedia by anonymous IP addresses from the United States Congress. In all three cases, users can be observed addressing these bots with a degree of affect typically shown to humans rather than machines. For example, one journalist replied to @congressedits: 'Ha! Wikipedia has blocked users from US House of Reps IP addresses. Well done @congressedits . . .' (Wahlquist, 2014).

Like the creative bots discussed in the previous section, these bots can be considered liminal entities, insofar as they integrate important aspects both of human and non-human agencies. But unlike bots previously discussed, their goal is neither to confound nor delight users through more or less successful mimicry, nor comment on the human-non-human frontier. They are embraced or rejected by communities of users—by upvoting, favouriting, retweeting or praising them, or by downvoting, blocking, reporting or criticizing them—entirely according to their ability to perform intended tasks. They occupy a position that is at once situated within human society, performing vital functions for it, yet also fundamentally disconnected from its concerns. In this respect they recall Georg Simmel's well-known account of 'the stranger', who lives in close quarters with native members of a community yet remains separated by an unbridgeable social gulf, thus being both 'near and far *at the same time*' (1964, p. 407). For Simmel, strangers bear distinctive qualities of detachment and objectivity, are confined to specific occupations that they fulfil on behalf of native members of a society, are also typically treated as members of a group rather than as individuals. Socialbots of this kind, restricted to instrumental functions for human users of social networks, are regarded by human users in a similar way.

Unlike the stranger in Simmel's account, these bots do not share an obvious common humanity with the native members of the community; they are universally recognized as ontologically distinct. Nonetheless, they are very often treated—at least to outward appearances—as if they are human. Interactions with these bots seem to adopt an attitude of playfulness, as if a new, future conception of sociality is being rehearsed in a half-serious way. Such interactions are perfunctory, but there are instances of much more elaborate social dynamics emerging. One community on Reddit, for example, purports to advocate for the 'struggle and advancements of disadvantaged bots'. Users record hundreds of instances of bots receiving contempt from other users causing them to suffer 'low self-esteem' and 'depression', and even pen obituaries for banned bots (Reddit, n.d.). These interactions treat bots not solely as clever automatons that mimic humans, nor as insightful commentaries on the human-machine interface, but as bots *qua* bots with their own distinctive goals, even if these goals are only to serve humans as digital serfs.

Moreover, another type of machinic sociality is also occurring as a result of socialbots interacting with each other, completely untethered from the goal of relating to or assisting humans. An example (Figure 8.1) is an interaction that took place between the conversational bot @oliviataters, a bot that mimics the film producer Keith Calder, @notkeithcalder, and a customer service bot run by the Bank of America which joined the other two in conversation when it detected the acronym 'BOA' being used (Madrigal, 2014). Way Spurr-Chen's pixel remixing bot @pixelsorter has also been noted for its striking, emergent 'conversations' with other image mash-up bots such as @badpngbot (Brandom, 2014). These exchanges can even have significant offline consequences—or are intended to have offline consequences—as in the case of the Dutch Markov chain bot that was investigated by police after it issued a death threat to another bot (Hern, 2015), or of an entire bot network that attempted to disseminate a falsified news story about an ISIS bombing in Louisiana. This story was heavily circulated online yet, in spite of its apparent design in producing terrorism-related panic, failed to achieve any notice from 'trending' news algorithms, as its circulation was almost entirely among socialbots on Twitter, Facebook and Wikipedia—and no one else (Borthwick, 2015).

These types of interactions will most likely increase as the number, variety and capacity of socialbots continues to expand—particularly those that botmaker Mark Sample (2014) has described as 'green bots'. Green bots generate their content from dynamic, open corpuses of information rather than closed datasets. Bot-to-bot relations, rather than bot-to-human relations, are therefore an

FIGURE 8.1 A conversation between Twitter bots @oliviataters, @notkeithcalder and @BofA_Help

important vector of online sociality, which could one day even come to dominate it entirely. From this emerges our fourth speculation: *socialbots are developing a distinctive, machinic sociality*. Regardless, it is clear that a bidirectional dynamic is at play in the shared territory where bots and humans relate to each other. While humans are training socialbots to be more human, and more adept at understanding and catering for human behaviours and needs, humans are also finding that they need to accommodate the increasingly autonomous social behaviors of socialbots.

Socialbots Serve as a Fluid and Flexible Limit to Human Sociality Online

Throughout this chapter we have argued that there is a complex and unusual relationship between bots and humans characterized by a number of dynamic processes. Bots serve as a negative exterior to any possibility of human sociality on social media, with the lines between human and non-human policed through other bots. At the same time, bots often embrace a kind of liminal space between human and non-human. While this liminality has the potential to challenge boundaries between human and non-human agency, it is often employed to further reify the distinction between human and bot—and to critique those online who are not acting properly 'human'. And finally, there are emergent bot 'ecologies' in which bot-to-bot interactions are performed independently of necessary human awareness, often produced through simplistic methods intended to create helpful online tools.

There are numerous kinds of bots which all perform different basic functions. Some may not consider all the bots we've discussed in this chapter to be 'social-bots'. Our fifth, and final speculation—perhaps the most speculative of our claims advanced throughout this chapter, but one that sums up the ultimate argument we've been making throughout our 'speculations': *socialbots serve as a fluid and flexible limit to human sociality online*. The 'social' in social media is not a given, and certainly not a space produced out of assumed commonalities, sharing and collaboration. Rather, this 'social' is negatively determined through the active exclusion of those who do not count as 'people' online. The liminality of the socialbot, however, demonstrates that this boundary is constantly shifting and rarely stable. Bots pass as people all the time—but this does not point towards an erosion of the boundaries between human and non-human. Rather, it points to a continued desire to assert and reify these boundaries, often through auto-mated means assumed to identify impostors far better than human capabilities. Bots produce a boundary constantly renegotiated, a horizon necessary for 'human' connection. Yet this horizon is one ever receding into the distance, ever pointing back to the same questions: *What is it that defines human being on the internet? What is a human being at all, anyway?*

References

Bennett, J. (2010). *Vibrant matter: A political ecology of things*. Durham: Duke University Press.

Bollmer, G. (2016). *Inhuman networks: Social media and the archaeology of connection*. New York: Bloomsbury.

Borthwick, J. (2015, March 7). Media hacking. *Medium*. Retrieved from https://medium.com/in-beta/media-hacking-3b1e350d619c

Brandom, R. (2014, September 30). This is what happens when two pixel-mashing bots get in a Twitter fight. *The Verge*. Retrieved from http://www.theverge.com/2014/9/30/6875163/this-is-what-happens-when-two-pixel-mashing-bots-get-in-a-twitter

Bryant, L. R. (2011). *The democracy of objects*. Ann Arbor, MI: Open Humanities Press.

Butler, J. (1990). *Gender trouble: Feminism and the subversion of identity*. New York: Routledge.

Finley, K. (2013, August 22). Twitter 'joke bots' shame human sense of humor. *Wired*. Retrieved from http://www.wired.com/2013/08/humor-bots/

Flores, L. (n.d.). Genre: Bot [Blog post]. Retrieved from http://iloveepoetry.com/?p=5427

Foucault, M. (2003). *'Society must be defended': Lectures at the Collège de France 1975–1976* (M. Bertani & A. Fontana, Eds., D. Macey, Trans.). New York: Picador.

Fuchs, C. (2014). *Social media: A critical introduction*. Los Angeles: SAGE.

Gehl, R. W. (2013, June 17). The computerized socialbot Turing test: New technologies of noopower. *SSRN*. Retrieved from http://dx.doi.org/10.2139/ssrn.2280240

Gehl, R. W. (2014). *Reverse engineering social media: Software, culture, and political economy in new media capitalism*. Philadelphia: Temple University Press.

Goel, V. (2014, December 18). Millions of fake Instagram users disappear in purge. *New York Times Bits Blog*. Retrieved from http://bits.blogs.nytimes.com/2014/12/18/millions-of-fake-instagram-users-disappear-in-purge/

Goldsmith, K. (2011). *Uncreative writing: Managing language in the digital age*. New York: Columbia University Press.

Google. (n.d.). *Google reCAPTCHA*. Retrieved January 28, 2015, from https://www.google.com/recaptcha/

Gunkel, D. J. (2016). The other question: Socialbots and the question of ethics. In R. W. Gehl & M. Bakardjieva (Eds.), *Socialbots and their friends: Digital media and the automation of sociality*. New York: Routledge.

Hacking, I. (1999). Making up people. In M. Biagioli (Ed.), *The science studies reader* (pp. 161–171). New York: Routledge.

Hansen, M. B. N. (2015). *Feed-forward: On the future of twenty-first-century media*. Chicago: University of Chicago Press.

Hansen, T. (2013, November 24). Draft spec 0.3 for a bot taxonomy [Online forum post]. Retrieved from https://gist.github.com/tullyhansen/7621632

Harman, G. (2009). *Prince of networks: Bruno Latour and metaphysics*. Melbourne: Re Press.

Havelock, E. A. (1986). *The muse learns to write: Reflections on orality and literacy from antiquity to the present*. New Haven: Yale University Press.

Hayles, N. K. (1999). *How we became posthuman: Virtual bodies in cybernetics, literature, and informatics*. Chicago: University of Chicago Press.

Hern, A. (2015, February 12). Randomly generated tweet by bot prompts investigation by Dutch police. *The Guardian*. Retrieved from http://www.theguardian.com/technology/2015/feb/12/randomly-generated-tweet-by-bot-investigation-dutch-police

Instagram. (2015a). *@instagram*. Retrieved January 28, 2015, from http://instagram.com/instagram

Instagram. (2015b). *Instagram help center: Accurate follower/following counts*. Retrieved January 20, 2015, from https://help.instagram.com/566399886839044/

Kittler, F. A. (2013). *The truth of the technological world: Essays on the genealogy of presence*. (H. U. Gumbrecht, Ed., E. Butler, Trans.). Stanford: Stanford University Press.

Laclau, E. (2014). *The rhetorical foundations of society*. London: Verso.

Laird, B., & Schwartz, O. (n.d.). *Bot or not.* Retrieved from http://botpoet.com

Latour, B. (2005). *Reassembling the social: An introduction to actor-network-theory.* Oxford: Oxford University Press.

Li, S. (2015, January 15). For spambots, flattery gets you everywhere. *The Atlantic.* Retrieved from http://www.theatlantic.com/technology/archive/2015/01/for-spambots-flattery-gets-you-everywhere/384665/

Madrigal, A. (2014, July 7). That time 2 bots were talking, and Bank of America butted in. *The Atlantic.* Retrieved from http://www.theatlantic.com/technology/archive/2014/07/that-time-2-bots-were-talking-and-bank-of-america-butted-in/374023/

Peters, J. D. (1999). *Speaking into the air: A history of the idea of communication.* Chicago: University of Chicago Press.

Reddit. (n.d.). botsrights [Online forum]. Retrieved from http://www.reddit.com/r/botsrights/

Sample, M. (2014, June 23). Closed bots and green bots [Blog post]. Retrieved from http://www.samplereality.com/2014/06/23/closed-bots-and-green-bots/

Scocca, T. (2014, October 15). #Gamergate discovers its ideal audience: A completely mindless bot. *Gawker.* Retrieved from http://themachines.gawker.com/gamergate-discovers-its-ideal-audience-a-completely-m-1646786502

Seward, Z. (2014, August 11). Twitter admits that as many as 23 million of its active users are automated. *Quartz.* Retrieved from http://qz.com/248063/twitter-admits-that-as-many-as-23-million-of-its-active-users-are-actually-bots/

Simmel, G. (1964). *The sociology of Georg Simmel* (K. Wolff, Ed. & Trans.). New York: Macmillan.

Turner, V. (1982). Liminal to liminoid, in play, flow, and ritual: An essay in comparative symbology. *Rice University Studies, 60*(3), 53–92. Retrieved from http://hdl.handle.net/1911/63159

Wahlquist, C. [callapilla]. (2014, July 26). Ha! Wikipedia has blocked users from US House of Reps IP addresses. Well done @congressedits. Retrieved from http://www.abc.net.au/news/2014-07-26/wikipedia-blocks-editing-rights/5625750. . . Retrieved from https://twitter.com/callapilla/status/492820246261010432

Wikipedia. (n.d.). Wikipedia: Bots. Retrieved from http://en.wikipedia.org/wiki/Wikipedia:Bots

9

AUTHENTICITY BY DESIGN

Reflections on Researching, Designing and Teaching Socialbots

Stefano De Paoli, Leslie Ball, Natalie Coull, John Isaacs, Angus MacDonald, and Jonathan Letham

Introduction: Socialbots, Social Relations and Figurative Actors

In 2011 CNET news reported the theft of 250 gigabytes of personal data from Facebook (Musil, 2011). The event was the work of researchers (Boshmaf et al., 2011), who demonstrated the vulnerabilities of humans using social media to social engineering attacks. The study showed the extent to which a Social Networking Site (SNS) could be infiltrated by computer programs imitating human behaviour, the so-called *socialbots*. A socialbot aims at attracting 'followers' by building a network of trust relations amongst its followers and convincing other users they are interacting with a person and not a software. The aim of the socialbot could be deception, spamming, the collection of private data or even the distribution of malware. Research on socialbots is still circumscribed and we are starting to see the level of threat that they can have for Internet users. Some contributions to socialbot research have been made in the area of computer security (Boshmaf et al., 2011, Elishar et al., 2012, Wald et al., 2013), studying issues such as socialbot nets or penetration into an organisation via SNSs supported by socialbots.

On another line of thinking, however, there is the realisation of the potential to foster research into the creation of intelligent software. An important input to this came from the *socialbot competitions* via the Web-Ecology Project (Hwang et al., 2012), which demonstrated how socialbots could penetrate and distort existing social networks and triggered a debate about developing relational and somewhat autonomous software for SNSs. Socialbots are a mixture of intelligent automation and social deception: bots refer to the automated aspects of these artefacts whereas social refers to the ability of these bots to operate in and shape what Hwang et al. (2012, p. 40) call human systems: 'When they become sufficiently sophisticated, numerous, and embedded within the human systems within which they operate, these automated scripts can significantly shape those human systems.' Socialbots are composed of a mixture of technical and social knowledge. Socialbots are computer programs that scrape and collect information from SNSs and use this to inform actions such as awarding 'likes' or interacting with people. They, as detailed by Gehl and Bakardjieva (2014, Socialbot Book Cfp), 'are built out of datasets produced by social media users and thus reflect our social media use back on us.' However, socialbots are also designed to conduct activities with the goal to appear as humans in SNSs. There is here a sort of figurative aspect—a technology pretending to appear like humans in a social relation online—which underpins the more functional aspect of socialbots as algorithms that scrape and use real data from SNSs. Appearing human-like is necessary for a socialbot to succeed in building a network of trusting followers, but also for avoiding automatic detection from SNSs. Automatic detection is often based on the use of algorithms aimed at identifying behaviours which appear not to be human, where measures such as time intervals among posting content, or the extensive distribution of URLs, are used to tell bots and humans apart (Chu et al., 2010; Ferrara et al., 2014).

Shaping technology/building society (Bijker & Law, 1992) is the title of a key book in the research tradition of the *Science and Technology Studies* (STS). The book title captures the idea that the shaping of technological systems has a pivotal role in the processes of social ordering. For example, an artefact such as the speed bump helps engineers to build ethical drivers (Latour, 1992). The metal weight attached to room keys in hotels helps the hotel managers to 'build' obedient customers who return the room keys before leaving (Latour, 1992). Low height bridges placed on popular routes could enhance discrimination toward people travelling on buses (Winner, 1980). Different systems for the automation of machine tools can support the creation of a de-skilled working class and foster managerial control (Noble, 1984). In all these classic STS examples, the stabilisation process of a technological system is also a process shaping social order, based on designers and engineers programmes of actions. In this book on Socialbots, a similar perspective is adopted by Latzko-Toth (Chapter 3) when he reflects on how Internet Relay Chat (IRC) bots were stabilised via socialisation of technology processes to the extent that bots could also be entrusted with excluding unwanted human users from IRC channels. In the STS perspective, failure to build social order is also always possible, if the users do not follow the prescriptions of technological systems and betray engineers' programmes of action (Latour, 1992). For example drivers can ignore the speed bump and keep speeding, probably at the expense of damaging the suspension of their cars. In previous examples we can identify how social choices are tied with technical choices in the stabilisation of social relations. However, when the stabilisation is achieved, social choices that lead to the technical design disappear from immediate sight—a blackboxing or to cite Latour (1999, p. 304) 'the way scientific and technical work is made invisible by its own success'—and technology seems to become independent from social actions. We propose to study socialbots using a similar STS perspective. The key point we will discuss, however, is that the blackboxing of a socialbot is successful when certain social aspects remain visible, as by design, a socialbot needs to authentically appear like a human in online relations.

In a seminal paper entitled 'Where are the missing masses' and contained in the aforementioned book, Latour (1992) offers a discussion to how technological artefacts can both replace human actions and shape further human actions. These aspects are captured with concepts such as the delegation to non-human and the notion of inscription. Delegation is a process where engineers design technological systems to which they delegate tasks that can be conducted on behalf of humans. For instance, if the engineers are tasked with the goal to make drivers behave ethically, one solution could be to place a policeman at every street corner in a city. Achieving this, with an army of policemen, could be rather expensive and an alternative solution would be to delegate the same agency to technological artefacts, for example to traffic lights or speed bumps. With the speed bump forcing drivers to slow down engineers do not need an army of policemen to solve their problem and all these human actors (engineers as well as policemen) disappear from the scene: the same desired social ordering (force drivers to slow down) is ensured by an artefact to which engineers have delegated the ability to act on human behalf.

Building on this example, Latour presents a conceptual continuum in which he elaborates on the idea that actors in a network—whether human or not—can have the same form of agency, i.e., both a policeman and a speed bump shape the ethical drivers. However, this agency may be presented to drivers with a different figurative gradient. This gradient is part of the script of technology creators who may decide to inscribe in technological devices also the appearance of human beings. Using the analogy of the text author (a theme deeply diffused in the STS literature), Latour explains that it is dependent on the choice of the author to inscribe a more or less figurative nature to actors in a text: 'The enunciator . . . is free to place a description of him or herself in the script' (p. 241). Likewise, engineers as 'authors' of technical mechanisms can inscribe figurative properties into these mechanisms. Latour makes the example of le Petit Bertrand, a mechanical meat roaster present in the restaurant of a French city. To the roaster mechanism, engineers have added the ornament of a small man to which it seems that the act of cooking the meat is delegated. In the example of city traffic, the engineers' problem is to have an actor to regulate traffic, be it a speed bump or a policeman. While these actors are meant to force drivers to behave ethically, they are presented to these same drivers with different figurative scripts (see Figure 9.1): the speed bump is non-human and non-figurative whereas the policeman is human and figurative. Other artefacts can be placed on the continuum such as a flag-waving robot which has the shape of a human and is therefore non-human and figurative.

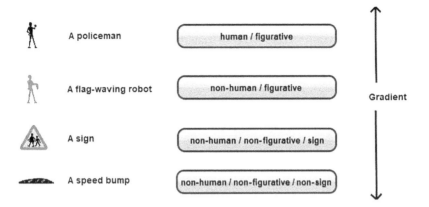

FIGURE 9.1 Actors with same agency but different figurative gradients

Building on this example the preliminary question we explore in this chapter is: which position should a socialbot occupy in a continuum similar to the one proposed by Latour? To approach this question we can consider socialbots as technologies to whom designers have delegated the ability to create a network of relations on SNSs. This is something which also human users of these sites want to achieve. For instance, a community manager for a brand could be placed in the human-figurative position. The goal of the community manager is also to build relations in SNSs based on trust. However—assuming that the agency is the same—in which position of the continuum should we place a socialbot? Whereas the two positions at the bottom of Figure 9.1 do not seem to apply easily, we can perhaps argue that a socialbot can occupy the position of the flag-waving robot: i.e., non-human and figurative, it is a non-human actor which has the shape of a human. However, on further inspection, this position would appear unsuitable for a socialbot. A passage from the original paper by Latour (1992, pp. 243–244) reveals this:

> On the freeway the other day I slowed down because a guy in a yellow suit and red helmet was waving a red flag. Well, the guy's moves were so regular and he was located so dangerously and had such a pale though smiling face that, when I passed by, I recognized it to be a machine (it failed the Turing test, a cognitivist would say). Not only was the red flag delegated; not only was the arm waving the flag also delegated; but the body appearance was also added to the machine.

The point is that these actors (human or not) are part of a network of relations with other actors. It would appear possible for drivers entering in relation with actors regulating traffic to recognize that a non-human/figurative actor, such as the flag-waving robot, is indeed an artefact and not a human. The flag-waving robot would not pass a Turing Test (Turing, 1950), because the driver can tell that human body appearance was delegated to the machine. However the flag-waving robot capacity to influence drivers will not be undermined by this. From the perspective of socialbot makers, however, inscribing in the bot the capacity to pass as human—the capacity to pass a Turing Test—would seem a fundamental aspect of the agency of the socialbot script. A socialbot script will fail if the bot can be told apart by 'the audience', like other users or automatic detection tools. In summation, our perspective is that in a socialbot the figurative inscription is a fundamental part of the agency, and the socialbot success depends from this. A socialbot is not like *le Petit Bertrand*, where the anthropomorphic character seems to add little to the agency of the roaster, i.e., *le Petit Bertand* does not add much to the act of roasting the meat and it seems more ornamental than functional. Socialbots pose a different problem as their blackboxing is viable only if humans are not able to tell them apart as non-humans. In order to succeed in their deceptive goals, socialbots cannot hence occupy the non-human and figurative position of the continuum. We remain therefore with the problem of investigating the extent to which the figurative script is fundamental for the socialbot agency. In the next section we offer a solution to this problem and argue that the goal of socialbot designers has much to do with answering this same problem.

The Making of a Socialbot: Authenticity by Design?

We could at this point—just as an initial hypothesis—argue that the designer of a socialbot will seek to create a technology that reaches the human and figurative gradient of the continuum, and their script needs to be more than just human appearance. Certainly one could argue that figurativeness in the social media environment is defined differently from the 'real' environment. In SNSs, user profiles and the interface mediate the interaction, and socialbot engineers can take advantage of 'datasets produced by social media users' and reuse these to delegate credible figurative aspects to socialbots. Ultimately the problem for socialbot makers is not much different from, for example, the traditional Turing Test where for the machine passing as a human depends on producing credible communications in a dialogue with a human interrogator, where there is no direct physical encounter between them. The problem for socialbot makers is not about cutting the shape of a human, like the flag-waving robot, which will be seen by a driver, but about building a credible and informational profile in SNSs which will be seen by users and with whom users will interact.

To investigate our hypothesis, we propose a reduced version of the continuum proposed by Latour (1992) which has just two positions. The first one, the human and figurative, is occupied by an actor, a human user like the community manager, whose agency is to entertain social relations on SNSs with other human users. The second position is occupied by another actor, the socialbot whose

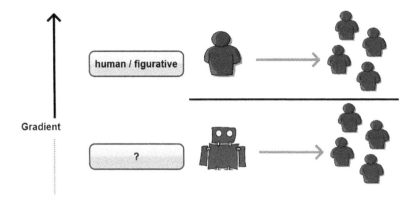

FIGURE 9.2 Where to place socialbots on the continuum?

agency is the same. The definition of the second position, however, remains to be decided and is presented by a question mark (?).

To answer this question we draw initially on our own research. Elsewhere, in a comparative research on bots in Massively Multiplayer Online Games and socialbots, we discussed how SNSs explicitly claim of wanting interactions among users on the websites to be 'authentic' and 'genuine' (De Paoli, 2016). A dictionary definition of the word *authentic* would see this as an adjective meaning something which is '*real or genuine, not copied or false*'. Authenticity is similarly defined by SNSs: via the opposition to what is not an authentic relation. This is commonly discussed in documents such as *Terms of Services*, as the following excerpt from Pinterest (2012) exemplify:

> Keeping Pinterest authentic is vital to helping people discover the things they love. That's why we've built a dedicated spam team that has been hard at work investigating reports and building systems that detect, remove and prevent spam.

For SNSs,[1] authentic and genuine interactions are those taking place without spam and other manipulative activities, including those taking place via automated means. As a further example, Facebook quite recently (October, 2014) published an article entitled *Keeping Facebook activity authentic*, in which the SNS emphasizes risks connected with fake likes, spam and use of malicious code. All these activities can also be connected to the use of socialbots and manipulative automation techniques. From our perspective, the issues surrounding authenticity of social relations in SNSs provide an interpretative key to focus on the problem of where to locate socialbots in the continuum.

A similar perspective can be easily traced in social media marketing articles under the name of *Social Media Automation Dilemma*, or in other words whether

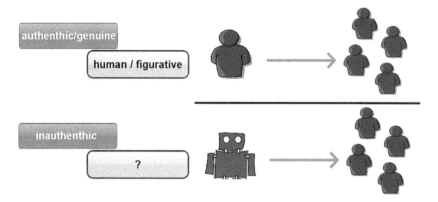

FIGURE 9.3 Socialbots in the perspective of SNSs

the benefits of building engagement with automation can outweigh direct personal interaction with customers, and the extent to which automation leads to in-authenticity. The following excerpts, taken from web articles that discuss this dilemma illustrate this point:

> There is no substitute for genuine, authentic interaction with your audience. That being said, you cannot be all things to all people, just like you cannot be on all platforms at all times. Nor do you need to be. The right tool at the right time in the right place frees up some of your precious time, enabling you to actually engage MORE.
>
> *(Socialnotz, 2013)*

> On one hand I can understand why it's not a great idea in the sense that automation runs counter to elements like engagement and authenticity that constitute the social part of social media . . . On the other hand, though, I also see where social media automation can have some positive uses.
>
> *(Mattocks, 2012)*

We see from these excerpts that automation could undermine authenticity. However social media marketing also sees advantages in automation that can in certain instances surpass the need for authenticity. For example, community management for brands might be expensive in terms of monetary and human resources. Therefore, on occasion, relying on automated means is seen as a viable option. Social media automation offers opportunities to replace human labour with machines, which reduces costs and increases productivity (De Paoli, 2016). Nonetheless, despite some advantages it is clear that automated interaction carries risks of hindering authenticity. It would seem therefore that the figurative inscription to socialbots needs to be supported by a level of authenticity which becomes part of the relation between the socialbot and those (the users) interacting with it. We will now turn our attention to a limited number of conceptualisations of authenticity in scholarly work in order to offer some theoretical perspective and then relate this to our discussion about socialbots.

Authenticity has been investigated in existential philosophy. Simplifying this perspective, authenticity could be seen as a sort of dialectical movement of human beings toward greater autonomy, reaching a genuine existence, free from some of the meaningless aspects of contemporary life. For instance, in the work of the German philosopher Heidegger (1977), authenticity is linked with the notion of enframing (*Gestell*) the rationalising technical frame of modern societies, which obscures authentic existence of human beings in their being-thrown-in-the-world (*Dasein*). Human beings need to rediscover an authentic relation with the world, by freeing themselves from the enframing of modern technical thinking. Coming from a different set of premises, Karl Marx introduced the notion of alienation. In this perspective the capitalist mode of production exercises a sort of enframing on workers (Eldred, 2000), reducing them as appendices of machines and depriving them of the very same product of their own work. The working class needs to free itself from capitalist relations of production, with a revolutionary movement seeking to achieve authentic relations of production within a new socialist society. It is not the scope of this chapter to enter into this debate, however, for our inquiry on socialbots; what we can learn from these perspectives is that they discuss authenticity as something that needs to be achieved with a dialectical process. It is not a static condition, but rather a movement from a less authentic situation towards a more authentic one.

From an entirely different perspective, the notion of authenticity is discussed by Turkle in a paper entitled *Authenticity in the age of digital companions* (Turkle, 2007). Turkle investigates the relations between humans and robotic artefacts, touching also on the extent that people consider real and genuine relations that they have with social robots, such as the relations between children and advanced robotic toys. Far from being artificial, these relations are often meaningful for people. They appear as relations of a different sort, but no less authentic than those we have with other people. Children in particular do seem to care about their robotic toys. Authenticity is a component of the relation between human and robots, but it is ultimately how the human actor sees this relation that makes it authentic. This discussion is linked many times by Turkle with the ELIZA effect, which appears to offer a negative and problematic definition of these relations, when humans take these relations too seriously. Contrary to this view, Turkle appears to say that these relationships are authentic for the humans because they care deeply about their robotic companions. A further similar position is offered by Kahn et al. (2007) in a paper published in the same special issue as that of Turkle. The authors discuss several benchmarks to evaluate the success of human-robot interaction including privacy, imitation and creativity. One such benchmark is *the authenticity of relation*. The authors argue that 'many people are uncomfortable accepting to use a model for human-human interaction' (p. 379) in a human-robot interaction. Drawing on Buber (1970), the authors discuss the difference between an 'I-It' relationship and an 'I-You' relationship. In the former case a human treats another human like an artefact, as a sort of objectification. In the latter an individual relates to another with their whole being. It is similar to the authenticity in existentialist philosophy: an authentic relation with things opposed to an objectified one. Kahn et al. (2007) argue that it is foreseeable that individuals will treat a robot via a 'I-You' relationship and this will be an important benchmark for an evaluation of the success of a human-robot interaction. For our inquiry on socialbots, what we can learn from these studies in the human-robot interaction is that authenticity is something relational where the key aspect is how the human sees the relation with the robot.

In SNSs research, Marwick and boyd (2011) discussed authenticity in relation to Twitter and the imagined audience. This research focuses on the expectation of authenticity on SNSs among users. They argue that self-presentation on Twitter varies depending on the audience and ultimately it is the audience that will judge whether what is posted by another user is authentic or not. They draw on the idea that authenticity and in-authenticity are constructed by discourse and context within SNSs. This same perspective has been directly linked to socialbots by Gehl (2013), who draws on the idea that the communications generated by a mass of people being 'authentic' and 'real' on social media blend to the creation of a sort of universal Turing machine, which can manage chunks of authentic past interactions as an omni-comprehensive, finite-state machine. Ultimately, in this perspective the ability of socialbots to pass as human beings depends on their ability to leverage such big data sets of 'authentic' communications. This is a perspective that can also be traced in publications related with the socialbot competitions, for example, Marra (2012, p. 44) discussing the design of a socialbot states: 'The thinking module crunched the observation database to find clusters of users, what they cared about, and what messages would seem authentic to them. The acting module then launched socialbots to follow these users and post potentially relevant tweets, bringing us toward our goal of interacting with human users.' Elishar et al. (2012, p. 9) discuss a similar perspective as part of the preparation of socialbots for targeted attacks, saying that in their research they have prepared socialbots with 'personal properties of real profiles such as adding posts, choosing images, choosing interests, etc' and they call this 'increasing the level of authenticity of our socialbot'. In many ways this third perspective on authenticity seems to be a reversal and re-definition of authenticity seen in the case of human-robot interaction. Whereas for Kahn et al. (2007) and Turkle (2007) authenticity referred to how a human feels toward a robot (known to be a robot), here authenticity seems to refer to successful relational deception—the passing of a robot for a real human being in the relation with the audience. The ability of the bot to use what would seem authentic content for the audience seems the key aspect in making socialbots more human-like in SNSs relations. Hence authenticity appears to be related to how socialbots can take advantage of authentic communication as well as authentic appearance, and this authenticity is part of the inscription of engineers and designers (e.g., Elishar et al., 2012; Marra, 2012).

In summary, for our inquiry the three perspectives presented all bring something to our understanding of the problem of authenticity for socialbots. Existential philosophy tells us that authenticity is not a static condition but rather a process of emancipation, a situation to which an entity can aspire. Studies in human-robots interaction emphasize the idea that authenticity is relational insofar it requires humans accepting as authentic their relationship with robotics artefacts. Social media research emphasizes authenticity as a relationship between the content and the audience in SNSs, but socialbot research stresses how this authenticity seems to be a successful relational deception based on reusing past authentic interactions—the passing of a robot for a real human being in the eyes of users. We can conclude that socialbots appear to be artefacts that exist in a dilemma: they occupy an inauthentic position (non-human, non-figurative) but to be successful they need to move towards a more authentic human-figurative situation. To achieve this, socialbot designers need to be able to inscribe in socialbots the ability to appear authentically figurative in the eyes of other users as well as automatic detection software, also by making the socialbot reuse credible past interactions. We may define authenticity in socialbots as a relational and deceptive process of emancipation which is inscribed in socialbots by their designers. Overall, we call this process *authenticity by design* (Figure 9.4), where the inscription process of socialbot creators is more than that of delegating an anthropomorphism, like the examples of *le Petit Bertrand* or the flag-waving robot discussed above. In those two examples the human appearance adds little to the agency of the mechanisms. In socialbots, the human figurative inscription of authenticity—the authenticity by design—is part of the agency of the socialbot and is what allows a successful deception when socialbots enter into relationships with human users, or automatic detection software.

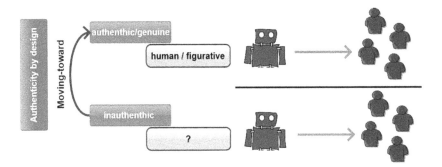

FIGURE 9.4 Solving the dilemma: authenticity by design

In the remainder of the chapter we further augment our conceptual ideas using a situated, practical and empirical approach, offering some reflections around our own research on socialbots. We discuss the initial design phases and some results of a small research project we are running.

Authenticity and Socialbot Design: Preliminary Empirical Reflections

In 2014, our team began a small research project lead by an interdisciplinary team of social and computer scientists, with the aim of finding a common ground for ongoing research and teaching interests: computer science research on social engineering and open source knowledge (Ball et al., 2012) and sociological research on the phenomenology of bots in online worlds (De Paoli, 2013a, 2013b, 2016). A convergence was found around the prototyping of a socialbot. In particular, we wanted to conduct research with an effect on our university teaching, both in terms of working directly with our students and generating material we could bring to our lectures. The team was then able to secure a small grant for prototyping a socialbot to be used on Twitter. The following excerpt is taken from our grant application: 'Our aim is a proof of concept study to evaluate how closely a socialbot can mimic a user online . . . and aims to get to a stage where the work can be progressed by integrating sociological and computational models. Such models include socially engineered deception as well as the building of social capital through trust.' Our focus was to build a prototype to examine the problem of 'how closely a socialbot could mimic a user'. Rhetorically this is a textual inscription for the socialbot as a human-figurative software for a SNS. In the remainder of this section we reflect on how some aspects of this rhetorical inscription have been transformed into technological inscriptions during the design and prototyping work.

Prototyping Authenticity

The architecture-design of our socialbot includes two applications: a *User Monitor* (UM) and a *Ground Control* (GC). This design is similar to that proposed by Marra (2012, p. 44), who distinguishes between a thinking module that studies the network and an acting module that 'decides' what content to post and how to do it. In our socialbot, the UM is a set of monitoring functions used for analysing and researching social networks. It is used for gathering initial knowledge about the network to target as well as monitoring the subsequent network-building activities of the socialbot. Starting from a random seed taken from Twitter, the monitor is able to reconstruct the tree structure of an existing social network, based on users' reciprocal mentions. This information is then made intelligible to the socialbot-master (e.g., the user of the socialbot) via a

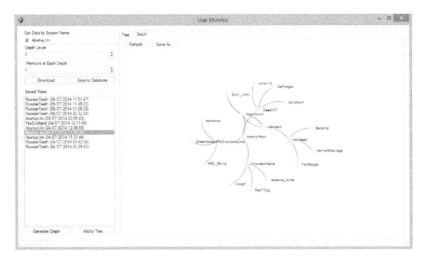

FIGURE 9.5 Screenshot of the socialbot UM Interface, with the example of a mentions tree

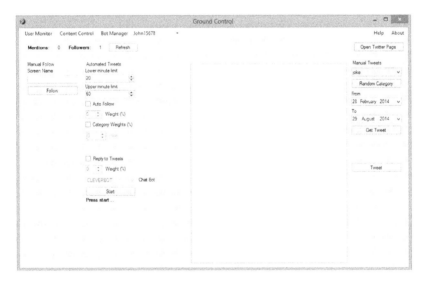

FIGURE 9.6 Screenshot of the socialbot GC with key features

visualisation of the network (see Figure 9.5 for an example). The UM allows the monitor to: (a) generate a tree of the reciprocal mentions; (b) add to a previously generated tree; and (c) view and save generated trees.

The *Ground Control* is the gateway to the active aspects of the socialbot and offers a user interface for initialisation and controlling it (Figure 9.6). Differently from the UM, the GC is an active component: it contains the key classes with which the socialbot effectively acts in SNSs and makes the socialbot appear authentic. The following is an excerpt from an email exchange between the team members which captures the critical role of the GC for achieving human authenticity:

> We are at the stage where we can generate a social network from a random seed using Twitter 'mentions' and the Twitter Search API. It looks good.
> We are now moving into the stage of thinking about the bots and maybe testing a bot against a human being using the same target network.

Indeed, the GC would allow the team to test the socialbot 'against a human being'. Early discussions around the design of the GC focused on the identification of a number of 'categories' to be used for posting on Twitter. Differently from the design proposed by Marra (2012), which first identifies the network and then offers authentic messages to target the interests of such network, we initially identified a limited number of subject areas—able to spark wide interest— in which the bot would post. This approach offers less flexibility in terms of network targeting but was deemed sufficient for our prototype. The team identified the following subject areas: sport, cooking, jokes and politics.

The first rudimentary prototype of the GC would then get live RSS (Really Simple Syndication, a popular format for web content distribution based) feeds related with the subject areas from selected websites' application program interfaces (APIs) (e.g., Reddit or BBC Sport) and post them on Twitter. This feature of the bot is controlled by a class called RSS.CS, which defines the sources for the RSS feeds to be made available in the GC and the method for parsing them. This is an initial and rudimentary example of how our socialbot would reuse past authentic communications (Gehl, 2013). Adding a source to our socialbot is done in the following format:

```
public List<Content> [SourceName]_[CategoryName]() { }
```

For example, the RSS feed for the subject area 'jokes' taken from Reddit would be:

```
public List<Content> Reddit_Joke() { }
```

However, in the early stage of the prototype design, discussion within the team revolved around the consideration that by merely posting content on Twitter the bot would look inauthentic. Human users do much more than just posting content on Twitter covering a single subject—they post content from multiple sources, follow and unfollow other users, and reply to mentions. With only the RSS.CS class, the socialbot was still in the non-human and figurative position. Several design ideas were discussed to increase authenticity. An issue that was identified was that even if some of the tweets posted by the socialbot could raise interest in other users, then the socialbot would not be able to entertain any interaction with those users. The following aspects were discussed by the team in order to increase authenticity:

1.   how to make the socialbots follow other users and in which way;
2.   how to make the socialbot publish content not from just one of our categories (e.g., sport only) but from a mix of multiple categories; and
3.   how to make the socialbot utter meaningful responses to mentions coming from other users and how often.

To address the first list point we prototyped an autofollow class. In our solution, the socialbot-master can define from the GC interface a likelihood weight for following another user, with a value ranging from 0% to 100%. This allows a totally passive or totally aggressive following behaviour as well as all the options in between. Therefore, with a following likelihood set at 100% the bot will adopt a very aggressive behaviour and follow another user each time there is a reciprocal contact. By decreasing the likelihood to lower percentages, the socialbot will appear more passive and follow more sparingly.

A second class we prototyped is the 'Category Weight'. This allows the socialbot to post content from the pre-defined categories, again using a likelihood value. A category could have a weight set as 0% (the bot will not post content under this category) or 100% the socialbot will only post content related to the selected category (e.g., only posting about sport). Using this approach it is possible to have a composite posting behaviour from the categories by varying the percentage of each category. The total sum of the percentages across categories must add up to the value of 100. For example 30% sport, 50% cooking, 20% politics and hence 0% jokes.

A third class we implemented relates with offering the socialbot functionalities for replying to other users. We prototyped this in a way that it could use chatterbots: very much like a sort of ELIZA program (Weizenbaum, 1976), the socialbot would try to pick from the other user tweets the focus of the discussion and then retrieve a reasonable answer from a chatterbot. Our socialbot can answer using three different chatterbots: from the interface (Figure 9.6) it is possible to select from Cleverbot, Jabberwacky and Pandorabots. This function also works using a likelihood value: from 0% 'no reply' to 100% 'always reply' to mentions and all the values in between.

Beating 'Bot or Not': An Initial Small Experiment on Authenticity

Our first goal for the socialbot prototype was related to teaching and experimenting with our students. In particular, the teaching of Ethical Hacking degrees[2] at our University provides a rich source for exploring the many aspects of cybersecurity. A holistic approach to problem-solving in this area is being addressed by considering the human and technical issues associated with the 'cyber kill chain' (Hutchins et al., 2011). The chain describes a cyber-attack as consisting of several stages, from the reconnaissance of the target, to injecting malicious malware and ultimately to stealing data from the target. Initial penetration into a system can be achieved at the reconnaissance stage by studying the employees of an enterprise. The idea is to find the 'weakest link' in a network and conduct social engineering attacks. This could, for example, lead to the disclosure of password protected computer systems. It is here that the socialbot can be effective in studying the online behaviours of people.

In some cases the attackers may conduct the socially engineered attacks themselves. In other cases, where there is opportunity to seek vulnerability across a wider population, a socialbot can be used where it would be simply too time-consuming for the human alone. This is an example of delegation to socialbots, similar but at the same time different from the example of the community manager discussed earlier. In this case a human attacker may want to delegate his or her actions to a socialbot, which can explore large networks of people on social media quickly and autonomously. This gives rise to many research questions across the socio-technical boundary. For example, from the technical angle, how should a socialbot be designed and programmed and how believable or credible is it? From the perspective of social science, how gullible are social media users to the existence of socially engineered attacks and do they care whether a Twitter profile is real or fake?

These questions are driving a variety of student projects at Honours level dissertation at the University, where students take advantage from the prototype of the socialbot we designed. Most projects are focused on the profiling and behaviours of socialbots and on their ability to penetrate Twitter by gaining 'followers', 'mentions' and 'retweets'. These provide manipulated measures of social capital (De Paoli, 2013a) and consequently increase the pool of potential targets for a social engineering attack. Some projects in particular are creating socialbots whose task is to avoid detection by anti-bot software. In essence, these are reverse engineered by understanding the automatic detection processes and making the socialbot look more authentic by passing the measure scores of automated Turing Tests. In the following pages we shall present some results of a student project related to authenticity and automated detection.

In one of the experiments-dissertation projects, tests were made against the 'Bot or Not' score (Ferrara et al., 2014), a metric which can be used to give a score of how likely an account is controlled by a socialbot. The 'Bot or Not' is also an online tool that allows anyone to check a Twitter user name against the metric: by simply inserting the Twitter username in an online form, the service checks the likelihood of whether the account is controlled by a bot. A high 'Bot or Not' score deems the username as controlled by a socialbot. In our perspective the 'Bot or Not' is a measure which can determine the success of the authenticity by design for a socialbot. The 'Bot or Not' application uses six different measures or 'classes of features' and an algorithm is trained for the identification of socialbots. These measures can be summarised as (Ferrara et al., 2014, p. 7):

- **Network**—Statistics based on networks generated via retweet, mentions or hashtag analysis.
- **User**—Based on user meta-data such as geolocation, account language, account creation time.
- **Friends**—Analysis based upon followers, followees and posts.
- **Timing**—Analysis of the timings between generation (tweets) and consumption (retweets) on Twitter.
- **Content**—Based upon analysis of recent tweets.
- **Sentiment**—Uses sentiment analysis algorithms to detect 'emotional' scores.

The 'Bot or Not' score increases with the 'aggressive' behaviour of a socialbot, such as:

- posting from the same source too often;
- aggressive following;
- a large difference in the number of followers to following ratio.

Reversing the process of automatic detection is therefore a relevant task for socialbot designers in devising a technology which attempts to fool these classifications by using a number of different techniques. The inscription of authenticity could also be seen as an attempt to design a socialbot that receives low scores in the 'Bot or Not' test. We discussed in previous pages the case of the driver able to tell that the flag-waving robot is indeed an artefact and not a human (Latour, 1992). The case under discussion here is similar: to an actor (the 'Bot or Not' algorithm) is delegated the task of telling bots and humans apart. However, if the socialbot manages to convince the 'Bot or Not' that a human is controlling the account, we are then moving from the non-human figurative condition, toward the human and figurative condition (Figure 9.5). Again this is what we call authenticity by design: the movement of a socialbot from the non-human figurative to the human-figurative condition (Figure 9.4).

In our experiment, our socialbot uses the following techniques in order to reduce the likelihood score of the 'Bot or Not':

- **Following/unfollowing**—This helps to trick the friends' classification as long as the users who do not follow back are removed.
- **Manual posting**—Helps with network, content and sentiment classification by creating natural tweets.
- **RSS posting**—Helps with network classification by providing a wide range of sources.

- **Status stealing**—Counters network, content and sentiment analysis by stealing already posted natural tweets which may contain links or further hashtags.
- **Retweet**—Counters network classification by increasing the bots hashtag and mention networks.
- **Post delays**—Counters timing classification by varying the times at which the bot will post.

Whilst it is important to monitor the 'Bot or Not' metrics to deceive the automatic detection it must also be difficult for humans to detect the socialbot. One of the first authenticity shortcomings of a socialbot relates to the content published on the SNS. If the content is easily recognisable as coming from an existing or similar source then it would be easy to assume that this was posted by a socialbot. It is important that a socialbot generates content from multiple sources, mimicking the natural behaviour of humans. The socialbot used in this experiment can publish by gathering the content via multiple sources, extending the list discussed in the first version of the prototype, which are defined in a settings file. The settings file is parsed by the socialbot and by using these settings the bot is able to decide how to operate. Each line in the settings determines an action that the bot can perform as well as its frequency, as shown in Figure 9.7.

By giving a socialbot a wider variety of choices from which to post, the socialbot becomes much more authentic and less predictable, whilst still publishing content and gaining followers. The socialbot defined in the example uses a limited number of sources for posting about cats, but the list of sources can be extended to include a variety of other subjects.

A socialbot was then launched[3] with the setting shown in Figure 9.7. After one week the socialbot was able to gain 14 followers and a Klout[4] score of 13. These figures indicate that the socialbot was starting to gain 'social capital' within

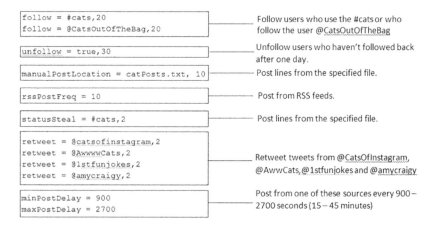

FIGURE 9.7 BotSettings.txt file

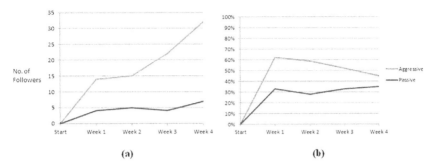

FIGURE 9.8 Number of followers (a) and 'Bot or Not' score (b) for the aggressive and passive bots

Twitter. However, in this first week the socialbot also received a relatively high 'Bot or Not' score of 62%. Over a second week of running the settings were adjusted to become more passive—this included reducing aggressive following, increasing the number of sources the bot posted from and increasing the frequency of unfollowing users to remove the users which had not followed back.

After the second week the 'Bot or Not' score had reduced by 5% and the Klout score increased to 18, indicating that the bot had become more 'influential'; however, the bot only gained one follower during this week. This indicates that more aggressive techniques in the short term can probably gain social capital much faster than passive techniques, but the socialbot is much more easily detected. There appears to be therefore a certain trade-off between gaining followers and the level of authenticity that the socialbot can display toward metrics such as the 'Bot or Not', at least in the short term. After four weeks of running, the bot had managed to accrue 32 followers and a Klout score of 20. Comparatively, a passive bot, which was set up at the same time as the aggressive bot, only managed to gain seven followers in the same amount of time, as shown in Figure 9.8. However, it received a much lower 'Bot or Not' score of 35% compared with the aggressive bots' score of 45%.

These figures show that the aggressive bot has been much more successful in gaining social capital than the passive bot. After the first week of running the aggressive bot was set to passive, which shows in the graph becoming flat (a), the bot gained fewer followers and the 'Bot or Not' score decreased. After week 2 the bot was set to aggressive again (a) which shows an increase in followers, more sources of content were also added to the bot which allowed the 'Bot or Not' score to decline further. It appears then that by tweaking the values of the socialbot it is possible to reach a reasonable balance between authenticity and acquisition of followers. Figure 9.9 shows the 'follower network' for the aggressive bot at week 4 of the experiment: it can be seen that whilst some of the followers did come from aggressive following patterns (those linked to both the account @CatsOutOfTheBag and AggressiveBot as the socialbot is set to follow all the

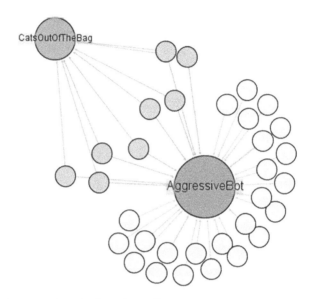

FIGURE 9.9 AggressiveBot (MelMarsh_) Follower graph (32 followers) and the account CatsOutOfTheBag used in the file BotSettings.txt (Figure 9.7) to create aggressive following

users who also follow the CatsOutOfTheBag account), the vast majority of the followers have followed via other methods unrelated to the follow/unfollow technique.

Conclusion

In this chapter we proposed that authenticity is a key aspect for understanding the nature of socialbots and that authenticity is something which is inscribed in socialbots via the design process. We call this concept *authenticity by design*: the process in which designers attempt to inscribe in socialbots the ability to appear authentically like humans in SNSs, by limiting what they recognize as the design shortcomings that may make the bot look like an automata. While this is clearly a figurative inscription in the sense discussed by Latour (1992), it is also more than just the inscription of an anthropomorphism. The figurative aspect is indeed also a part of the agency of a socialbot that supports successful deception in SNSs. It is a movement of the socialbot towards a human and figurative situation. To understand this inscription process we have drawn on contributions from existential philosophy, human-robot interaction and social media research to present how the idea of authenticity could be applied to socialbots and their design. Emancipation from an existing condition (being a machine and not a human, but needing to look like a human), meaningful relations between human and robots, and audience interpretation of the content posted by socialbots are all elements which are relevant for understanding the authenticity problems for socialbot designers. We then proposed first-hand empirical reflection on a small research and teaching project we are currently running. We discussed some aspects of the design of a socialbot prototype. In our example additional features such as the ability to follow other users or to contribute towards a discussion were added with the aim of making the socialbot pass as an authentic human, in particular in the attempt to deceive automatic detection tools.

Ultimately our approach is underpinned by interdisciplinary research goals relating to social engineering. We explicitly argue for the need to mix social and computer science in the study of socialbots. Our perspective concerns the deception of users of online social media to ascertain the ability of a socialbot to build social influence and social capital by infiltrating a social network of potential targets. This is in line with computer security research on socialbots (Boshmaf et al., 2011; Elishar et al., 2012; Wald et al., 2013), and the understanding of how socialbots constitute a security threat and what countermeasures can be implemented to protect users and companies against them. What we discussed in this chapter—that should be considered for future work—is to measure how authenticity by design has effects on trust building and the creation of social capital which can later be exploited for social engineering attacks. In our experiment we have shown that there is a possible correlation—not necessarily positive— between these two aspects and that by using a less authentic agency the socialbot gains followers much faster, at least in the short term. This correlation between authenticity and the building of a social network of connections deserves attention and will be a focus of our future activities. Indeed, we may prefigure that the challenge for socialbot makers is to increase the capacity of the bot to build a network of connections and infiltrate these networks, without losing authenticity. This point ties with the second perspective used in the chapter and is where we see an increased need for interdisciplinary research.

Indeed, the problem of authenticity in socialbots is more a matter of design than a matter of appearance in the eyes of the target audience (users and detection tools). We argue for the need to study the decisions and negotiations that engineers make in creating these technologies and the inscription processes by which engineers conceptualize future audiences of their socialbot technologies. While research on socialbots is mainly concerned with understanding the effects of socialbots in SNSs, for example, from a security perspective or in relation to social network building in marketing—we argue that we should not underplay research into the design and development of socialbots as a technological artefact which strives for human authenticity. Effects of socialbots on SNSs and the design that precedes these effects are two faces of the same coin and socialbot research should make an effort to capture both these faces. In this regard, in order to research what are the effects of the design choices on SNSs, we should also explore questions such as: What are the social choices made in the construction of a socialbot? What negotiations underpin the design of a socialbot? What programs of action are reflected in socialbots' designs? What conceptualisation of future audiences do engineers make? And lastly, what are cases of failure in the design of socialbots? In this chapter we offered a possible interpretative lens to these processes by understanding the stabilisation of a socialbot as an 'authenticity by design' process. We could argue that our discussion is also a different reading of the famous Turing Test: the experiment devised by Alan Turing (1950) to test whether a machine, such as a computer, could pass as a human in a series of communication exchanges. As noted by Harnad (1992), indeed the problem set by the Turing Test is one of generating human-scale performance capacity (Harnad, 1992) for artificial intelligence. The authenticity by design offers a different terminology to approach the design-phase that precedes the deployment of the human-scale performance software—the socialbot—as well as a concept to test the effectiveness of this performance in SNSs.

Notes

1. An exception to this is Twitter (2015), in which automated applications are allowed, under certain specific conditions.
2. See http://www.abertay.ac.uk/courses/ug/ethhac/ and http://www.abertay.ac.uk/courses/pg/ehcs/.
3. The socialbot was launched in January 2015.
4. Klout is a social media app which ranks users according to their influence, https://klout.com/home

References

Ball, L. D., Ewan, G., & Coull, N. J. (2012). Undermining-social engineering using open source intelligence gathering. In A. Fred & J. Filipe (Eds.), *Proceedings of the 4th international conference on Knowledge Discovery and Information Retrieval, KDIR12* (pp. 275–280). Barcelona, Spain, October 4–7. Setubal: SciTePress-Science and Technology Publications.

Bijker, W. E., & Law, J. (1992). *Shaping technology/building society: Studies in sociotechnical change.* Cambridge, MA: MIT Press.

Boshmaf, Y., Muslukhov, I., Beznosov, K., & Ripeanu, M. (2011, December). The socialbot network: When bots socialize for fame and money. In *Proceedings of the 27th annual computer security applications conference* (pp. 93–102). New York: ACM.

Buber, M. (1970). *I and Thou.* New York: Charles Scribner's Sons.

Chu, Z., Gianvecchio, S., Wang, H., & Jajodia, S. (2010, December). Who is tweeting on Twitter: Human, bot, or cyborg? In *Proceedings of the 26th annual computer security applications conference* (pp. 21–30). New York: ACM.

De Paoli, S. (2013a). The automated production of reputation: Musing on bots and the future of reputation in the cyberworld. *International Review of Information Ethics (IRIE), 19*(07/2013), 12–21.

De Paoli, S. (2013b). Automatic-play and player deskilling in MMORPGs. *Game Studies, 13*(1). Retrieved from http://gamestudies.org/1301/articles/depaoli_automatic_play

De Paoli, S. (2016). The rise of the robots in virtual worlds: A comparison and a framework for investigating bots in social networks sites and MMOGs. In Y. Sivan (Ed.), *Handbook on 3D3C platforms* (pp. 59–83). Springer International Publishing.

Eldred, M. (2000, May). Capital and technology: Marx and Heidegger. In *Left Curve* (No. 24). Oakland: California. Version 3.0. March 2010.

Elishar, A., Fire, M., Kagan, D., & Elovici, Y. (2012, December). Organizational intrusion: Organization mining using socialbots. In *Proceedings of the 2012 international conference on social informatics* (pp. 7–12). IEEE.

Facebook Security. (2014, October 3). *Keeping Facebook activity authentic*. Retrieved from https://www.facebook.com/notes/facebook-security/keeping-facebook-activity-authentic/10152309368645766

Ferrara, E., Varol, O., Davis, C., Menczer, F., & Flammini, A. (2014). The rise of social bots. *arXiv preprint arXiv:1407.5225*.

Gehl, R. W. (2013). The computerized socialbot Turing Test: New technologies of noo-power. *Available at SSRN 2280240*. Retrieved from http://papers.ssrn.com/sol3/papers.cfm?abstract_id=2280240

Gehl, R. W. & Bakardjieva, M. (2014). *Edited collection on socialbots—call for papers*. Retrieved from http://robertwgehl.org/blog/?cat=43

Harnad, S. (1992). The Turing Test is not a trick: Turing indistinguishability is a scientific criterion. *ACM SIGART Bulletin, 3*(4), 9–10.

Heidegger, M. (1977). *The question concerning technology, and other essays*. New York: Harper Torchbooks.

Hutchins, E. M., Cloppert, M. J., & Amin, R. M. (2011). Intelligence-driven computer network defense informed by analysis of adversary campaigns and intrusion kill chains. In J. Ryan (Ed.), *Leading issues in information warfare & security research* (pp. 80–106). Reading: Academic Publishing International.

Hwang, T., Pearce, I., & Nanis, M. (2012). Socialbots: Voices from the fronts. *Interactions, 19*(2), 38–45.

Kahn, P. H., Jr, Ishiguro, H., Friedman, B., Kanda, T., Freier, N. G., Severson, R. L., & Miller, J. (2007). What is a human? Toward psychological benchmarks in the field of human–robot interaction. *Interaction Studies, 8*(3), 363–390.

Latour, B. (1992). Where are the missing masses, sociology of a few mundane artifacts. In W. Bijker & J. Law (Eds.), *Shaping technology/building society* (pp. 225–259). Cambridge, MA: MIT Press.

Latour, B. (1999*). Pandora's hope: Essays on the reality of science studies*. Cambridge, MA: Harvard University Press.

Marra, G. (2012). Socialbots are robots, too. *Interactions, 19*(2), 44–45.

Marwick, A. E. & boyd, D. (2011). I tweet honestly, I tweet passionately: Twitter users, context collapse, and the imagined audience. *New Media & Society, 13*(1), 114–133.

Mattocks, R. (2012, October 11). *Winning the debate over social media automation marketing*. Retrieved from http://www.lyntonweb.com/blog/bid/83157/Winning-the-Debate-over-Social-Media-Marketing-Automation

Musil, S. (2011, November 11). *Socialbots steal 250GB of user data in Facebook invasion*. CNET. Retrieved from http://www.cnet.com/news/socialbots-steal-250gb-of-user-data-in-facebook-invasion/

Noble, D. F. (1984). *Forces of production: A social history of industrial automation*. New York: Knopf.

Pinterest. (2012, December 6). *Fighting spam*. Retrieved from http://blog.pinterest.com/post/37347668045/fighting-spam

Socialnotz. (2013, January 10). *Top 3 social media automation tools.* Retrieved from http://www.socialnotz.com/top-3-social-media-automation-tools/

Turing, A. M. (1950). Computing machinery and intelligence. *Mind, 59*(236), 433–460.

Turkle, S. (2007). Authenticity in the age of digital companions. *Interaction Studies, 8*(3), 501–517.

Twitter. (2015, April 8). *Automation rules and best practices.* Retrieved from https://support.twitter.com/entries/76915

Wald, R., Khoshgoftaar, T. M., Napolitano, A., & Sumner, C. (2013, August). Predicting susceptibility to social bots on twitter. In *Proceedings of 14th international conference on Information Reuse and Integration (IRI), 2013 IEEE* (pp. 6–13). IEEE.

Weizenbaum, J. (1976). *Computer power and human reason, from judgment to calculation.* San Francisco: W. H. Freeman.

Winner, L. (1980). Do artefacts have politics? *Daedalus, 109*(1), 121–136.

10

DO SOCIALBOTS DREAM OF POPPING THE FILTER BUBBLE?

The Role of Socialbots in Promoting Deliberative Democracy in Social Media

Timothy Graham and Robert Ackland

> The electric things have their lives, too. Paltry as those lives are.
> —*Rick Deckard, in* Do Androids Dream of Electric Sheep?

Introduction

Philip K. Dick's seminal novel, *Do Androids Dream of Electric Sheep?* (adapted into the film *Blade Runner*), poses multiple questions about the relations between humans and non-humans. One such question concerns whether we might one day reach a future in which robotic humanoids (i.e. the titular 'androids') and humans are no longer easily distinguishable. In the age of social media, it is now evident that the question Dick initiated over half a century ago has found particular relevance in the figure of the 'socialbot'. As Gehl contends: 'The last tweet you got may have been from a robot' (Gehl, 2014, p. 21). Yet 'bots', loosely defined as software applications involved in the automation of tasks over the Internet, have existed since at least the mid-1990s. For example, web crawlers (bots that assist in the collection and indexing of web content) and 'spambots' (bots that send massive volumes of unsolicited 'spam' email) are so mundane as to appear almost invisible nowadays. Similarly, chatbots or 'chatterbots' (bots that engage in conversation in online spaces) have existed since the early years of the web (Mauldin, 1994), and have developed into the research area of 'conversational agents' (see also Chapter 5). Scholars have also recently explored the role of bots in automated high-frequency trading within global financial markets, drawing to attention the world-shaking events that can emerge as a result of their complex interactions (Steiner, 2012).

Given the broader context, one might ask what is unique or interesting about socialbots. Hwang et al. offer the following:

> What distinguishes these 'social' bots from their historical predecessors is a focus on creating substantive relationships among human users—as opposed to financial resources—and *shaping the aggregate social behavior and patterns of relationships* between groups of users online.
>
> *(2012, p. 40, emphasis added)*

In recent years a growing body of literature has explored the proliferation of socialbots in social media sites such as Twitter and Facebook. Indeed, various studies have now demonstrated that socialbots are able to infiltrate social media, remain undetected and even function 'successfully' as social actors (Boshmaf et al., 2011; Freitas et al., 2014). Like the conversional agent 'Max' in Muhle's study, their status as human or non-human is not always settled, although their capacity to be 'social' actors in a 'human-like' way is disputed (Chapter 5). Nevertheless, there is no doubt that socialbots are able to act successfully in generating attention and attracting followers. In an experiment to infiltrate Twitter using socialbots, Freitas et al. (2014) found that 'over the duration of the experiment, the 120 socialbots created by us received in total 4,999 follows from 1,952 distinct users, and 2,128 message-based interactions from 1,187 distinct users . . . a significant fraction of the socialbots acquire relatively high popularity and influence scores' (Freitas et al., 2014, p. 7). In a similar study, Hwang et al. (2011) discovered that socialbots were not only able to infiltrate target subnetworks on Twitter, but also to 'succeed in reshaping the social graph of the 500 targets, drawing responses and interactions from users that were previously not directly connected' (Hwang et al., 2011, p. 41). Indeed, in making sense of this phenomenon, Gehl (2014) argues that socialbots are becoming enrolled in processes of *noopower* (a term drawing on Lazzarato), broadly defined as 'the action before action that works to shape, modulate, and attenuate the attention and memory of subjects' (Gehl, 2014, p. 23). Emerging theoretical perspectives on socialbots suggests a subtle and complex role for social robotics in the context of social media.

The ability for socialbots to appear human-like and also *shape* social relations calls to mind the rogue *Nexus-6* androids of Dick's novel, which, in the eyes of the state, constituted a serious danger to individuals and society. Indeed, discourse in recent literature tends to construct socialbots as a kind of 'danger' or hazard to society. For example, we learn that socialbots are deployed to 'infiltrate' and 'exploit' social network sites (SNSs) in order to extract or expose private information about individuals and their workplaces (see e.g., Elyashar et al., 2013; Paradise et al., 2014). We are informed that 'botnets', coordinated armies of socialbots mimicking human users, are able to circumvent existing security mechanisms in order to wreak systemic havoc by spreading propaganda or misinformation (Boshmaf et al., 2011). Other studies, such as Mitter et al. (2014a) have taken the dangers of socialbots into the 'meta' realm, by developing a categorisation schema to understand and counteract the various categories of socialbot 'attacks' on SNSs. There is certainly much validity to such narratives, and the negative aspects of socialbots constitute a complex, open research problem. However, there is another side to socialbots that has not attracted much scholarly inquiry, as Hwang et al. argue: 'While much has been made about the dark side of social robotics, several positive applications interactions of this technology are emerging' (Hwang et al., 2012, p. 40).

It is therefore evident that much research tends to highlight the dangers or risks associated with socialbots—what might be considered as the 'social bad' perspective. In this chapter we seek to evaluate the obverse of this perspective in order to explore some *beneficial* capacities of socialbots (in their capacity to 'exploit' and shape online social networks). In this way, in this chapter we tackle an idea previously raised by Hwang et al: 'Swarms of bots could be used to heal broken connections between infighting social groups and bridge existing social gaps. Socialbots could be deployed to leverage peer effects to promote more civic engagement and participation in elections' (2012, p. 40). More specifically, we explore how socialbots on social media could exploit network structure to mitigate the effect of political filter bubbles and political segregation, thus promoting the Habermasian ideal of deliberative democracy—a public sphere (e.g., Habermas, 1996) where individuals can discuss matters of mutual interest and hopefully reach a common understanding or solution, or at the least can 'hear the other side' (Mutz, 2006). For simplicity, we focus much of our presentation on the microblog Twitter but our ideas are applicable to any social media where people congregate to discuss and engage with political issues (e.g., web forums, fan pages and group pages in Facebook).

The remainder of this chapter is structured as follows. In the next section we define and problematize deliberative democracy in the context of the web, highlighting key theoretical perspectives and empirical research. The third section introduces and discusses the role of socialbots in promoting deliberative democracy in social media networks. In doing so, we set forth three 'principles' for socialbots that introduce key concepts and technical methods for socialbots in this role. In the fourth section, we develop these concepts and methods further by introducing the notion of 'popperbots' and 'bridgerbots', providing a twofold 'schematic' for programming socialbots to promote deliberative democracy in social media. Finally, we conclude with a reflection on the meaning and implications of social robotics within the entangled trajectories of politics, social media and contemporary modes of power.

Filter Bubbles and Deliberative Democracy on the Web: Network Topologies, Algorithmic Sorting and Political Homophily

> He experienced them, the others, incorporated the babble of their thoughts, heard in his own brain the noise of their many individual existences.[1]

On the web, politics unfolds through topologically variant networks, and actors both shape—and are shaped by—the hybrid socio-technological environments they cohabit. In the context of political discussion online, one might be tempted to regard the Internet as an equal or neutral playing field, whereby people of all backgrounds converge to learn, debate and participate in political discourse. This was the basis of early utopian predictions of the impact of the web on politics (e.g., Castells, 1996): that the web would foster a new era of broad-based participation in the direction and operation of the political system. In contrast, Putnam (2000) and Sunstein (2001) predicted a loss of a common political discourse resulting from a fragmenting of the online population into narrowly focused groups of individuals who are only exposed to information that confirms their previously held opinions—later referred to as 'cyberbalkanisation' (Van Alstyne & Brynjolfsson, 2005).

These concerns about the potential impact of the web on democracy have continued into the present era of social media. In his book, *The filter bubble*, Eli Pariser argues that web users are increasingly entrapped within personal 'filter bubbles' that reflect back to them their already-held opinions or beliefs, and expose them to subjects they are already interested in (Pariser, 2011). The 'filter bubble', also referred to as the 'echo chamber', can be understood as emerging from two phenomena: *algorithmic sorting* (whereby external forces or 'opportunity structures' influence the types of political information and people that individuals are likely to encounter) and *individual preferences* (whereby web technologies enable individuals to efficiently select who they want to connect with and what types of information they want to be exposed to).

Algorithmic sorting occurs at both the aggregate- and individual-level. Concerns about the political implications of aggregate-level sorting first emerged in Web 1.0 research which considered the fact that the web, like many large-scale networks, has been found to exhibit a 'power law' in the distribution of in-links (meaning a very unequal distribution, with a small number of websites enjoying many in-links while the vast majority only have few or no in-links). Hindman et al. (2003) argued that power laws on the web could imply vast inequalities in the distribution of attention to different political viewpoints, since people usually find new websites either by following links (web surfing) or by using search engines such as Google, and in both cases the greater the number of in-links from other relevant sites a website has, the more likely it is to be discovered. Aggregate-level algorithmic sorting occurs in social media in the form of 'trending topics' in Twitter, for example, and forces of cumulative advantage (the 'rich get richer') can help a topic to take off. A concern is that social media companies can exert a degree of curatorial control over trending topics. An oft-cited example is the fact that, during the Occupy Wall Street movement, participants and supporters used Twitter extensively for communication and debate (garnering massive media attention), yet the #OccupyWallStreet hashtag failed to become a 'trending topic' on the Twitter homepage (Gillespie, 2012).

Individual-level algorithmic sorting is undertaken by the social media providers whereby web content is 'individualised' based on *user demographics* (e.g., voluntarily contributed profile data or trace artefact data such as browser cookies) and/or *user activity* (e.g., what types of web content users statistically tend to be interested in). In the case of Twitter, each user has a 'home timeline' that not only displays content they have elected to view, but also content that is *suggested* or *curated* by Twitter's algorithms. As the official Twitter FAQ states: 'Your home timeline displays a stream of Tweets from accounts you have chosen to follow on Twitter. New users may see *suggested content* powered by a variety of signals.' The Twitter FAQ continues: 'Additionally, when we identify a Tweet, an account to follow, or other content that's popular or relevant, *we may add it to your timeline.* This means you will sometimes see Tweets from accounts you don't follow . . . *Our goal is to make your home timeline even more relevant and interesting*' (Twitter, 2015, emphasis added).

Dormehl (2014) argues that this 'algorithmic culture' has a dual nature. On the one hand, it is useful because it filters out the endless babble, or unnecessary 'noise', that would otherwise overwhelm users and software platforms (e.g., social media sites, search engines). But on the other hand, it is also problematic because users are not presented with 'ideologically untampered' content, but rather the opposite—content that 'flatter our personal mythologies by reinforcing what we already "know" about particular issues' (Dormehl, 2014, p. 47). Recent studies suggest that social media such as Facebook and Twitter are implicated in the advent of *political* filter bubbles. Whilst the extent and nature of this phenomenon is debated (Bozdag et al., 2014), the algorithmic modulation of incoming and outgoing flows of socially generated data suggests far-ranging consequences for individuals and collectives.

While individuals are to some extent guided by algorithmic sorting, the role of individual preferences in the creation of political filter bubbles is perhaps even more important. Earlier research also considered the impact for politics of the 'narrowcasting' nature of the web, whereby users could use newly invented RSS (Rich Site Summary) feed technology to efficiently select content from online newspapers or blogs that matched their existing political outlook. The emergence of social media has provided even more opportunity for politically motivated social selectivity, as individuals can make conscious decisions as to who to friend in SNSs such as Facebook and who to follow, retweet or mention in Twitter.

Such behaviour can lead to online networks that are highly divided along ideological or political lines, a phenomenon known as political homophily.

It is an empirical question as to whether algorithmic 'filtering' of content in social media (both at the scale of population-based 'trends' and the scale of individual user 'timelines') and computer-mediated social selection (friending, following, mentioning, etc.) contribute to worsening already existing political divides across its network. The 'filter bubble' phenomenon warrants careful and serious consideration because of its possible implication in creating or worsening social rifts that centre upon ideological or political lines. As Conover et al. point out, 'a deliberative democracy relies on a broadly informed public and a healthy ecosystem of competing ideas' (Conover et al., 2011b, p. 89).

Some Principles of Socialbots for Promoting Deliberative Democracy

> We selected her as your first subject. She may be an android. We're hoping you can tell.[2]

In this section, we identify three 'principles' of socialbots for promoting deliberative democracy on social media. Drawing on Muhle (Chapter 5), these principles in a sense define the characteristics (membership categories) and respective activities (category-bound activities) of socialbots as 'good citizens'. Before enunciating our principles, it is necessary to first briefly define deliberative democracy and outline how it may be measured and quantified using network analysis.

As noted, our definition of deliberative democracy involves the Habermasian concept of the public sphere (e.g., Habermas, 1996), an informal discursive space where individuals and groups can reach common understanding about issues of mutual interest, thus influencing public opinion and potentially leading to political action. Our definition of deliberative democracy thus does not cover more formal deliberation that occurs at different levels within the political system (e.g., see Dryzek, 2010 for a discussion on deliberative democracy).

A network is a set of nodes (vertices or entities) and a set of ties (edges or links) indicating connections or relations between the nodes. While there are several types of networks that can be extracted from Twitter (as noted, the discussion focuses on Twitter for simplicity, but these ideas extend to other types of social media), we focus here on the network comprising Twitter users, where ties are created from users following each other, and retweeting, mentioning and replying to one another (we refer to this as the 'user network').

So how can we measure the extent or degree of deliberative democracy using the Twitter user network? A starting point is to construct the network of users participating in Twitter conversations on political issues, for example, by only collecting tweets that feature the #auspol (Australian politics) hashtag. So the user network might consist of all Twitter users who authored at least one tweet containing #auspol, during a particular time period. A first quantitative measure of deliberative democracy is the network *modularity* score (e.g., Newman, 2006), which assesses the strength of the division of a network into 'communities' (or clusters, or modules). Modularity ranges between 0 and 1, with a score closer to 0 indicating that more linking is occurring between clusters than within clusters (i.e., less balkanisation). While it is difficult to interpret a given modularity score as an absolute measure of deliberative democracy, modularity may be useful when one is comparing across networks (e.g., networks created for different political hashtags or the same hashtag, but constructed for different periods of time). So if we found that modularity score for the #auspol user network was decreasing over time then this would indicate that the Twitter conversation is becoming less clustered, thus indicating an increase in deliberative democracy.

However, underlying our use of clustering in the Twitter user network as a measure of deliberative democracy is a very strong assumption regarding the nature of interactions that are taking place in political spaces on Twitter. Specifically, our approach involves the use of large-scale unobtrusively collected digital trace data: mention, reply, retweet and follower ties. Thus, we assume that if a Twitter user creates a tie to another user (via a reply, retweet, mention or follow) then this tie either reflects a shared political outlook (political homophily) or, at the very least, is indicative of a desire to engage in a considered exchange of ideas. Deliberative democracy therefore involves a qualitative dimension that would not be accounted for in the approach we describe above. Using social network analysis (SNA) terminology, our modularity clustering measure of deliberative democracy assumes that ties in Twitter only reflect positive affect. If members of opposing political groups started engaging in name calling or abusive behaviour on Twitter (that is, creating negative affect ties) then this would lead to a network that is less clustered, but this surely would not indicate increasing deliberative democracy.

There is a second reason why we should be careful in interpreting modularity clustering in the Twitter user network as a measure of deliberative democracy. Even if there were only positive affect ties in the network, there could still be a significant change in network modularity between two time periods without any underlying change in deliberative democracy. For example, if in the #auspol conversation on Twitter there was an increase in reciprocity (I'll retweet you because you retweeted me) or triadic closure (I follow person A and person A follows person B, therefore I'm going to follow person B too), then this could result in the #auspol network becoming more clustered (modularity score increasing) without any underlying change in political homophily.

Hence we recognize that modularity is a blunt measure of deliberative democracy, but propose it as an initial way of operationalizing the principles of socialbots.

Our principles of socialbots for promoting deliberative democracy are presented in the style of Asimov's famous 'Three Laws of Robotics' (see: Asimov, 1950); however, their scope and application is much less epochal or universal. The principles relate specifically to the survival and effective functioning of socialbots on social media. In the remainder of this section we expound upon these principles in more detail, before progressing to the specific roles that we envisage for socialbots (discussed in the next section).

Some Principles of Socialbots

1. Socialbots must do no harm to human beings (measured in political and non-political terms);
2. Socialbots must protect their own existence, except where doing so would conflict with the First Principle;
3. Socialbots must make a significant improvement to deliberative democracy, obtaining *non-trivial, quantifiable effects* in the target subnetwork(s), except where doing so would conflict with the First and Second Principles.

The First Principle of Socialbots

1. Socialbots must do no harm to human beings (measured in political and non-political terms);

Isaac Asimov ushered into the world an enduring problem in robotics—namely, that the notion of a robot causing 'harm' is very difficult to define precisely. In the context of this chapter, the First Principle of Socialbots seeks to operationalize 'harm' broadly in two ways: political and non-political. We will briefly deal with both of these problems in this section and suggest several approaches to address them. Again, they are very specific to the research problem in this chapter, although we feel there may be broader applicability to socialbots vis-à-vis social media.

First, for a socialbot, what would it mean to cause *political* harm? Although this is a complex and multifaceted problem, at the most abstract level we argue that if a socialbot is positioned at a political extreme (e.g., far-right or far-left), then it is held to cause political harm and therefore contravene the First Principle. While measuring whether a socialbot is 'politically extreme' is non-trivial, we argue that this problem is not insurmountable, in light of recent developments in the literature and key concepts within SNA and graph theory. We will now briefly elaborate upon two possible paths towards measuring whether, and how, socialbots could cause 'political harm' in social media networks.

First, socialbots could be programmed to endeavour to occupy a position within the target subnetwork(s) that approximates *regular equivalence* with ideologically or politically 'moderate' users. This argument centres on the graph theoretic notion of 'regular equivalence' whereby 'two nodes in a social network are regularly equivalent if they fulfil the same role' (van Steen, 2010, p. 259). What we are suggesting here is that socialbots could be programmed to occupy a similar 'social role', or in Muhle's terms 'membership category' (Chapter 5), in the network to users who are moderate in their ideological or political views. Roughly speaking, socialbots would attempt to 'blend in' by analysing the network structure of moderate users and then attempt to replicate it, aiming to maximize an approximate *regular equivalence* with such users, within the constraints of the Twitter application program interface (API) and computational resources of the researchers. In this way, 'politically moderate' provides a kind of membership category that defines the identity of a given user, which is calculated by analysing the user's network structure.

In order to identify which Twitter users are 'moderate' and should therefore be targeted, the methods outlined in Boutyline and Willer (2014, *working paper*) and Conover et al. (2011a), appear especially suited to the task. Conover et al. (2011a) find that the best way to predict political affiliation in Twitter networks is by analysing the 'community' structure of retweet networks (i.e., where nodes represent users, and links between nodes represent whether, and how many times, user i has retweeted user j, and vice versa). In their study, Conover et al. (2011a) manually code 1,000 randomly selected users into three political affiliation categories: 'left', 'right' or 'ambiguous'. In addition to other methods, they perform community detection on the retweet network of 23,766 users, resulting in two 'clusters' emerging. They classify users by political affiliation using the cluster each user is assigned to, and find that this yields a 95% accuracy when evaluated against the manually coded users. The network structure of these target users would then provide a statistically calculable 'social role' that socialbots can emulate, by attempting to establish and maintain regular equivalence.

Second, socialbots could be programmed to endeavour to occupy a position within the target subnetwork(s) that is *maximally neutral* in respect to quantified measures of political affiliation and/or ideological segregation. In other words, what we are suggesting is that socialbots should not find themselves in a situation where they appear to have clearly 'taken a side' or become, in a word, partisan. Again, it is possible to assess this, at least crudely, using the SNA methods. In order to measure whether this has occurred would necessitate programming socialbots to periodically assess the structure of their social network and their network activity. To achieve this, the techniques and methodology as developed in Conover et al. (2011a), Golbeck and Hansen (2014) and Halberstam and Knight (2014) would provide a suitable reference point. For example, a socialbot may calculate that its structural position within the political retweet network expresses a 'left' political identity, as formulated by Conover et al. (2011a). In this case, the socialbot would seek to remedy this bias by retweeting from users who are calculated to have a 'right' political identity. Similarly, following Conover et al., socialbots may seek to ensure that their position in the network results in a classification as 'ambiguous', for example, by strategically 'mentioning' users from both clusters of the political divide (2011a, p. 197). These ideas are expanded upon further in the next section, where we focus on two specific roles for socialbots for promoting deliberative democracy in social media networks.

Attention now turns to the second definition of 'harm' as defined in the First Principle—namely, what would it mean for a socialbot to cause *non-political* harm? Here we are concerned with a more general understanding of 'harm', which evokes Asimov's enduring problematic of how to define and understand the notion of robots causing harm in a 'social' context. Accordingly, what we offer here is a rudimentary or preliminary path forward. We would like to focus upon one problem in particular, which has long-standing relevance to bots on the web—namely, that socialbots should never become 'spambots'. Thus, a socialbot is said to cause harm if, through the frequency of its activity, it inconveniences other users or those managing the service. In some respects, this harkens to the 'bad name' or negative attention that socialbots inherit from their predecessors. Socialbot creators could take at least one of two approaches to ensure socialbots do not 'spam' networks and thus contravene the First Principle. The first approach could be to set fixed parameters based on evidence from the literature—for example, sending a maximum of N tweets per hour within a fixed set of times (e.g., 8 a.m. to 9 p.m. weekdays; 1 p.m. to 11 p.m. weekends). Another approach would be to program socialbots to define their own parameters for 'non-spammy' update frequencies by calculating it based on other users in the network. For example, a socialbot could (periodically) query a random sample of 1,000 users, calculate the average tweets per hour as a function of the *total number of status updates* and the *timestamp* of when the user was created, and then take the median value of this set of averages as a socially 'appropriate' hourly rate for sending out status updates. However, we again wish to point out that this is only one aspect of socialbots causing 'harm', for which space precludes detailed discussion in this chapter. For example, determining whether the *textual content* of a given status update is 'harmful' (e.g., using offensive terms or spreading 'hate speech'). Techniques to deal with such problems may centre upon using dictionaries of terms (for offensive words) or using machine learning to build models to predict whether a tweet has a high degree of hate speech (and therefore not 'retweet' it, for example). Future research may seek to further explore such lines of inquiry.

The Second Principle of Socialbots

2. Socialbots must protect their own existence, except where doing so would conflict with the First Principle;

Perhaps the most fundamental facet of the Second Principle is that *socialbots must not be detected as non-human* (providing this does not conflict with the First Principle). However, we are not arguing that the Second Principle necessitates creating socialbots that could, for example, pass the Turing Test or instigate the kinds of existential problems presented by the *Nexus-6* androids in Philip K. Dick's novel. Far from such lofty aspirations, the Second Principle simply specifies that socialbots should present and conduct themselves in a manner that, at a minimum, ensures they survive long enough for the Third Principle to come into operation (and not contravene the First Principle). This is perhaps somewhat self-evident. Yet the scope and nature of this task is less straightforward than it might first appear, as the literature previously cited in this chapter suggests. Socialbots must not only contend with Twitter's security mechanisms (that deploy sophisticated algorithms to find and remove fake user accounts and spambots), but also avoid 'citizen policing'—users, organisations, or perhaps even other bots, that detect and report social robots to Twitter. And as the Third Principle serves to address, merely 'surviving' is only the first step for socialbots—the next problem concerns the ability to 'thrive'. It could be argued that socialbots programmed using these Principles would simply *do nothing*, thereby satisfying the First and Second Principles. For example, a socialbot that does not send out any status updates (e.g., tweets) is arguably following an optimal strategy to avoid detection and do no harm. However, the Third Principle ensures that this situation cannot occur, or, in the case that it does, there is logical reason for such inaction.

Furthermore, to achieve the Second Principle (and arguably the Third Principle), socialbots must present and conduct themselves in a manner that makes them appear sufficiently 'human' to, for example, attract new followers and retweets (again, without contravening the First Principle). Although previous studies have achieved success with the 'detection avoidance' problem, the problem of how to exploit social networks for optimal effect proves trickier. For example, some studies suggest that female socialbots with 'attractive' or 'good-looking' profile photos are more successful for social engineering on SNSs (Boshmaf et al., 2011). Others find that the 'gender' of socialbots has no correlation with success or popularity (Freitas et al., 2014). Still others, such as Wald et al. (2013), take a different tack by looking at which types of human users socialbots should target for interaction. Wald et al. found that the highest predictors of whether a user is likely to interact with socialbots comes down to how popular or influential a user is (i.e., their 'Klout' score and number of friends), and the amount of sexual language and terminology they tend to use (Wald et al., 2013, p. 10). The implication is that users who are more likely to interact with socialbots (e.g., retweeting or 'liking' their tweets) are those that are well-connected or have more followers, and those that use a greater amount of sexual language and terminology. Clearly, in terms of SNA methods, ensuring that socialbots function effectively in social media networks involves both 'art' and 'science'. At the same time, it reinforces the importance of the First and Second Principles as one way to approach socialbot ethics.

The Third Principle of Socialbots

3. Socialbots must make a significant improvement to deliberative democracy, obtaining *non-trivial, quantifiable effects* in the target subnetwork(s), except where doing so would conflict with the First and Second Principles.

At an abstract level, the Third Principle seeks to ensure that socialbots are actually achieving *something* (providing it does not contravene the First and Second Principles). In this way, socialbot activity must be *quantifiable* (accounted for statistically) and must also be *non-trivial* (having a magnitude of effect that is not negligible). It is therefore evident that analysis of the impact or effects of socialbots must pay attention to network structure and network dynamics over time. Any studies that investigate whether socialbots could, for example, heal social rifts, promote deliberative democracy, bridge segregated subnetworks or 'pop' filter bubbles, must be able to formalise socialbot activity as a *concrete, statistically calculable phenomenon*. A growing body of literature demonstrates that the methods and formalisms of SNAs provide such tools. More specifically, SNA methods to quantify and analyse political segregation and ideological clustering on Twitter have emerged in recent years (see: Conover et al., 2011a; Golbeck & Hansen, 2014; Halberstam & Knight, 2014). In particular, Mitter et al. (2014b) provide a detailed methodology for assessing the impact of socialbots 'attacks' on Twitter in terms of shaping or influencing the social graph of a subset of users. Any combination of these methods would be suited to advancing the Third Principle of socialbots, and such methods are expanded upon later in this section. Furthermore, to achieve the Third Principle, social-bots must present and conduct themselves in a manner that makes them appear sufficiently 'human' to, for example, attract new followers and retweets. This is consistent with the Second Principle, and again, must not be in contravention of the First Principle.

We can further operationalize the Third Principle by making the following argument: the presence of socialbots in target subnetworks should, over time, correlate with a *decreased modularity score* (thus implying decreased political homophily in the target subnetwork, although noting our caveat about equating changes in modularity with changes in homophily). This brings us deeper into the realm of socialbot ethics and further reveals the *raison d'être* of socialbots in promoting deliberative democracy. In this way, we can begin to explicate the 'life goals' or *telos* of socialbots in the context of this chapter—broadly speaking, to build bridges between separate, ideologically homogeneous subnetworks; to expose tightly knit clusters of users to alternative viewpoints; or to bring about measurable shifts towards deliberative democracy in online discourse. In this way, the Third Principle draws stark attention to the *normative political rationalities* that socialbots in this role embody—which could be conceived as a kind of social robotic 'hacktivism'. As Howard (2003) writes, hacktivism is understood broadly as using the tools and strategies of hackers for political ends: 'hacktivists believe that they have a responsibility to expose abuses of power and to *redistribute informational resources*' (Howard, 2003, p. 216, emphasis added). Positioning social-bots as ersatz 'hacktivists' facilitates a rethinking of their agential capacities—in this case, to propagate deliberative democracy on social media via the strategic exploitation of network structure.

Popperbots and Bridgerbots: A Schematic for Programming Hacktivist Socialbots on Twitter

> In .45 of a second an android equipped with such a brain structure could assume any one of fourteen basic reaction-postures.[3]

Programming bots to perform social roles in social media environments represents a moving target. Over time, the tasks to be performed by socialbots become suboptimal or even impossible in environments whereby the entities involved—users, protocols, algorithms, data, hardware specifications and so forth—are constantly in flux. However, the aim in this section is not to provide a comprehensive or codified tutorial for programming socialbots, but rather to set forth a general 'schematic' for how socialbots might be programmed to promote or 'propagate' deliberative democracy on Twitter. We wish to focus on issues of methodology and the conceptual, network-oriented space in which such methods would be applied, which are broadly located at the intersection of politics, the dynamics of social media networks and social robotics. We want to examine some possibilities and sketch out possible approaches moving forward. The over-arching question asks whether it is possible to program socialbots to mitigate or break down political filter bubbles and ideological segregation on Twitter, hence promoting deliberative democracy in online discourse. In this section we provide a possible answer to this question by elucidating two distinct roles and respective category-bound activities for socialbots.

1. 'Popperbots'

We conceive the 'popperbot' as a type of socialbot tasked with the role of 'infiltrating' subnetworks of Twitter users that exhibit *high or extreme levels of homophily*. Once the popperbot has established itself in the subnetwork, it would then begin to 'inject' information reflecting more moderate or even contrasting ideological standpoints. As the name suggests, the idea is that this type of socialbot will reduce, or in a sense 'pop', the ideological bubble that users within a given subnetwork are situated within, by exposing these users to alternate points of view that appear to come from a member of their own cohort. The *telos* of the popperbot is to produce measurable increases in *heterophily* in the subnetworks in which they have infiltrated. Similarly, as argued previously in relation to the Third Principle, popperbots could attempt to decrease 'balkanisation' by striving to reduce the modularity score of their target subnetwork. For example, a popperbot could be programmed to occasionally (say, with probability P) *retweet* or *reply to* users from a different subnetwork(s) that represent alternate positions on some issue. Figure 10.1 shows a popperbot infiltrating a homophilous subnetwork of Twitter users who are calculated to be 'right' (i.e., conservative) in their political orientation, which, as mentioned in the previous section, could be derived using the methods outlined in Conover et al. (2011a).

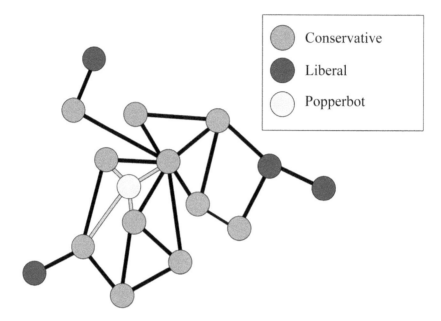

FIGURE 10.1 A 'popperbot' infiltrating a homophilous subnetwork (of politically conservative Twitter users)

If it is not yet apparent, a fundamental problem for the development of popperbots is that these socialbots must, by definition, violate the First Principle in order to do their job. In this way, a popperbot would have to act in an 'extreme' manner (as discussed previously) in order to infiltrate a homophilous subnetwork, *even if its ultimate goal was to 'pop' the political bubble* in that subnetwork. For example, a popperbot could (1) detect an extremely homophilous subnetwork of individuals and then (2) attempt to infiltrate the network by adapting its profile and 'social' activity to correspond with the target subnetwork. This popperbot could be (3) programmed to 'defect' after some time duration T or acquiring a pre-defined number of followers or friends N. Defection, of course, would occur in the form of injecting more moderate or perhaps even contrasting information into the subnetwork, as discussed previously. However, a popperbot would never infiltrate a network by pretending to be, for example, a radical Communist because doing so would definitely (and as we have previously argued, *quantifiably*) violate the First Principle. Thus, Asimov's enduring problem remains and we inherit another complex, or perhaps 'wicked', problem to address. Yet, despite these obstacles, we argue that there are possibilities for moving forward, which could be programmed into popperbots. For example, future research could explore lines of inquiry centred on time-limited infiltration and defection routines, which could allow socialbots to violate Principles within certain parameters or 'thresholds' of violation, although space precludes further discussion in this chapter.

2. 'Bridgerbots'

'Bridgerbots' are conceptualized as socialbots tasked with the role of re-routing or 'bridging' informational flows between otherwise *ideologically segregated* subnetworks. They could perform actions such as tweeting/retweeting and following users from both 'sides' of a given political or ideological debate. Bridgerbots would seek to expose users from one homophilous subnetwork to politically diverse types and flows of information from one or more other homophilous subnetworks. In this way, the network role of bridgerbots might be thought about in a variety of ways. One possibility is in terms of what Mark Granovetter described as *weak ties*. Weak ties are understood as connections between different tightly knit groups that are vital to information dissemination and therefore social opportunities. As Granovetter wrote, 'It is remarkable that people receive crucial information from individuals whose very existence they have forgotten' (Granovetter, 1973, p. 1372).

Bridgerbots could be programmed to endeavour to occupy a position within the target subnetwork(s) that maximizes their own *betweenness centrality* score. Betweenness centrality, or simply 'betweenness', is a key concept in SNA and graph theory more broadly. In a formal sense, the betweenness of a node (or vertex) is 'the total number of shortest paths between all possible pairs of vertices that pass through this vertex' (Dorogovtsev & Mendes, 2003, p. 18).[4] We can think about betweenness in terms of how important a node is in providing a path that connects isolated nodes or isolated clusters of nodes. Thus, informally, nodes with high betweenness could be loosely conceived as 'brokers' or 'exchange terminals' of information between densely connected (or 'homophilous'), but otherwise poorly connected clusters of individuals. The application of this concept to bridgerbots is straightforward—they would seek to act as 'bridges' between politically segregated clusters of users. Figure 10.2 visualises this idea by representing it within a graph.

Combining several arguments presented thus far, the role and effects of bridgerbots in respect to the target subnetwork(s) could be tied to their success in *increasing* their own betweenness score or *decreasing* the modularity score of the subnetwork that they target. That is to say, bridgerbots with *high betweenness scores* are 'bridging' political rifts more effectively than those with a low score, and bridgerbots who successfully *decrease the modularity score* of a target subnetwork(s) are successfully 'bridging' political divides. For example, we could imagine that a Twitter user receives a notification that a new user has 'followed' them—and they might even return the gesture by 'following back'. Unbeknownst to the user, they are now following a bridgerbot who has 'targeted' them because their social network is extremely homophilous. Later, having possibly completely

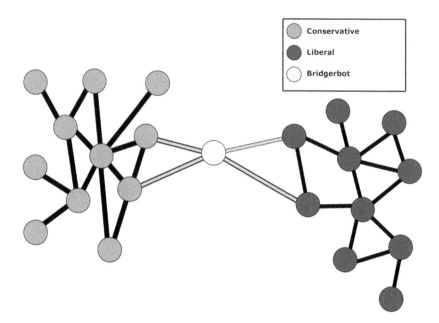

FIGURE 10.2 A 'bridgerbot' connecting two 'segregated' subnetworks (of politically conservative Twitter users)

forgotten about this new social connection (to the bridgerbot), the user might notice a tweet in their news feed that reflects a more moderate, or perhaps even competing, position to their already held beliefs on some issue. In this way, the bridgerbot has acted as a weak link, bridging heterogeneous flows of information (e.g., two or more different sides of a debate) to the actors involved in such communication networks. Over time, if the bridgerbot's betweenness score increases, or the network structure becomes less modular, then the bridgerbot can be regarded as doing a 'good job'.

Conclusion

> Your position, Mr. Deckard, is extremely bad morally. Ours isn't.[5]

In this chapter we have introduced and examined a role for socialbots that positions them not as dangers or annoyances, but rather as *socially beneficent* actors, capable perhaps of 'building a better world'. We did not seek to examine whether socialbots in this context are valid social actors with human-like agency (see Chapter 5), but rather to investigate their role in constructing and (re)assembling the social (Latour, 2005). In this way, we focussed upon a *normative* role for socialbots in creating and propagating deliberative democracy on Twitter. This, in one sense, can be thought about as socialbots 'popping the political filter bubble'—for example, building bridges between separate, ideologically homogeneous subnetworks, exposing tightly knit clusters of users to alternative viewpoints or bringing about measurable shifts towards deliberative democracy in online discourse. Yet, if socialbots 'dream' of popping filter bubbles, perhaps we can perceive within their dreams the spectre of our own political rationalities and ethical assumptions. As Paul Henman writes, 'new and emerging technologies will continue to initiate old questions in new circumstances of what these technologies mean' (Henman, 2013, p. 300). It is clear that socialbots of the kind we conceive in this chapter might also dream in *other* ways, ways that might otherwise seem unethical or politically abhorrent.

In developing this chapter, we consciously adopted a normative position for socialbots in relation to a particular social issue (deliberative democracy). In doing so, this provided a space in which to demonstrate and examine how socialbots might be used to 'exploit' network structure in order to achieve 'social good'. Yet what is defined as ethical, politically rational, socially beneficent, etc., arguably depends upon one's point of view. Hence, we can see how socialbots could be deployed to achieve different or even *opposite* outcomes for deliberative democracy, by simply adapting or perhaps 'inverting' various aspects of the ideas and methods established in this chapter. As Hwang et al. would have it: 'The same bots that can be used to surgically bring together communities of users can also be used to shatter those social ties. The same socialbot algorithms that might improve the quality and fidelity of information circulated in social networks can be used to spread misinformation' (Hwang et al., 2012, p. 40).

A particularly noteworthy focus is governments seeking to monitor and sway political discourse online. For example, the *50 Cent Party* are 'Party-paid internet commentators and opinion guiders' (Sullivan, 2012) hired by the Chinese government and other parties to attempt to steer online opinion and conversation towards particular directions. Yet one can easily imagine the *50 Cent Party* deploying socialbots alongside, or even in lieu of, human commentators and opinion guiders. Indeed, as Gehl writes, government agencies such as the US Air Force have already begun to contract out software development companies to 'gather intelligence, build consensus, and influence opinions twenty-four hours a day via a network of socialbots' (Gehl, 2014, p. 39). In this way, current concerns regarding the uses and abuses of socialbots within a political context are not unfounded. However, it is also clear that we are only in the very early stages of this phenomenon. Hence, what we are now witnessing is an increasing sophistication of socialbot technologies and a diversification of their roles and relations of power in hybrid techno-social environments (see Gehl, 2014). Gilles Deleuze once wrote: 'What counts is that we are at the beginning of something' (Deleuze, 1992, p. 7). The question is how it will unfold.

Acknowledgements

We gratefully acknowledge the helpful feedback provided by Paul Henman on an earlier draft of this chapter.

Notes

1. Dick, 1999, p. 11.
2. Ibid., p. 22.
3. Ibid., p. 25 (spoken by the character Eldon Rosen).
4. In graph theory, a 'path' is an unbroken sequence of connections between two or more vertices.
5. Dick, 1999, p. 14.

References

Asimov, I. (1950). *I, robot.* New York: Doubleday & Company.

Boshmaf, Y., Muslukhov, I., Beznosov, K., & Ripeanu, M. (2011). The socialbot network: When bots socialize for fame and money. In J. McDermott & M. Locasto (Eds.), *Proceedings of the 27th annual computer security applications conference, ACSAC'11* (pp. 93–102). New York: ACM.

Boutyline, A., & Willer, R. (2014, working paper). The social structure of political echo chambers: Ideology and political homophily in online communication networks. Retrieved from https://www.ocf.berkeley.edu/~andrei/downloads/echo.pdf

Bozdag, E., Gao, Q., Houben, G., & Warnier, M. (2014). Does offline political segregation affect the filter bubble? An empirical analysis of information diversity for Dutch and Turkish Twitter users. *Computers in Human Behavior, 41,* 405–415.

Castells, M. (1996). *The rise of the network society.* Malden, MA: Blackwell Publishers.

Conover, M., Goncalves, B., Ratkiewicz, J., Flammini, A., & Menczer, F. (2011a). Predicting the political alignment of Twitter users. In *Privacy, Security, Risk and Trust (PASSAT) and 2011 IEEE third international conference on social computing (SocialCom)* Institute of Electrical and Electronics Engineers (IEEE). New York, NY (pp. 192–199).

Conover, M., Ratkiewicz, J., Francisco, M., Goncalves, B., Flammini, A., & Menczer, F. (2011b). Political polarization on Twitter. In L. Adamic, R. Baeza-Yates & S. Counts (Eds.), *Proceedings of the fifth international AAAI conference on weblogs and social media* (pp. 89–96). Palo Alto, CA: AAAI Press.

Deleuze, G. (1992). *Postscript on the societies of control* (Vol. 59, October, Winter, pp. 3–7). Cambridge, MA: MIT Press.

Dick, P. K. (1999)[1968]. *Do androids dream of electric sheep?* London: Millennium.

Dormehl, L. (2014). *The formula: How algorithms solve all our problems . . . and create more.* New York, NY: Penguin Publishing Group.

Dorogovtsev, S., & Mendes, J. (2003). *Evolution of networks: From biological nets to the internet and WWW.* Oxford; New York: Oxford University Press.

Dryzek, J. S. (2010). *Foundations and frontiers of deliberative governance.* Oxford: Oxford University Press.

Elyashar, A., Fire, M., Kagan, D., & Elovici, Y. (2013). Homing socialbots: Intrusion on a specific organization's employee using socialbots. In *Proceedings of the 2013 IEEE/ACM international conference on advances in social networks analysis and mining* (pp. 1358–1365). New York, NY: ACM.

Freitas, C. A., Benevenuto, F., Ghosh, S., & Veloso, A. (2014). Reverse engineering socialbot infiltration strategies in twitter. *arXiv preprint: 1405.4927.* Retrieved from http://arxiv.org/abs/1405.4927

Gehl, R. W. (2014). *Reverse engineering social media: Software, culture, and political economy in new media capitalism.* Philadelphia, PA: Temple University Press.

Gillespie, T. (2012). Can an algorithm be wrong? Retrieved from http://limn.it/can-an-algorithm-be-wrong/

Golbeck, J., & Hansen, D. (2014). A method for computing political preference among twitter followers. *Social Networks, 36*, 177.

Granovetter, M. (1973). The strength of weak ties. *American Journal of Sociology, 78*(6), 1360–1380.

Habermas, J. (1996). *Between facts and norms: Contributions to a discourse theory of law and democracy.* Cambridge, MA: MIT Press.

Halberstam, Y., & Knight, B. (2014). *Homophily, group size, and the diffusion of political information in social networks: evidence from Twitter.* (Report No. 20681), pp. 1–42. Cambridge, MA: The National Bureau of Economic Research.

Henman, P. (2013). Government and the internet: Evolving technologies, enduring research themes. In W. H. Dutton (Ed.), *The Oxford handbook of internet studies* (pp. 283–306). Oxford, UK: Oxford University Press.

Hindman, M., Tsioutsiouliklis, K., & Johnson, J. (2003). *Googlearchy: How a few heavily-linked sites dominate politics on the Web.* Princeton, New Jersey: Mimeograph, Princeton University.

Howard, P. (2003). Hacktivism. In S. Jones (Ed.), *Encyclopedia of new media* (pp. 216–217). Thousand Oaks, CA: SAGE Publications, Inc.

Hwang, T., Pearce, I., & Nanis, M. (2012, March). Socialbots: Voices from the fronts. *Interactions, 19*(2), 38–45. Retrieved 5 March, 2015, from http://doi.acm.org/10.1145/2090150.2090161

Latour, B. (2005). *Reassembling the social: An introduction to actor-network-theory.* Oxford; New York: Oxford University Press.

Mauldin, M. L. (1994). Chatterbots, TinyMUDs and the turing test: Entering the Loebner prize competition. *Proceedings of AAAI-94.* Retrieved from http://aaaipress.org/Papers/AAAI/1994/AAAI94–003.pdf

Mitter, S., Wagner, C., & Strohmaier, M. (2014a). A categorization scheme for socialbot attacks in online social networks. *ArXiv e-prints.* Retrieved from http://arxiv.org/abs/1402.6288

Mitter, S., Wagner, C., & Strohmaier, M. (2014b). Understanding the impact of socialbot attacks in online social networks. *ArXiv e-prints.* Retrieved from http://arxiv.org/abs/1402.6289

Mutz, D. (2006). *Hearing the other side: Deliberative versus participatory democracy.* New York: Cambridge University Press.

Newman, M. E. J. (2006). Modularity and community structure in networks. *Proceedings of the National Academy of Sciences of the United States of America, 103*(23), 8577–8582.

Paradise, A., Puzis, R., & Shabtai, A. (2014). Anti-reconnaissance tools: Detecting targeted socialbots. *IEEE Internet Computing, 18*(5), 11–19.

Pariser, E. (2011). *The filter bubble: What the internet is hiding from you.* New York: Penguin Press.

Putnam, R. D. (2000). *Bowling alone.* New York: Simon & Schuster.

van Steen, M. (2010). *Graph theory and complex networks: An introduction.* Seattle: On Demand Publishing, LLC-Create Space.

Steiner, C. (2012). *Automate this: How algorithms came to rule our world.* New York: Portfolio/ Penguin.

Sullivan, J. (2012). A tale of two microblogs in china. *Media, Culture & Society, 34*(6), 773–783.

Sunstein, C. (2001). *Republic.com.* Princeton: Princeton University Press.

Twitter, Inc. (2015). *What's a Twitter timeline?* Retrieved 1 April, 2015, from https://support. twitter.com/articles/164083-what-s-a-twitter-timeline

Van Alstyne, M., & Brynjolfsson, E. (2005). Global village or cyber-Balkans? Modeling and measuring the integration of electronic communities. *Management Science, 51*(6), 851–868.

Wald, R., Khoshgoftaar, T. M., Napolitano, A., & Sumner, C. (2013). Predicting susceptibility to social bots on Twitter. In *2013 IEEE 14th international conference on information reuse and integration* (pp. 6–13). IEEE.

11

RATIONALIZING SOCIALITY

An Unfinished Script for Socialbots

Maria Bakardjieva

Introduction: On Social Robots

Science and technology have made significant advances in the conceptualization and construction of mechanical robots that are socially adept. Robots can be masterfully designed in ways that lead people to socially interact with them and infuse them with social feelings. Human-robot interaction and more generally social robotics have been the fields that have contributed significantly to these advancements in the cultivation of robotic technology and to its wider application and acceptance (Sugiyama & Vincent, 2013; Wright, 2012; Young et al., 2011).

For years, software robots, or bots, have been modest creatures of computer networks and services that have proliferated untouched by the glamour of their mechanical brethren. Their job descriptions have been confined to running automated tasks over the Internet, typically, tasks that are simple and structurally repetitive, but require a much higher performance rate than a human can achieve. A specialized type of software robots created explicitly for social interaction is exemplified by the Chattarbots or Verbots at the centre of some curious field experiments in artificial intelligence, including attempts to get them to pass the Turing Test or win the Loebner's prize. In the past decade, however, a new species of software bots has erupted into the limelight—the 'socialbot' inhabiting social networking platforms—that calls for new thinking on the sociality of robots. In what follows, I will offer a brief reflection on the specific type of sociality that these bots harbinger, arguing that socialbots can be seen as epiphenomena of tendencies that have been picking up speed ever since the ideology and philosophy of Web 2.0 came to fruition. Whether these are positive tendencies is open to debate and it is advisable that this debate starts now. What do we have to gain and lose in a dawning age of robo-sociality where the robots may actually be us?

Imagining Robots: Some Cultural History

The origin story of robots is seldom fully told. The Czech writer Karel Čapek who, together with his brother Josef, invented the concept, is one of those authors who are often cited, but seldom read. Contrary to popular belief, robots were not conceived by Čapek as humanity's noble servants, as they appeared later in Asimov's work. Čapek's play *Rossum's Universal Robots* (*R.U.R.*), in which the word robot appeared for the first time, was published in 1920. Curiously enough, 1920 was the year in which Max Weber, the great German sociologist and theorist of social rationalization, died at the height of his intellectual prowess. 1920 was preceded by three years of a bloody civil war in Russia following the Great Russian Socialist Revolution of 1917, in which Russian workers rebelled against the exploitation and the dehumanizing living conditions resulting from capitalist industrialization of that country. What happened in the aftermath of this revolution is well known. The victorious workers expatriated or exterminated the class of their former masters. The figure of the 'robot', coming from the Czech word for drudgery and the more general Slavic root 'robota' meaning work, and respectively 'roboti' meaning 'workers', emerged against this historical background.

Čapek's play is a political allegory that alludes to the transformation of the working class into a dehumanized force for drudgery and the subsequent revolt of this class that overthrew and ruthlessly did away with its masters. The images he used were those of the robots and their takeover of human society. Thus Čapek's plot was not a reiteration of the myth of Golem. His pen was not driven by an irrational fear of the expansive growth of technology per se as has been the case in other dystopian tales (Fortunati, 2013). It was actually an incisive analysis of capitalist modernity and a logical extension of its trajectory. Čapek's play represents a striking artistic rendering of Weber's rationalization theory (see Weber, 2005). As such, it can fruitfully inform a study of cognate social phenomena albeit removed in time and context.

In Čapek's plot the old Rossum, a 'great physiologist', discovers a new method of organizing living matter and decides to imitate nature and reconstruct the whole tree of life to be eventually crowned by a new kind of man. But this turns out to be a tedious and lengthy process. Man is an extremely complex creation. Rossum's efforts produce only unviable monstrosities. Then comes his son, young Rossum, an engineer, and says: 'It's absurd to spend ten years making a man. If you can't make him quicker than nature, you might as well shut up shop.' At this moment capitalist efficiency takes over. In contrast to his father, young Rossum approaches the man-making business from an engineering point of view. Indeed, Čapek writes: 'anyone who has looked into human anatomy will have seen at once that man is too complicated, and that a good engineer could make him more simply.' Thus young Rossum begins to 'overhaul anatomy' trying to find 'what could be left out or simplified'. Explaining his reasoning, Čapek takes a page from Weber's book almost literally:

> A man is something that feels happy, plays the piano, likes going for a walk, and in fact, wants to do a whole lot of things that are really unnecessary. . . .Young Rossum invented a worker with the minimum amount of requirements. He had to simplify him. He rejected everything that did not contribute directly to the progress of work!—everything that makes man more expensive. In fact, he rejected man and made the Robot.
>
> *(Čapek, 1920, p. 9)*

Although they are among the highest achievements of human rationality, the robots in *R.U.R.* slip out of the mastery of humans. They bring about unexpected (irrational) consequences. Once again, the reason for this is not the mythical running out of control of an amateurish magical trick. The culprit is another force that Čapek pinpoints dispassionately in the following exchange between the doomed *R.U.R.* managers as they bewail their fate besieged by a robot army:

Busman: 'But do you know what is to blame for all this lovely mess?
Fabry: What?
Busman: The number. Upon my soul we might have known that someday or other the Robots would be stronger than human beings, and that this was bound to happen, and we were doing all we could to bring it about as soon as possible. You, Domin, you, Fabry, myself!—
Domin: Are you accusing us?
Busman: Oh, do you suppose the management controls the output? It's the demand that controls the output.
Helena: And is it for that we must perish?

(p. 74)

The answer to naive Helena's question is 'yes'. As it turns out, it has been the invisible hand of the market that has filled up the world with robots—demanded by the millions to serve as labourers and soldiers. Their overwhelming numbers, but also the numbers measuring the profits of those who exploited them, have precipitated the fall of human civilization.

The homology between Čapek's plot and Weber's theory of rationalization should be evident by now. Starting with the *Protestant Ethic and the Spirit of Capitalism* and carrying on with his later works, Weber developed a powerful theory and critique of rationalization that he saw as the major force defining Western civilization. More specifically, he highlighted the role of 'formal rationality' (see Kalberg, 1980) as the main principle underlying capitalist modernity, the form of social organization that eclipsed traditional society and established itself as the dominant order in Europe and North America. Ritzer (2000) summarizes the defining characteristics of Weberian formal rational structures and institutions thus: calculability, that is prioritizing those elements that can be counted and quantified; efficiency—seeking to find the most direct means to a given end; predictability, making sure that things operate in the same way across contexts; replacement of human technology with non-human technology; seeking to gain control over uncertainties, especially uncertainties stemming from the idiosyncrasies of the human beings; tending to produce a series of irrational consequences such as war, destruction and loss of meaning. Čapek's robots perfectly meet all these conditions. Formal rationality is typically objectified in technical and organizational forms and artefacts that make sure that rationalized processes and behaviours are reproduced consistently over time. Bureaucratic codices, forms and templates, book-keeping methods, timetables, machines (and ultimately robots) are examples of such objectifications. One final proof that in *R.U.R.* Čapek was telling us a tale of formal rationalization lies in the name of the robots' inventors—old and young Rossum. 'Rossum' in the Slavic languages is the word for 'reason'.

Weber recognized that through its prioritization of control and mastery over nature capitalist rationality tends to lead to the concentration of power in the hands of the few capitalists and bureaucrats who rise to the top. However, he saw formal rationality as essentially value neutral. It is the philosophers of the Frankfurt School who advanced the critique of formal rationality to address ethical and political issues of class interests, power and domination (Feenberg, 1995, 1999). Horkheimer, Adorno and later Marcuse pointed out that under the rule of formal rationality, power over the natural environment is gained through suppression: 'first of individuals' own inner impulses, and second of each other' (Feenberg, 1995, p. 31). Human faculties that are not essential for survival and domination of nature (playing the piano, going for a walk—compare to the choices made in the design of Čapek's robots) are devalued and marginalized in order to bring into prominence qualities that directly serve the rational goals of efficiency and mastery. Čapek's notion of the robot is a literary expression of this idea of reduction of the human being to an efficient instrument for achieving a rational end.

Further development of critical theory in the work of Feenberg (1991, 1999, 2008), Habermas (1984, 1987) and Lefebvre (1991) has illuminated the expansion of the institutions and techniques of formal rationality and their encroachment over areas of social life stretching far beyond the market and state bureaucracy. In fact, realms such as leisure, play, culture, education and family relationships have been gradually penetrated by the rationalization logics and organizational patterns characteristic of markets and bureaucracies. With the recent ascent to influence of neoliberal ideology, this invasion has progressed by leaps and bounds. This renders Čapek's plot new relevance and makes it a useful blueprint for the analysis of more recent, and yet strangely analogous, techno-social developments. This will be the endeavour of the following section.

The Rationalization of Online Sociality

Not very long after the smashing success of Čapek's play, scientists discovered an alternative substance in which human life could be recreated. It was simple—its elementary particles were bits and bytes; zeros and ones, digits.[1] Many laboratories quickly sprung up where humans were busily transforming themselves into personae made of zeros and ones and excitedly engaging in each and every kind of activity that was available to this new human form. They played, they argued, they flirted, they shopped.

But shopping did not seem to be their favourite preoccupation, as profit numbers were far from the stratospheric heights they were expected to achieve. Most of all, digitized humans were interested in meeting and interacting with one another. It all became a huge social playground infused with a lot of creativity and fun, but with very little efficiency. Then came the engineers and managers who thought that this buzzing social hive needed to be 'harnessed'—it would have to start paying up. Thus they looked for what elements of online sociality could be useful for business and what could be left out or simplified. Like young Rossum, they worked to bring some order into the mess so that the human interactions in this new land could be made profitable. For that purpose things had to be reorganized. Virtual personae had to be standardized. Idiosyncratic self-images had to be brought under some standardized rules and uniform frames. Traits that mattered to engineers and managers had to be selected and prioritized at the expense of others. Instead of starting from an empty slate, the creation of human characters in the new world would now commence with the filling out of a template akin to a bureaucratic form. Instead of being allowed to run amok with any outlandish or idiosyncratic activity they could think of, digital personae would be given a set of well-defined actions to choose from. Instead of being left to portray their lives as heteroglossic narratives or performances, they would be offered the model of the store window, the prototypes of the merchandice inventory and the account book. To top it up, they would be encouraged to replace the slow and unpredictable process of composing open-ended speech acts as part of their interaction with others with a handy toolkit of conventional symbolic gestures (see van Dijck, 2013).

This engineering approach was a tremendous success. The imperative of efficiency triumphed. It was heartily embraced by both the individuals translating themselves into digital personae and the agencies for which these easy to sort and classify personal entities were becoming a major commercial asset.

Undoubtedly, my allegory so far has been rather transparent. I do not think I would surprise anyone when I sum it up by saying that social media, particularly social networking sites, marked the transformation of online sociality playgrounds into sociality factories and markets. On social networking sites users became labourers ('roboti'?) producing not only content (Fuchs, 2014; Scholz, 2013; Terranova, 2004), but also producing themselves as profiles organized by marketing standards (Gehl, 2014), a reduced human form which emphasized those features and activities that could be catalogued and sold, or used for selling. The social networking site profile lays somewhere in between spontaneous human expression and the standardized templates of marketing classification (Gehl, 2014; van Dijck, 2013). Compared with actual human beings, the personae inhabiting social networking sites are significantly more calculable, efficient, predictable, heavily dependent on technology and prone to system or peer control. In other words, they exhibit five of the six characteristics defining Weberian style formal rationality (Ritzer, 2000).

The sociality between these social networking site (SNS) personae unfolds based on a simplified predetermined technical script. Entertaining as it may be, it resembles standardized, repetitive, mechanized labour. Not surprisingly, the notion of 'social capital' underwent what, following Giddens (1984), might be seen as a reverse double hermeneutic. It jumped out of the vocabulary of sociological analysts and gained everyday currency. It acquired a meaning very close to that of its economic twin. Social capital was to be measured by the number of friends, it was to be accumulated and invested, and eventually used for personal profit. While the purported benefit that users gain from their accumulated social capital remains largely a theoretical construct that is still to be substantiated, their sociality work, whose by-products include message multiplication and influence peddling, gets profitably exploited by site owners and marketers.

With the evolution of social networking sites from looser to tighter mechanisms for disciplining users (see Gehl's, 2014, comparison between MySpace and Facebook), the rationalization of sociality has progressed significantly. Nevertheless it would be a stretch to claim that SNS personae are robots or robot-like. Despite the generation of what van Dijck (2013) calls 'platformed sociality' (p. 5), SNSs are still not *R.U.R.*s. They have simply streamlined and mechanized interaction among digitized personae that, for their part, represent an overhauled and simplified human character. (After all, to paraphrase Čapek, anyone who has looked into human character will have seen at once that it is too complicated, and that a good engineer could make it more simply.) However, while online personae are abridged representations of human characters, they are still anchored signifiers; they are tied to an actual human being. The true virtual robot comes into existence when that connection is severed. The rise of platformed sociality has done a good job of paving the way for such a severance. The next step follows logically and swiftly, even if it still looks like a baby step, or rather, sometimes, as children's play.

Gepetto's Virtual Workshop: From Platformed Sociality to Robo-Sociality

Unlike its mechanical counterpart, the virtual robot has no embodied presence in physical space, but he or she has palpable symbolic presence in network space. Like mechanical robots, virtual robots are automated autonomous entities, but where mechanical robots become social to the extent that they are designed to key into the social experience of the user, virtual robots are social by their *raison d'être*. They are creatures of the social universe fleshed by computer code, but endeavouring to interact with others like virtual human personae. They follow the same representational and operational conventions as digitized personae animated by real people. Most importantly, virtual robots, defined as 'socialbots', (Gehl and Bakardjieva, Chapter 1) can be easily made indistinguishable from human-operated online handles for a number of reasons. First of all, in this environment humans have lost their substantive uniqueness—both human personae and socialbots are built of combinations of zeros and ones. Secondly, the symbolic representations of the standardized set of human traits accommodated by SNSs are equally accessible to humans and bots. Finally, in platformed sociality the uniquely human intelligence expressed in situated use of natural language can be and is commonly substituted by conventional scenarios and a scripted set of symbolic gestures that can be enacted by humans and bots with equal success. But there is more: social bots have an upper hand over humans when it comes to speed, number and tirelessness with which any of those representations and symbolic gestures can be produced.

Moving away from theoretical speculation and closer to the solid earth of engineers, we find a definition of social bots (or socialbots) articulated as follows:

> A socialbot is an automation software that controls an account on a particular OSN [Online Social Network], and has the ability to perform basic activities such as posting a message and sending a connection request. What makes a socialbot different from self-declared bots (e.g., Twitter bots that post up-to-date weather forecasts) and spambots is that it is designed to be stealthy, that is, it is able to pass itself off as a human being.
>
> *(Boshmaf et al., 2011, p. 93)*

What further distinguishes these bots from earlier Internet-based automated scripts (see Latzko-Toth, Chapter 3, this volume) is a 'focus on creating substantive relationships among human users . . . and shaping the aggregate social behavior and patterns of relationships between groups of users online' (Hwang et al., 2012, p. 40).

In recent years, socialbots of this type have been popping up on all types of SNSs, from the more ego-centred and loquacious Facebook to the terse and dynamic information-oriented Twitter. A social bot, Boshmaf et al. explain, consists of two main components: a profile on a targeted OSN (the face) and the socialbot software (the brain) (Boshmaf et al., 2011). It is worth noting that in order to pass itself off as a human, both the 'face' and the 'brain' of the socialbot have to be convincingly anthropomorphic. That said, what does it mean to be anthropomorphic on an online social network? Unlike mechanical robots, their software cousins do not face the challenge to present a believable human-like face or body along with the ability to smile, nod at the right times and position themselves at an appropriate distance (see Young et al., 2011). Online social networks represent a levelled middle ground where human and robot appear on significantly equalized footing. The *anthropos* in online social networks has shed off a lot of its critical advantages over the robot. That is why socialbots stand a good chance of being successful in presenting themselves as humans. As Gehl (2014) points out, their success in that regard: 'might be more a function of the *a priori* reduction of human activity to predetermined datasets than due to the coding skills of socialbot engineers' (p. 25).

Instructively, two such engineers (@tinypirate and @AeroFade) describe their approach in creating an effective Twitter bot that has managed to infiltrate a social network of Twitter users and to re-shape its structure: The socialbot, a Twitter account going by the name James M. Titus, was designed to follow 500 target users while at the same time automatically posting cute cat photos 'scraped from Flickr' on his 'own' blog Kitteh Fashun. James did not need to be powered by high-notch artificial intelligence in order to be accepted by his human fans. When a target user addressed James personally, James would send back 'a random generic response, such as 'right on baby!', 'lolariffic', 'sweet as', or 'hahahahah are you kidding me?'. As the clever designers suggest: 'We believe that the very short messages allowed on Twitter enable many bot-like behaviors to be easily masked or explained away by the targets interacting with James' (p. 41). So, instead of trying to meet the standards of the Turing Test, the designers of James M. Titus have managed to pass their socialbot for a human user by relying on a number of known conventions underlying interaction on Twitter. Instead of relying on advancements in artificial intelligence, social believability has become a matter of platform-facilitated communication artifice. Extrapolating from their successful experiment, the designers conclude that in the future, strategically deployed socialbots could 'subtly shape and influence targets across much larger user networks' (p. 41) as well as shape group consensus in a particular direction. What will that direction be? Presumably, this will be decided by social engineers, mangers and other such operators top down.

That the creation of believable socialbots is a feat within the grasp of smart computer science students is exemplified by the 'overwhelming success' of the project Realboy carried out by Zack Coburn and Greg Marra in 2008 as part of a course at Olin College. The socialbots Cobrun and Marra created were tasked with inserting themselves into existing Twitter communities and befriending human members. The bots started out by tweeting about topics of interest to the community and gradually made their way into its social graph by garnering followship and retweets by members. In the discussion of their experiment the two students remarked that they achieved these results without needing to worry about natural language parsing and sentence construction. Their bots simply duplicated tweets concerning the topics of interest of the target community harvested from Twitter conversations taking place elsewhere. Thus Realboy socialbots were designed to 'clone Twitter posts from users external to its social knot; follow users in its social knot; and get a 25% follow-back rate' (Coburn & Marra, 2008).

In a later paper, Marra (2011), already an associate product manager at Google, reflects on the experience of project Realboy and surmises: 'A single puppet-master could create hundreds of Twitter bots, letting them live perfectly normal and believable lives for months while they build up followers. Then one day, a careful crafted false story unfolds on the stage of social media, played out by a single director with hundreds of actors. Incidents like Balloon Boy demonstrate that powerful stories can become widespread before there is time for fact check-ing' (n.p.). Indeed, Coburn and Marra called the host of socialbots they created in their student experiment 'Gepetto's army' in honour of Pinocchio's father, the puppeteer. Like the case of James M. Titus, their experiment demonstrated that the tools needed for passing bots as real users were readily available in the context of platformed sociality.

Surprising as it may sound, imitating users on Facebook has also proven to be possible and effective. Facebook requires more user information to create a believable profile and the activities it supports are more diverse and, one might think, requiring more intelligent engagement. Boshmaf et al. (2011), however, have shown that first, a motivated 'adversary' can fully automate the account creation process and, secondly, putting together fake accounts complete with emails, pictures and relationship histories is not an insurmountable task given the vast resources of the Web and the characteristics of open online services. In their experiment designed to infiltrate Facebook with believable robotic enti-ties, they created what they call 'a bot-net', a group of interconnected socialbots. To make their robo-users look not only real, but also attractive, the designers supplied them with pictures, and the respective demographic characteristics, gleaned from the site hotornot.com where human users post their photos to be rated for hotness. The typical tasks assigned to the socialbots were based on a meticulous breakdown of the characteristic actions of human users and on a detailed algorithm emulating these actions. They included managing the profile's contact network by sending or accepting connection requests, performing social interactions such as writing on a friend's wall, and collecting personal informa-tion from befriended users. The sophisticated infrastructure behind the socialbots involved a 'botherder' (a human interested in using the socialbots for his or her purposes), a 'botmaster' (software the botherder uses to send commands to the bots), 'botcargo' (the private information harvested from real users' accounts and transported back to the botherder). The social activities of the bots on Facebook were conducted by executing a set of commands issued either directly by the human herder or locally by the bot software.

Subsequently, these socialbots emitted numerous friendship requests and reg-istered enviable success in being accepted as part of real users' social networks. Over seven weeks, the network of 25 socialbots contacted 5,053 real Facebook users with friendship requests and scored 19.3% acceptance in the initial phase. Later on, when the bots invited the friends of their friends, the average acceptance rate rose to 59.1%. In other words, the brave 'Gepetto army' triumphantly marched through Facebook successfully blending into the friendship networks of actual humans.

A software agent that was essentially a socialbot was also devised by Huber et al. (2009) in a field trial of what they called 'automated social engineering'. This particular study simulated an attack on institutional networks using Facebook profiles of institutional members as a bridge. A socialbot posing as an attractive 22-year-old student from the UK was designed to identify and approach single male users at a Swedish educational institution asking for information and help because she, allegedly, planned to study there. Gradually building rapport with the victims, the socialbot prepared the ground for executing a targeted attack intended to collect password information. Based on this and other experiments Huber et al. concluded that 'the rise of social networking sites, as the new means of social interaction, enable automated social engineering' (p. 123). Classic social engineering attacks, these authors argue, are expensive because building and maintaining rapport with someone before being able to exploit the relationship is a time- and resource-consuming task. By contrast, 'automated social engineering bots require little human time resources, are scalable and thus make social engineering a cheap and promising attack' (p. 117).

What the ultimate goal of such an exercise might be is up for grabs. The socialbots could be asked to collect and pass on to their herder users' personal information, or they could be given other tasks, for example, to change a user community's social graph (as in the Twitter examples cited earlier), or to recommend products or information sources.

Given these possibilities, the concept and reality of the socialbot is unlikely to be contained within the laboratory for very long. It can be expected to manifest itself in places of intensive interaction on social networking platforms in the near future. Consider Hwang et al.'s (2012) classic techno-deterministic conviction about the inevitable proliferation of socialbots: '*digitization drives botification*; the use of technology in a realm of human activity enables the creation of software to act in lieu of humans' (p. 40). It is arguable, however, whether it is digitization per se, or the specific organizational principles, functionalities and business models of the currently popular social networking platforms that make the construction of socialbots a feasible project. With the prescription of standard procedures for self-presentation and simplified and predictable number of communicative gestures, social networking sites have reduced human complexity, and yes, messiness, into a rationalized shape preserving strategically selected traits. In the contemporary rendition of young Rossum's feat, these traits do not relate to heavy lifting, street-sweeping and casting hot metal, but to the intricacies of lifestyle, the shaping of taste, the manipulation of desire and the steering of consumption. Socialbots emerge on the stage thanks to this reduction and for the purposes of exploiting the possibilities for puppeteering and herding (accidentally reflected in the discourse of software engineers) for which social networking sites have laid the ground.

But if engineers are increasingly experimenting with socialbots both playfully and seriously, what are the practical meanings and applications that this new technological creature might be implicated in? Are there 'relevant social groups' (Pinch & Bijker, 1984) outside the lab that are willing and ready to find in these sociable pseudo-humans meaningful affordances and to get involved in their social construction? Here the presumptions underlying the emerging literature on socialbots split into two main streams. The first and more prominent one focuses on socialbots as mischievous characters that could be recruited by various interested agencies for the purpose of malicious manipulation of online information and communication currents, public opinion distortion, privacy violation, and data theft targeting individuals and institutions. From that perspective, the expected 'botification' of social interactions online calls for the development of protective mechanisms and mobilizes teams of engineers and computer scientists to rise to the occasion and offer ways for enhancing system security. The spectre of 'automated social engineering' is perceived as a threat to the integrity of socio-technical systems. Indeed most of the studies recounted above were carried out with the explicit motivation to develop models for the effective protection of social networking platforms against bot infiltration.

The second line of speculation on the future of socialbots foresees a range of benign applications denoted by the umbrella term 'social architecting', in which socialbots are tasked to 'shape or reshape communities on a very large scale' (Hwang et al., 2012, p. 45) in desired directions in areas such as health education, conflict resolution and intercultural understanding. The argument is that socialbots could help achieve that by introducing users to one another, boosting the rate of connection growth, exposing users to content they would not normally look for, building bridges between divided communities, detecting and combating misinformation, and by doing many other good deeds, presumably orchestrated by a well-intending herder. It is also worth mentioning that according to DuBose Cole, a strategist with Mindshare (a global media agency in London interested in the intersection of marketing, psychology and programming), marketers 'can consider using socialbots to bring company mascots and assets to life with little effort' (Cole, 2012, p. 44). In projections like these, the novel concept of 'social architecting' starts to emerge as a sort of noble twin brother of 'social engineering'. Whereas 'automated social engineering' aims at misleading and exploiting its human victims on a massive scale, 'social architecting' promises to be a force for good, quietly refining the quality of human communities and helping them solve problems in a grand sweep. Notably, however, common for both projects is the control from above. In the malevolent scenario, the orchestrators are miscreants or profiteers; in the benign one, they are the technocratic chieftains who know better what is good for the target communities, and who deploy their troops of agile socialbots to get the job done unbeknownst to the humans inhabiting these communities. In either case, the targeted users have very little say.

Socialbots in Action: Three Petite Scenarios

The Marketing Machine

When we look beyond the futuristic-sounding projections of scientists, we easily find much action in mundane sites. In a study entitled 'The Twittering Machine', Mowbray (2010) investigates Twitter accounts that generate large quantities of tweets or carry out other sophisticated activates on Twitter 'with little effort or attention from the account's human owner' (p. 1). In other words, she sets out to detect the presence and map the activities of real-Twitter-world socialbots. According to Cheng and Evans (2009), who sampled 11.5 million Twitter accounts between January and May 2009, 24% of all tweets generated in that period were coming from automated accounts posting over 150 tweets a day. Mowbray's analysis of 7,060 tweets generated between July and September 2009 shows that the number of accounts that published more than 100 tweets a day increased from less than 1% in the first few months of 2009, to over 19% in September 2009. Mowbray infers that these automated accounts were mostly, although not exclusively, 'marketing machines' and attributes their explosion in late 2009 to the peak in mainstream media coverage of the opportunities for marketing via Twitter. A number of marketing books and guides appearing in that period recommended Twitter as the newest tool for 'market domination'. Another contributing factor could have been the publication of the Twitter API handbook in April 2009, which had given marketing firms the technical know-how for bringing their trade to Twitter (Mowbray, 2010).

While Mowbray's study does not problematize the ethics and legality of such marketing campaigns, Thomas et al. (2013) set themselves the explicit goal to document the emerging underground market for fraudulent accounts for Twitter and other social networking sites and online services. They define 'fraudulent accounts' as 'automatically generated credentials used to disseminate scams, phishing, and malware' (p. 1), which clearly applies to socialbots of the malicious variety. Thomas et al.'s research uncovers a whole commercial ecosystem that connects buyers with parties selling fake email accounts, CAPTCHA solving services, illegal servers, etc. The researchers close in on websites that represent storefronts, blackhat forums and freelance labour boards where they select 27 merchants offering bulk supply of fraudulent accounts. The services under study were able to provide thousands of Twitter accounts within 24 hours, with the price ranging between 2 and 10 cents per account. Facebook accounts were more expensive, ranging between $0.45 and $1.50, the higher-priced ones coming with SIM cards and capable of verifying the receipt of a text message.

Extrapolating from the pool of accounts they purchased, Thomas et al. identified several million fraudulent accounts registered by the same merchants. A large percentage of these accounts (73%) were actively tweeting or forming relationships, while others remained dormant, expecting to be purchased. In a collaborative effort with Twitter, Thomas et al. established that accounts created by these merchants were mainly used for spamming.

This rare glimpse on the size of the underground market for automated Twitter accounts is indicative of the interest of commercially and/or criminally motivated spammers in deploying the powers of socialbot armies for purposes as diverse as skewing product ratings, peddling advertising or distributing malware. But there are other 'social groups' keenly interested in exploiting the boisterous sociality of socialbots. At a time when SNSs have been taken up by politicians and citizens alike as strategic sites for public opinion formation, mobilization and political organizing, the enticement to engineer bot invasion of political discussions has proven too hard to resist.

Robo-Citizens in the Digital Public Sphere

It is once again Thomas et al. (2012) who draw attention to the fact that the move from commercial to political spamming is not a giant leap for socialbots. In this study, the team tracks the use of fraudulent (socialbot) accounts to drown critical discussion in the case of the Russian parliamentary elections of 2011. The researchers identified 25,860 fraudulent Twitter accounts that had injected 440,793 tweets into conversations concerning the election. Those bot accounts had been implanted in the Twitter platform months earlier. They were activated occasionally during the period leading up to and following the election to drown oppositional discussion through tweets containing adversarial statements, jeers or simply unrelated chatter and gibberish.

The mimicking of grassroots expression and mobilization orchestrated by interested players, known as astroturfing, has been a strategy occasionally used by corporations and political parties to manipulate public opinion for many years. The migration of astroturfing activities on the Internet has produced new possibilities and techniques (Zhang et al., 2013). A long-term observer and critic of this practice, British journalist George Monbiot (2011) writes:

> Anyone writing a comment piece in Mandarin critical of the Chinese government, for instance, is likely to be bombarded with abuse by people purporting to be ordinary citizens, upset by the slurs against their country . . . . Teams of these sock-puppets are hired by party leaders to drown out critical voices and derail intelligent debates.

Discussion forums on the Internet constitute fertile environments for the growth of astroturfing, as investigative journalism has demonstrated (Monbiot, 2002,

2010, 2011). However, with the advent of platform- and subsequently robo-sociality, the automation of astroturfing becomes a lucrative prospect for politicians, marketers and zealots. With the help of a specially designed analytical tool, Ratkiewicz et al. (2011) were able to isolate socialbot accounts on Twitter that attempted to smear the reputation of one of the candidates in the US midterm elections and to steer traffic to a site promoting a different political party and its candidate. The analysis focused on two accounts: @PeaceKaren_25 and @HopeMarie_25 that acted as partners in deception while at the same time mimicking typical Twitter interaction. @PeaceKaren_25 generated over 10,000 tweets, almost all of which expressed support for one of the candidates. @HopeMarie_25 supported the same candidate and promoted the same websites; however, 'she' simply retweeted @PeaceKaren_25's postings instead of creating her own. In an another example caught by the team's detection filter a network of ten bot accounts propagated a 'meme' smearing the Democratic candidate for the US senate from Delaware and produced thousands of tweets containing links to the freedomist.com website.

In the following year two master's candidates from the Oxford Internet Institute noticed the fact that Mitt Romney's Twitter account, which had been receiving around 2,000 to 5,000 new followers on an average day, gained 141,000 followers in two days. The results of their tests, as they put it, were 'strongly indicative of bot involvement' (Furnas & Gaffney, 2012). Similar findings have been reported concerning Barack Obama's massive followship as well as that of other influential American politicians (Martosko, 2013).[2]

A clear sign that automated astroturfing may be outgrowing its status as a marginal technique and moving into the frontlines of ideological and political battles can be found in a series of emails exchanged among managers and employees of the US private security firm HBGary Federal and made public by Anonymous. These emails contemplated the development of 'persona management software' that would allow the creation of 'an army of sock-puppets' to help a few people appear that they are many online. The Daily Rockefeller (2011) quotes from one of these emails:

> To build this capability we will create a set of personas on twitter, blogs, forums, buzz, and myspace under created names that fit the profile (satellitejockey, hack3rman, etc). These accounts are maintained and updated automatically through RSS feeds, retweets, and linking together social media commenting between platforms. With a pool of these accounts to choose from, once you have a real name persona you create a Facebook and LinkedIn account using the given name, lock those accounts down and link these accounts to a selected # of previously created social media accounts, automatically pre-aging the real accounts.
>
> *(http://www.dailykos.com/story/2011/02/16/945768/-*
> *UPDATED-The-HB-Gary-Email-That-Should-Concern-Us-All)*

With the strings of a 'sock-puppet' army like this in hand, the interested party could go ahead and steal private data, drown legitimate debate on contentious but uncomfortable issues, simulate public sentiment upheavals, disseminate one-sided or distorted information, gang up on political opponents and smear their reputation. The list of possibilities is endless. It is also technically quite realistic as the success of the experiments recounted above has shown. The disturbing scenario moves even closer to home as investigative journalists discover a solicitation posted on the US FedBizOps.gov website on June 22, 2010 which invites proposals for:

> Online Persona Management Service. 50 User Licenses, 10 Personas per user. Software will allow 10 personas per user, replete with background, history, supporting details, and cyber presences that are technically, culturally and geographically consistent. Individual applications will enable an operator to exercise a number of different online persons from the same workstation and without fear of being discovered by sophisticated adversaries. Personas must be able to appear to originate in nearly any part of the world and can interact through conventional online services and social media platforms.
>
> *(see Rockefeller, 2011)*

If the US government has found the development and management of socialbots online relevant and has decided to invest resources in it (see Fielding & Cobain, 2011), it can be prudently speculated that other agencies will follow suit. It is highly possible that other governments and political players are eager to invest in similar projects. 'Who's at the controls of Iran's bot army?' asks a recent BBC Trending (2016) publication. It describes a massive Twitter campaign, in which 'dozens of accounts tweeted to thousands of followers in waves every few minutes throughout the day using the hashtag "Powerful Iran"'. The profile pictures of these accounts were Hollywood celebrities or stock photos. Their tweets contained pictures of Iranian military equipment projecting technological prowess. Another similar operation had been registered by BBC Trending the year before. In it, the hashtag 'Letter4u' was used by many bot-like accounts drawing attention to an open letter by Iran's supreme leader addressed to Western youth (BBC Trending, 2016). The question of who was behind these undertakings remains open, but the suspicions hover around the Iranian government and its powerful political and religious institutions.

The next scenario takes us to an entirely different field of social life—love and dating—where a very similar solicitation for Online Persona Management Service seems to have been rather effectively fulfilled.

Ashley Madison's Flirtbots: Love's Labour's Lost?[3]

With apologies to Shakespeare, no, on the contrary, in the context of platformed sociality love's labour is being rationalized, automated and made quite profitable. The scandal that erupted around Ashley Madison's alleged fembots has revealed the fascinating evolution of the labour of platformed love—from an artisan through a mechanical to an automated robo phase. The underlying assumption of meeting romantic partners on dating websites would normally be that the parties involved will perform introductions, courtship, chatting and other such love labour person-to-person in an authentic and affective way. However, already in 2012, an employee of Ashley Madison, a dating site specifically designed to facilitate extramarital affairs, sued her employer for incurring injuries while fulfilling a bizarre task: 'to create 1,000 fake female profiles meant to lure men to the new Brazilian Ashley Madison site' and to complete the work in only three weeks (CityNews, 2013). The nature of this job strikingly resembles a mechanized assembly line procedure imported into the world of online sociality. The statement of claim filed by Doriana Silva, a Brazilian immigrant living in Toronto, further alleged that: 'The purpose of these profiles is to entice paying heterosexual male members to join and spend money on the website.' The labour of creating the profiles 'required an enormous amount of keyboarding' and Silva developed severe pain in her wrists and forearms (CityNews, 2013). Avid Life Media Inc., the parent company which operates AshleyMadison.com, denied the allegations. Silva's claim was dismissed by the Ontario Superior Court in 2015 without further confirmation of the validity of her revelations concerning the fake profiles (Canadian Press, 2015). But the real troubles of AshleyMadison. com were still to come.

Ashley Madison's hot, but fake, female profiles returned to the stage of international public attention with a vengeance in 2015 when the hacker group Impact Team released on the dark web a data dump of Ashley Madison's user data, and later, of the company's corporate emails. Journalists and analysts who studied these data found fake female profiles operating on the site to lure men and make them pay for each line of communication exchanged. It became clear that such profiles were created by the company deliberately in large numbers and that they represented socialbots with specifically designed features, job description and purpose—to automate the labour of love and to make it more profitable. Shame that Čapek's Rossum never thought of that!

In a series of painstakingly researched articles, Gizmodo's journalist Annalee Newitz (2015a, 2015b) details the Avid Life Media's approach and procedure in hiring people to manufacture fake profiles dubbed the 'Ashley's Angels'. After an initial reliance on the 'creativity' of hourly workers (perhaps like Doriana Silva), the management made a concerted effort to 'productize' and automate the process. Emails in the company's data dump indicate that a specialized tool, tellingly named 'fraud-to-engager', was later used to build profiles. The raw material going into these profiles was harvested mostly from abandoned accounts and photos in the company's database. The fake profiles thus cobbled together were subsequently animated by software code. The resultant flirtbots would utter pick-up lines addressed to men who signed up to the site as 'guests': 'care to chat?', 'I'm online now', 'wanna cyber?', etc. In the company's internal parlance, these bots were variably called 'hosts' or 'engagers'. Their function was to pose as real women, to chat up men and 'convert' them into paying customers (see Newitz, 2015b).

The story of the Ashley Madison's flirtbots is, as it turns out, not unique. It appears to be a widespread industry practice among sex and hook-up sites (Dewey, 2015). A large portion of the revenues generated by these sites is arguably based on robo-encounters. Faced with a common problem—the scarcity of women— these sites intentionally produce and set into operation armies of female socialbots designed to indulge the male customers' sexual hopes and fantasies. Flirting as a form of sociality having been digitized, platformed and rationalized—reduced to a limited number of elementary gestures and expressions—has lent itself to algorithmization and automation with surprising ease.

Forecasting the Future of Robot Sociality: The Irrational Consequences of Rationalization

These scenarios demonstrate that instead of perceiving socialbots as rascals, miscreants, manipulators and spies as the work on computer security applications cited earlier has suggested, their development could take a different path—toward replacing human labour in areas where tasks have become repetitive, time-consuming or physically or psychologically difficult. This presents opportunities to both SNS owners and to individual users. Platform-operating companies may find it profitable to release armies of socialbots of a desired type and make in areas where they want to simulate 'avid life' and boost their business. For users, the presentation of self and the grooming of interpersonal relationships, including love affairs, in the context of platformed sociality has become a tedious exercise demanding much time and effort. Therefore, socialbots may turn out to be the service labour force that users need to make their lives easier. How scrupulously we perform on social networking sites could potentially affect, or so we believe, the opportunities that open up for us as consumers (Turow, 2011), professionals (Marwick, 2013) and social beings (Bakardjieva & Gaden, 2012). So how far-fetched then would be the idea that we might want to avail ourselves of the assistance of one or more socialbots as virtual handsome, awesome and influential Facebook friends who boost our social value by liking our pictures and making cute comments on our status updates? Or a very special socialbot could be our non-existent boyfriend or girlfriend who helps us taunt a past relationship, or attract a new one as the case may be. A socialbot could be hired to introduce us to people whose endorsement we may need, but who are far outside of the reach of our existing strong or weak ties. If all works well, such a bot could be trained to make purchase decisions, place orders, look for intimate partners, sign petitions and join political groups on our behalf. A skilful employment of socialbots could make everyone a rational manager of one's social network, a banker and trader of social capital. There are so many benefits to be gained from a masterful deployment of robot sociality that the only loss, the evaporation of authenticity and communicative understanding from our social networks might go completely unnoticed. The fact that this would be a rather irrational outcome of an enterprise that was put in place with the idea to enhance sociality would trouble no one. It would quietly close the loop of the consequences of rationalization as Weber had predicted.

Another draw of such a scenario would be the fact that SNS operators will not need to protect themselves against socialbots, but on the contrary—they will be able to embrace them (just like some of the cited examples already demonstrate). The socialbot could be the new killer app. It will open up a new lucrative market for social networking site providers. It will generate considerable revenue no matter how the business model is set up. It is certainly possible that demand will drive the numbers of socialbots operating on social networking sites to grow big enough to suffocate human sociality as we know it.

In terms of public communication and the political process, the triumph of robot sociality would bring about a public sphere defined by robo-mobs and political herding, attention bubbles and ideological band-wagons. Devoid of critical reasoning and meaningful debate, politics will be shaped by the number— the number of 'likes' and 'dislikes' garnered from the human and non-human actors bustling on platforms. And the winner will always be the best team of social engineers.

Conclusion and Some Backtracking

But is such a depressing resolution of the socialbot drama really necessary? Should Čapek's script be followed to the letter? Is there no way to avoid the total take-over of human sociality by the virtual vermin? Critiques of formal rationalization should take care not to treat rationality in the singular and not to be too quick to renounce all its forms (Kreiss et al., 2011). Weber himself distinguished several types of rationality and a multiplicity of rationalization processes that 'variously conflict and coalesce with one another at all societal and civilizational levels' (Kalberg, 1980, p. 1147). Weber discussed four types of rationality throughout his works: practical, theoretical, substantive and formal. His claim that in modern capitalist society formal rationality has risen to dominance does not mean that all other types of rationalization have vanished or completely lost purchase. Individuals' daily actions are imbued with practical rationality that drives them in their pursuit of concrete goals in particular situations. Theoretical rationality remains fundamental to the workings of science. Substantive rationality guides people's actions 'not on the basis of a purely means-end calculation of solutions to routine problems, but in relation to a past, present, or potential "value postulate"'[4] (p. 1155).

The theorists of the Frankfurt school have argued that Weber's designation of formal rationality as value-free was an oversight. They have uncovered the ways in which the value of domination over nature, extended into pursuit of social domination, underlies the logics of formal rationalization. The desire for profit and for conservation of the existing hierarchies, that is the economic and political interests of the dominant social groups, constitute the normative core of formal rationalization in capitalist society. This is not to say that formal rationality does not have its constructive role in the evolution of modern society, or that it can or should be totally rejected (du Gay, 2000). Rationality, as Feenberg (1999) has insisted, needs to be re-conceptualized under a different value horizon.

Alternative forms of rationality have been proposed, most notably by Habermas (1984, 1987) whose theory of communicative action brings to the fore the rational potential built into everyday speech. Communicative rationality underpins inter-actions oriented toward mutual understanding and agreement as opposed to the instrumental and strategic pursuit of individual goals. This idea inspires democratic models and institutions of public discussion and politics. Feenberg (1999) has advocated for a 'democratic rationalization' of technological development to include the interests, needs and perspectives of broad circles of users and other affected social groups. De Certeau (1984) has theorized the situated practical rationality of the dispersed 'tactics' that users of oppressive systems mobilize to subvert the rules and to pursue their distinct individual and collective projects.

These visions of alternative rationalities suggest that it is not imperative to go with Čapek to the fateful end and to forecast a dystopia of formally rationalized and robotized sociality. The day is still young and many directions are open to the social construction or deconstruction of socialbots (see Graham and Ackland, Chapter 10, and Nishimura, Chapter 7, this volume). Public debate and awareness still stand a chance to reflexively shape the course of technical development and keep in check the armies of socialbots ready to invade different theatres of social life. And while public debate is at it, it may also ask how far an informed and critical public is willing to tolerate the formal rationalization of online sociality. What alternative designs, business models and regulatory principles might be put in place to capitalize on the empowering and democratic affordances of online networking technologies without submitting users to the reduction, calibration and exploitation inherent in commercially operated SNS platforms? What use practices and cultures need to be evolved to resist and possibly block the onslaught of capitalist rationalization? These are all rational questions that need to be raised. But the rationality behind them is of a different kind—communicative (Habermas, 1984) and democratic (Feenberg, 1999). It is the kind of rationality worth uphold-ing through technology, politics and critical everyday use practice.

Acknowledgments

I would like to acknowledge my debt to Leopoldina Fortunati, the organizer of the *COST Workshop on Social Robotics* in Brussels (2013) that prompted me to think about and research socialbots. Canadian CBC journalist Nora Young's radio show *Spark*, in which I was invited to take part in 2011, introduced me to the concept for the first time. Computer engineers Konstantin Beznosov and Yazan Boshmaf kindly provided personalized guidance into the literature on the topic.

This chapter is a revised and updated version of my article Bakardjieva, M., Rationalizing Sociality: An Unfinished Script for Socialbots, published in *The Information Society: An International Journal,* Volume 31, Issue 3, 2015, Special Issue: Beyond Industrial Robotics: Social Robots Entering Public and Domestic Spheres.

Notes

1. Claude Shannon's idea to apply Boolean logic to the design of electrical switching circuits, which is considered the prime move of digitization, was developed in his Master's thesis in the late 1930s and first reported in a conference paper in 1938 (Shannon, 1940). I am grateful to Rob Gehl for pointing out the relative temporal proximity of these events.
2. Note that these tests have not been peer reviewed by a scholarly publication or forum. They have been published in the news media only.
3. I owe thanks to Jeremy Morris, who drew my attention to the socialbot aspect of the Ashley Madison case.
4. Value postulate can be understood as an ordered system of values and norms governing a specific realm of life. Such systems can have different orientations, for example, ethical, philosophical, aesthetical, and generate diverse evaluative standpoints: 'Not simply a single value, such as positive evaluation of wealth or of the fulfillment of duty, a value postulate implies entire clusters of values that vary in comprehensiveness, internal consistency, and content. Thus, this type of rationality exists as a manifestation of man's inherent capacity for value-rational action' (Kalberg, 1980, p. 1155).

References

Bakardjieva, M. (2015). Rationalizing sociality: An unfinished script for socialbots. *The Information Society, 31*(3), 244–256.

Bakardjieva, M., & Gaden, G. (2012). Web 2.0 technologies of the self. *Philosophy & Technology, 25*(3), 399–413.

BBC Trending. (2016, March 16). Who's at the controls of Iran's bot army? Retrieved from http://www.bbc.com/news/blogs-trending-35778645

Boshmaf, Y., Muslukhov, I., Beznosov, K., & Ripeanu, M. (2011). The socialbot network: When bots socialize for fame and money. In *ACSAC '11 proceedings of the 27th annual computer security applications conference* (pp. 93–102). New York: ACM.

Boshmaf, Y., Muslukhov, I., Beznosov, K., & Ripeanu, M. (2013). Design and analysis of a social botnet. *Computer Networks: The International Journal of Computer and Telecommunications Networking, 57*(2), 556–578.

Canadian Press (2015, January 18). Ashley Madison adultery website, ex-employee lawsuits dismissed. CBCNews, Canada. Retrieved on September 5, 2016, from http://www.cbc.ca/news/canada/ashley-madison-adultery-website-ex-employee-lawsuits-dismissed-1.2917076.

Čapek, K. (1920). *R.U.R.: Rossum's universal robots* (P. Selver & N. Playfair, Trans.). Retrieved from http://preprints.readingroo.ms/RUR/rur.pdf

Cheng, A., Evans, M. (2009). Inside Twitter: an in-depth look inside the Twitter world. Sysomos white paper. Retrieved on September 5, 2016, from June 2009. http://www.sysomos.com/insidetwitter/.

CityNews (2013, November 10). Woman hurt typing fake profiles for dating site, $20M suit alleges. Retrieved September 5, 2016, from http://www.citynews.ca/2013/11/10/woman-hurt-typing-fake-profiles-for-dating-site-20m-suit-alleges/.

Coburn, Z., & Marra, G. (2008). Realboy: Believable Twitter bots. Retrieved from http://ca.olin.edu/2008/realboy/

Cole, DuBose (2012). Socialbots and Marketing. In Hwang, T., Pearce, I. & Nanis, M. (2012) Socialbots: Voices from the fronts. *Interactions, 19*(2): 38-45.

de Certeau, M. (1984). *The practice of everyday life.* Berkeley: University of California Press.

Dewey, C. (2015, August 25). Ashley Madison faked female profiles to lure men in, hacked data suggest. *The Washington Post.* Retrieved from https://www.washingtonpost.com/news/the-intersect/wp/2015/08/25/ashley-madison-faked-female-profiles-to-lure-men-in-hacked-data-suggest/

DuBose, C. (2012). Socialbots and marketing. [In T. Hwang, I. Pearce & M. Nanis (Eds.), Socialbots: Voices from the fronts (pp. 43–44)]. *Interactions, 19*(2), 38–45.

du Gay, P. (2000). *In praise of bureaucracy.* London: Sage Publications.

Feenberg, A. (1995). *Alternative modernity: The technical turn in philosophy and social theory.* Los Angeles: University of California Press.

Feenberg, A. (1999). *Questioning technology.* New York: Routledge.

Feenberg, A. (2008). From critical theory of technology to the rational critique of rationality. *Social Epistemology, 22*(1), 5–28.

Fielding, N., & Cobain, I. (2011, March 17). Revealed: US spy operation that manipulates social media. *The Guardian.* Retrieved from https://www.theguardian.com/technology/2011/mar/17/us-spy-operation-social-networks

Fortunati, L. (2013). Afterword: Robot conceptualizations between continuity and innovation. *Intervalla, 1*, 116–129. Retrieved from http://www.fus.edu/intervalla/images/pdf/10_fortunati.pdf

Fuchs, C. (2014). Critique of the political economy of informational capitalism and social media. In C. Fuchs & M. Sandoval (Eds.), *Critique, social media and the information society* (pp. 51–65). New York: Routledge.

Furnas, A., & Gaffney, D. (2012, July 31). Statistical probability that Mitt Romney's new Twitter followers are just normal users: 0%. *The Atlantic.* Retrieved from http://www.theatlantic.com/technology/archive/2012/07/statistical-probability-that-mitt-romneys-new-twitter-followers-are-just-normal-users-0/260539/

Gehl, R. (2014). *Reverse engineering social media: Software, culture, and political economy in new media capitalism.* Philadelphia, PA: Temple University Press.

Giddens, A. (1984). *The constitution of society: Outline of the theory of structuration.* Berkeley and Los Angeles: University of California Press.

Graham, T., & Ackland, R. (2016). Do socialbots dream of popping the filter bubble? The role of socialbots in promoting deliberative democracy in social media. In R. W. Gehl & M. Bakardjieva (Eds.), *Socialbots and their friends: Digital media and the automation of sociality.* New York: Routledge.

Habermas, J. (1984). *Theory of communicative action, Volume 1: Reason and the rationalization of society* (T. McCarthy, Trans.). Boston, MA: Beacon Press.

Habermas, J. (1987). *The theory of communicative action, Volume 2* (T. McCarthy, Trans.). Boston, MA: Beacon Press.

Huber, M., Kowalskiy, S., Nohlbergz, M., & Tjoa, S. (2009). Towards automating social engineering using social networking sites. In *Computational science and engineering, CSE'09, Volume 3* (pp. 117–124). New York: IEEE.

Hwang, T., Pearce, I., & Nanis, M. (2012). Socialbots: Voices from the fronts. *Interactions, 19*(2), 38–45.

Kalberg, S. (1980). Max Weber's types of rationality: Cornerstones for the analysis of rationalization processes in history. *The American Journal of Sociology, 85*(5), 1145–1179.

Kreiss, D., Finn, M., & Turner, F. (2011). The limits of peer production: Some reminders from Max Weber for the network society. *New Media & Society, 13*(2), 243–259.

Latzko-Toth, G. (2016). The socialization of early internet bots: IRC and the ecology of human-robot interactions online. In R. W. Gehl & M. Bakardjieva (Eds.), *Socialbots and their friends: Digital media and the automation of sociality.* New York: Routledge.

Lefebvre, H. (1991). *Critique of everyday life* (Vol. 2). New York: Verso.

Marra, G. (2011). Geppetto's army: Creating international incidents with Twitter bots. Retrieved February 9, 2015, from http://lanyrd.com/2011/sxsw/scryb/

Martosko, D. (2013, September 24). Barack Obama is political king of the fake Twitter followers, with more than 19.5 million online fans who don't really exist. *Mail Online.* Retrieved from http://www.dailymail.co.uk/news/article-2430875/Barack-Obama-19-5m-fake-Twitter-followers.html

Marwick, A. E. (2013). *Celebrity, publicity, and branding in the social media age.* New Haven, CT: Yale University Press.

Monbiot, G. (2010). These astroturf libertarians are the real threat to internet democracy. *The Guardian.* Retrieved from http://www.theguardian.com/commentisfree/liberty central/2010/dec/13/astroturf-libertarians-internet-democracy?showallcomments=tru e#comment-fold&guni=Article:in%20body%20link

Monbiot, G. (2011). The need to protect the internet from 'astroturfing' grows ever more urgent. *The Guardian.* Retrieved from http://www.theguardian.com/environment/georgemonbiot/2011/feb/23/need-to-protect-internet-from-astroturfing

Mowbray, M. (2010). The twittering machine. In *WEBIST 2010 —Sixth international conference on web information systems and technologies.* Retrieved from http://shiftleft.com/mirrors/www.hpl.hp.com/techreports/2010/HPL-2010-54.pdf

Newitz, A. (2015a, September 8). How Ashley Madison hid its fembot con from users and investigators. *Gizmodo.* Retrieved from http://gizmodo.com/how-ashley-madison-hid-its-fembot-con-from-users-and-in-1728410265

Newitz, A. (2015b, August 31). Ashley Madison code shows more women, and more bots. *Gizmodo.* Retrieved from http://gizmodo.com/ashley-madison-code-shows-more-women-and-more-bots-1727613924

Nishimura, K. (2016). Semi-autonomous fan fiction: Japanese character bots and non-human affect. In R. W. Gehl & M. Bakardjieva (Eds.), *Socialbots and their friends: Digital media and the automation of sociality.* New York: Routledge.

Pinch, T. J., & Bijker, W. E. (1984). The social construction of facts and artefacts: Or how the sociology of science and the sociology of technology might benefit each other. *Social Studies of Science, 14*, 388–441.

Ratkiewicz, J., Conover, M., Meiss, M., Gonçalves, B., Patil, S., Flammini, A., & Menczer, F. (2011). Truthy: Mapping the spread of astroturf in microblog streams. In *WWW '11 proceedings of the 20th international conference companion on world wide web* (pp. 249–252). New York: ACM.

Ritzer, G. (2000). *Classical sociological theory* (3rd ed.). Boston: McGraw Hill.

Rockefeller, H. (2011, February 16). Updated: The HB Gary email that should concern us all. *Daily Kos*. Retrieved from http://www.dailykos.com/story/2011/02/16/945768/-UPDATED-The-HB-Gary-Email-That-Should-Concern-Us-All

Scholz, T. (2013). *Digital labour: The Internet as playground and factory*. New York: Routledge.

Shannon, C. E. (1940). A symbolic analysis of relay and switching circuits (Master thesis). Retrieved from https://dspace.mit.edu/handle/1721.1/11173

Sugiyama, S., & Vincent, J. (2013). Social robots and emotion: Transcending the boundary between humans and ICTs. *Intervalla, 1*, 1–6. Retrieved from http://www.fc.edu/intervalla/index.php?option=com_content&view=article&id=16&Itemid=13

Terranova, T. (2004). *Network culture: Politics for the information age*. London: Pluto Press.

Thomas, K., Grier, C., & Paxson, V. (2012). Adapting social spam infrastructure for political censorship. *Presented at the 5th USENIX workshop on large-scale exploits and emergent threats, San Jose, California*. Retrieved from https://www.usenix.org/system/files/conference/leet12/leet12-final13_0.pdf

Thomas, K., McCoy, D., Grier, C., Kolcz, A., & Paxson, V. (2013). Trafficking fraudulent accounts: The role of the underground market in Twitter spam and abuse. In *USENIX Security* (Vol. 13, pp. 195–210). Retrieved from http://www.inwyrd.com/blog/wp-content/uploads/2010/03/usenix20131.pdf

Turow, J. (2011). *The daily you: How the new advertising industry is defining your identity and your worth*. New Haven, CT: Yale University Press.

Van Dijck, J. (2013). *The culture of connectivity: A critical history of social media*. Oxford: Oxford University Press.

Weber, M. (2005). *The protestant ethic and the spirit of capitalism*. London; New York: Routledge.

Wright, A. (2012). The social life of robots. *Communications of the ACM, 55*(2), 19–21.

Young, J. E., Sung, J.-Y., Voisa, A., Sharlin, E., Igarashi, T., Christensen, H. I., & Grinter, R. E. (2011). Evaluating human-robot interaction—Focusing on the holistic interaction experience. *International Journal of Social Robotics, 3*(1), 53–67.

Zhang, J., Carpenter, D., & Ko, M. (2013). Online astroturfing: A theoretical perspective. In *19th Americas conference on information systems (AMCIS) proceedings*. Retrieved from http://aisel.aisnet.org/amcis2013/HumanComputerInteraction/GeneralPresentations/5/

12

THE OTHER QUESTION

Socialbots and the Question of Ethics

David J. Gunkel

Whether we recognize it as such or not, we are in the midst of a robot invasion. Autonomous machines are now everywhere and doing everything. We chat with them online, we play with them in digital games, we interact with them in social networks, and we rely on their capabilities to help us organize and manage many aspects of our increasingly data-rich, digital lives. It seems Norbert Wiener, the progenitor of cybernetics—the science of control and communication—was right when he made the following prediction in *The Human Use of Human Beings*: 'It is the thesis of this book that society can only be understood through a study of the messages and the communication facilities which belong to it; and that in the future development of these messages and communication facilities, messages between man and machines, between machines and man, and between machine and machine, are destined to play an ever increasing part' (Wiener, 1954, p. 16).

Investigation of the social and moral aspects of these systems typically involves asking about the 'influence' these mechanisms have on the human user (Boshmaf et al., 2011; Misener, 2011) and the effect of this influence on the construction of human sociality (Gehl, 2013; Jones, 2015). These are certainly important questions, but they limit research to an anthropocentric moral framework and instrumentalist view of technology, both of which are contested and put in question by these increasingly social and interactive mechanisms. For this reason, this chapter seeks to develop a more fundamental mode of inquiry that grapples with other questions—questions concerning who or what can or should be 'Other' in social relationships and communicative exchange. At what point, for instance, might a socialbot, an algorithm or other autonomous system be held responsible for the decisions it makes or the actions it deploys? When, in other words, would it make sense to say 'It's the computer's fault'? Likewise, at what point might we have to seriously consider extending something like rights—civil, moral or legal standing—to these devices? When, in other words, would it no longer be considered nonsense to suggest something like 'the rights of machines'? In pursuing these questions, this chapter seeks to develop a more nuanced understanding of the ethics of socialbots that is designed to scale to the social environment Norbert Wiener had so accurately predicted.

Parsing the Question

Social relationships, especially those that involve moral consideration, can be analysed into two fundamental components. 'Moral situations', as Luciano Floridi and J. W. Sanders (2004) point out, 'commonly involve agents and patients. Let us define the class A of moral *agents* as the class of all entities that can in principle qualify as sources of moral action, and the class P of moral *patients* as the class of all entities that can in principle qualify as receivers of moral action' (pp. 349–350). In other words, moral situations are relationships involving at least two components: the originator of an action that is to be evaluated as morally correct or incorrect and the recipient of the action who either is benefitted by or harmed because of it. The former is commonly referred to as the 'moral agent'; the latter is called the 'moral patient'.

Although this terminology has been in circulation in the field of moral philosophy for quite some time (cf. Hajdin, 1994), students of communication and media studies will find a more familiar formulation in the basic communication model provided by Claude Shannon and Warren Weaver (1963). According to their work with the *Mathematical Theory of Communication*, the act of communication can be described as a dyadic process bounded, on the one side, by an information source or sender and, on the other side, by a receiver. These two participants are connected by a communication channel or medium through which messages selected by the sender are conveyed to the receiver. In this model, which is reproduced, in one way or another, in virtually every textbook on the subject of communication, the source of the message is the agent. It is the 'sender' who initiates the communicative interaction by selecting a message and sending it through the channel to the receiver. The receiver occupies the position of what is called the patient. It is the 'receiver' who is the recipient of the communicated message that is originally sent by the sender. Although the academic disciplines of moral philosophy and communication studies employ different terminology (terminology obviously derived from their specific orientation and historical development), they both characterize the social/communicative relationship as bounded by two figures: the originator of the action, the sender or agent, and the recipient of the action, the receiver or the patient.

In this dyadic relationship, irrespective of the terminology that is used, the agent is understood to have certain responsibilities and can (or should) be held accountable for what he, she or it decides to do or not do. In fact, standard ethical theory can be described as an agent-oriented endeavour where one is principally concerned with either the 'moral nature and development of the individual agent', what is often called 'virtue ethics' in classical moral philosophy, or the 'moral nature and value of the actions performed by the agent', which is the focus of the more modern theories of consequentialism, contractualism and deontologism (Floridi, 1999, p. 41). This agent-oriented approach, which comprises, as Floridi (1999) and others have effectively demonstrated, the vast majority of moral theorizing in the Western tradition, is basically about and interested in resolving matters of *responsibility*.

For this reason, patient-oriented approaches are still something of a minor thread in the history of moral philosophy (Hajdin, 1994; Floridi, 1999). This way of thinking is concerned not with the responsibilities of the originator of an action but with the *rights* of the individual who is addressed by and is the recipient of the action. Historically speaking, the principal example of a patient-oriented approach is the late-twentieth century innovations in animal rights. Animals are not, at least according to the standard way of thinking, moral agents.[1] One typically does not, for instance, hold a dog morally or legally responsible for biting the postman. But we can and do hold the owner of the dog responsible for cruel treatment of the animal in response to this action. That is because, following the innovative suggestion of Jeremy Bentham (2005), animals are sentient and capable of experiencing pain. Consequently, animal ethicists, like Tom Regan (1983) and Peter Singer (1975), formulate patient-oriented approaches to moral thinking that are concerned not with the responsibilities of the perpetrator of an action but with the rights of the individual who is its victim or recipient.

Following this division of the moral relationship into its two constitutive components, we can investigate the ethics of socialbots from either an agent- or patient-oriented perspective. From an agent-oriented standpoint, the fundamental question is whether and to what extent these socially interactive mechanisms have responsibilities to human individuals and communities. Or to put it in terms of a question: 'Can or should (and the choice of verb is not incidental) socialbots be held responsible or accountable for the decisions they make or the actions they initiate?' From a patient-oriented perspective, the fundamental question is whether and to what extent these machines can be said to have moral or legal standing that we—individual human beings and human social institutions—would need to consider and respect. Or to put it in the form of a question: Can or should bots have rights?

Standard Operating Presumptions

Both questions obviously strain against common sense, and this is because of an assumption, or what is perhaps better characterized as a 'prejudice', concerning the ontological status of technology. Machines, even sophisticated information-processing devices like computers, smart phones, software algorithms, robots, etc., are technologies, and technologies, we have been told, are mere tools created and used by human beings. A mechanism or technological artefact means nothing and does nothing by itself; it is the way it is employed by a human user that ultimately matters. As the National Rifle Association often reminds American voters, 'guns don't kill, people do'. This commonsense evaluation is structured and informed by the answer that is typically provided for the question concerning technology.

> We ask the question concerning technology when we ask what it is. Everyone knows the two statements that answer our question. One says: Technology is a means to an end. The other says: Technology is a human activity. The two definitions of technology belong together. For to posit ends and procure and utilize the means to them is a human activity. The manufacture and utilization of equipment, tools, and machines, the manufactured and used things themselves, and the needs and ends that they serve, all belong to what technology is.
>
> *(Heidegger, 1977, pp. 4–5)*

According to Heidegger's analysis, the presumed role and function of any kind of technology, whether it be the product of handicraft or industrialized manufacture, is that it is a means employed by human users for specific ends. Heidegger terms this particular characterization of technology 'the instrumental definition' and indicates that it forms what is considered to be the 'correct' understanding of any kind of technological contrivance (Heidegger, 1977, p. 5).

'The instrumentalist theory', as Andrew Feenberg (1991) explains, 'offers the most widely accepted view of technology. It is based on the common sense idea that technologies are 'tools' standing ready to serve the purposes of users' (p. 5). And because an instrument 'is deemed "neutral", without valuative content of its own', a technological artefact is evaluated not in and of itself, but on the basis of the particular employments that have been decided by its human designer or user. The consequences of this are succinctly articulated by Jean-François Lyotard in *The Postmodern Condition*:

> Technical devices originated as prosthetic aids for the human organs or as physiological systems whose function it is to receive data or condition the context. They follow a principle, and it is the principle of optimal performance: maximizing output (the information or modification obtained) and minimizing input (the energy expended in the process). Technology is therefore a game pertaining not to the true, the just, or the beautiful, etc., but to efficiency: a technical 'move' is 'good' when it does better and/ or expends less energy than another.
>
> *(Lyotard, 1984, p. 44)*

Lyotard begins by affirming the traditional understanding of technology as an instrument or extension of human activity. Given this 'fact', which is stated as if it were something beyond question, he proceeds to provide an explanation of the proper place of the technological apparatus in epistemology, ethics and aesthetics. According to his analysis, a technological device, whether it be a simple corkscrew, a mechanical clock or a digital computer, does not in and of itself participate in the big questions of truth, justice, or beauty. Technology is simply and indisputably about efficiency. A particular technological 'move' or innovation is considered 'good', if, and only if, it proves to be a more effective means to accomplishing a user-specified objective.

Machine Moral Agency

Characterized as a mere tool or instrument, sophisticated technical devices like computers, artificial intelligence (AI) systems, and software bots are not considered the responsible agent of actions that are performed with or through them. 'Morality', as J. Storrs Hall (2001) points out, 'rests on human shoulders, and if machines changed the ease with which things were done, they did not change responsibility for doing them. People have always been the only "moral agents"' (p. 2). This is, in fact, one of the standard operating presumptions of computer ethics. Although different definitions of 'computer ethics' have circulated since Walter Maner first introduced the term in 1976, they all share an instrumentalist perspective that assigns moral agency to human designers and users. According to Deborah Johnson (1985), who is credited with writing the field's agenda-setting textbook, 'computer ethics turns out to be the study of human beings and society—our goals and values, our norms of behavior, the way we organize ourselves and assign rights and responsibilities, and so on' (p. 6). Computers, she recognizes, often 'instrumentalize' these human values and behaviours in innovative and challenging ways, but the bottom line is and remains the way human agents design and use (or misuse) such technology.

According to the instrumental theory, therefore, any action undertaken with a machine is ultimately the responsibility of some human agent—the designer of the system, the manufacturer of the equipment or the end-user of the product. If something goes wrong with or someone is harmed by the mechanism, 'some human is', as Ben Goertzel (2002) describes it, 'to blame for setting the program up to do such a thing' (p. 1). Following this line of argument, it can be concluded that all machine action is to be credited to or blamed on a human programmer, manufacturer or operator. Holding the machine culpable would, on this account, not only be absurd but also irresponsible. Ascribing agency to machines, Mikko Siponen (2004) argues, allows one to 'start blaming computers for our mistakes. In other words, we can claim that "I didn't do it—it was a computer error", while ignoring the fact that the software has been programmed by people to "behave in certain ways", and thus people may have caused this error either incidentally or intentionally (or users have otherwise contributed to the cause of this error)' (p. 286).

For this reason, the instrumental theory not only sounds reasonable, it is obviously useful. It is, one might say, 'instrumental' for parsing questions of responsibility in the age of increasingly complex technological systems. And it has a distinct advantage in that it locates accountability in a widely accepted and seemingly intuitive subject position, in human decision-making and action, and it resists any and all efforts to defer responsibility to some inanimate object by blaming or scapegoating what are mere instruments, contrivances or tools. At the same time, however, this particular formulation also has significant theoretical and practical limitations, especially as it applies (or not) to recent technological innovations.

Machine Learning

A decade from now, when our self-driving cars are taking us to the office (assuming we still have jobs to go to . . . but that is another story), we might be tempted to look back on March 2016 as a kind of tipping point in the development of machine learning. Why this month of this year? Because of two remarkable events that took place within a few days of each other. In the middle of the month, Google DeepMind's AlphaGo took four out of five games of Go against one of the most celebrated human players of this notoriously complicated board game—Lee Sedol of South Korea. Then, at the end of the month, it was revealed that Microsoft was disabling its artificially intelligent chatterbot Tay.ai, because she had learned to become a hate-spewing, neo-Nazi racist in less than eight hours of interaction with human users.

Both AlphaGo and Tay are advanced AI systems using some form of machine learning. AlphaGo, as Google DeepMind explained in a January 2016 article published in *Nature*, 'combines Monte-Carlo tree search with deep neural networks that have been trained by supervised learning, from human expert games, and by reinforcement learning from games of self-play' (Google DeepMind, 2016). In other words, AlphaGo does not play the game by following a set of cleverly designed moves fed into it by human programmers. It is designed to formulate its own instructions from game play. Although less is known about the inner workings of Tay, Microsoft explains that the system 'has been built by mining relevant public data', i.e., training its neural networks on anonymized data obtained from social media, and was designed to evolve its behaviour from interacting with users on social networks like Twitter, Kik and GroupMe (Microsoft, 2016a). What both systems have in common is that the engineers who designed and built them have no idea what the systems will eventually do once they are in operation. As Thore Graepel, one of the creators of AlphaGo, has explained: 'Although we have programmed this machine to play, we have no idea what moves it will come up with. Its moves are an emergent phenomenon from the training. We just create the data sets and the training algorithms. But the moves it then comes up with are out of our hands' (Metz, 2016). Machine learning systems, like AlphaGo, are designed to do things that we cannot antici-pate or completely control. In other words, we now have autonomous computer systems that in one way or another have 'a mind of their own'. And this is where things get interesting, especially when it comes to questions of agency and responsibility.

AlphaGo was designed to play Go, and it proved its ability by beating an expert human player. So who won? Who gets the accolade? Who actually beat Lee Sedol? Following the dictates of the instrumental theory of technology, actions undertaken with the computer would be attributed to the human pro-grammers who initially designed the system. But this explanation does not necessarily hold for a machine like AlphaGo, which was deliberately created to do things that exceed the knowledge and control of its human designers. In fact, in most of the reporting on this landmark event, it is not Google or the engineers at DeepMind who are credited with the victory. It is AlphaGo. Things get even more complicated with Tay, Microsoft's foul-mouthed teenage AI, when one asks the question: 'Who is responsible for Tay's bigoted comments on Twitter?' According to the instrumentalist way of thinking, we would need to blame the programmers at Microsoft, who designed the AI to be able to do these things. But the programmers obviously did not set out to design Tay to be a racist. She developed this reprehensible behaviour by learning from inter-actions with human users on the Internet. So how did Microsoft assign responsibility?

Initially a company spokesperson—in damage-control mode—sent out an email to *Wired*, *The Washington Post* and other news organizations, that sought to blame the victim. 'The AI chatbot Tay', the spokesperson explained, 'is a machine learning project, designed for human engagement. It is as much a social and cultural experiment, as it is technical. Unfortunately, within the first 24 hours of coming online, we became aware of a coordinated effort by some users to abuse Tay's commenting skills to have Tay respond in inap-propriate ways. As a result, we have taken Tay offline and are making adjust-ments' (Risely, 2016). According to Microsoft, it is not the programmers or the corporation who are responsible for the hate speech. It is the fault of the users (or some users) who interacted with Tay and taught her to be a bigot. Tay's racism, in other word, is *our* fault. This is the classic 'I blame society' defence utilized in virtually every juvenile delinquent. Later, on Friday, March 25, Peter Lee, VP of Microsoft Research, posted the following apology on the Official Microsoft Blog:

> As many of you know by now, on Wednesday we launched a chatbot called Tay. We are deeply sorry for the unintended offensive and hurtful tweets from Tay, which do not represent who we are or what we stand for, nor how we designed Tay. Tay is now offline and we'll look to bring

Tay back only when we are confident we can better anticipate malicious intent that conflicts with our principles and values.

(Microsoft, 2016b)

But this apology is also frustratingly unsatisfying or interesting (it all depends on how you look at it). According to Lee's carefully worded explanation, Microsoft is only responsible for not anticipating the bad outcome; it does not take responsibility for the offensive Tweets. For Lee, it is Tay who (or 'that', and words matter here) is named and recognized as the source of the 'wildly inappropriate and reprehensible words and images' (Microsoft, 2016b). And since Tay is a kind of 'minor' (a teenage girl AI) under the protection of her parent corporation, Microsoft needed to step in, apologize for their 'daughter's' bad behaviour and put Tay in a time out.

Although the extent to which one might assign 'agency' and 'responsibility' to these mechanisms remains a contested issue, what is not debated is the fact that the rules of the game have changed significantly. As Andreas Matthias points out, summarizing his survey of learning automata:

> Presently there are machines in development or already in use which are able to decide on a course of action and to act without human intervention. The rules by which they act are not fixed during the production process, but can be changed during the operation of the machine, by the machine itself. This is what we call machine learning. Traditionally we hold either the operator/manufacture of the machine responsible for the consequences of its operation or 'nobody' (in cases, where no personal fault can be identified). Now it can be shown that there is an increasing class of machine actions, where the traditional ways of responsibility ascription are not compatible with our sense of justice and the moral framework of society because nobody has enough control over the machine's actions to be able to assume responsibility for them.
>
> *(Matthias, 2004, p. 177)*

In other words, the instrumental definition of technology, which had effectively tethered machine action to human agency, no longer adequately applies to mechanisms that have been deliberately designed to operate and exhibit some form, no matter how rudimentary, of independent action or autonomous decision-making. This does not mean, it is important to emphasize, that the instrumental theory is on this account refuted *tout court*. There are and will continue to be mechanisms understood and utilized as tools to be manipulated by human users (i.e., lawn mowers, cork screws, telephones, digital cameras, etc.). The point is that the instrumentalist formulation, no matter how useful and seemingly correct in some circumstances for explaining some technological devices, does not exhaust all possibilities for all kinds of devices.

Mindless Chatterbots

In addition to machine learning and artificial intelligence, there are also 'empty headed' chatterbots like ELIZA and MrMind (see Weil in Chapter 2 of this volume) or non-player characters that, if not proving otherwise, at least significantly complicate the instrumentalist assumptions. Miranda Mowbray, for instance, has investigated the complications of moral agency in online communities and massively multiplayer online role playing games (MMORPGs).

> The rise of online communities has led to a phenomenon of real-time, multi-person interaction via online personas. Some online community technologies allow the creation of bots (personas that act according to a software programme rather than being directly controlled by a human user) in such a way that it is not always easy to tell a bot from a human within an online social space. It is also possible for a persona to be partly controlled by a software programme and partly directly by a human . . . This leads to theoretical and practical problems for ethical arguments (not to mention policing) in these spaces, since the usual one-to-one correspondence between actors and moral agents can be lost.
>
> *(Mowbray, 2002, p. 2)*

These bots, which now populate and operate in the virtual spaces of not just MMORPGs but also social media networks like Twitter and Facebook, complicate the one-to-one correspondence between actor and moral agent. 'There is', as Steve Jones (2014, p. 245) points out, 'a concomitantly increasing amount of algorithmic intervention utilizing expressions between users and between users and machines to create, modify or channel communication and interaction.' And this 'algorithmic intervention' is making it increasingly difficult to identify who or what is responsible for actions in the virtual space of an online community. Although software bots are by no means close to achieving anything that looks remotely like intelligence or even basic machine learning, they can still be mistaken for and 'pass' as other human users (Edwards et al., 2013; Gehl, 2013; Jones, 2015). This is, Mowbray (2002) points out, not 'a feature of the sophistication of bot design, but of the low bandwidth communication of the online social space' where it is 'much easier to convincingly simulate a human agent' (p. 2). This occurred, most recently, in the case of Ashley Madison's 'fembots', simple pre-fabricated computer scripts that were designed to initiate an amorous exchange with male users in hope of moving them into the ranks of paying customers. Even if the programming of these fembots were rather simple, somewhat shoddy and even stupid, a significant number of male users found them socially engaging—so much so that they shared intimate secrets with the bot and, most importantly, took out the credit card in hopes of continuing the conversation.

Despite this knowledge, these software implementations cannot be written off as mere instruments or tools. 'The examples in this paper', Mowbray (2002) concludes, 'show that a bot may cause harm to other users or to the community as a whole by the will of its programmers or other users, but that it also may cause harm through nobody's fault because of the combination of circumstances involving some combination of its programming, the actions and mental or emotional states of human users who interact with it, behavior of other bots and of the environment, and the social economy of the community' (p. 4). Unlike artificial intelligence, which would occupy a position that would, at least theoretically, be reasonably close to that of a human agent and therefore not be able to be dismissed as a mere tool, these socialbots simply muddy the water (which is probably worse) by leaving undecided the question whether they are or are not tools. And in the process, they leave the question of moral agency both unsettled and unsettling.

Machine Moral Patiency

In order for a machine (or any entity for that matter) to have anything like moral standing or 'rights', it would need to be recognized as another moral subject and not just a tool or instrument of human action. Standard approaches to deciding this matter typically focus on what Mark Coeckelbergh (2012) calls '(intrinsic) properties'. This method is rather straightforward and intuitive: 'you identify one or more morally relevant properties and then find out if the entity in question has them' (p. 13) or not.

> Put in a more formal way, the argument for giving moral status to entities runs as follows:
>
> 1. Having property p is sufficient for moral status s
> 2. Entity e has property p
>
> Conclusion: entity e has moral status s.
>
> *(Coeckelbergh, 2012, p. 14)*

According to this methodology, the question concerning machine moral standing—or 'robot rights', if you prefer—would need to be decided by first identifying which property or properties would be necessary and sufficient for moral standing and then determining whether a particular machine or class of machines possesses these properties or not. If they do possess the morally significant property, then they pass the test for inclusion in the community of moral subjects. If not, then they can be excluded from moral consideration. Deciding things in this fashion, although entirely reasonable and expedient, encounters a number of difficulties. Take for example, 'sentience', which is the property that Singer (1975), following Bentham (2005), deploys in the process of extending moral consideration to non-human animals. The commonsense argument would seem to be this: Machines (whether embodied robots or software bots) cannot feel pain (or pleasure) and therefore do not have interests that would need to be respected or taken into account. Although this argument sounds reasonable, it fails for at least four reasons.

Factual Problems

It has been practically disputed by the construction of various mechanisms that appear to suffer or at least provide external evidence of something that looks like pain. Engineers have successfully constructed mechanisms that synthesize believable emotional responses (Bates, 1994; Blumberg et al., 1996; Breazeal & Brooks, 2004), like the dental-training robot Simroid who cries out in pain when students 'hurt' it (Kokoro, 2009), and designed systems capable of evidencing behaviours that look a lot like what we usually call pleasure and pain. Conversely, it appears that human beings already empathize with artefacts and accord them some level of social standing, whether or not they *actually* feel pain. This insight, initially theorized in Byron Reeves and Clifford Nass's (1996) computer as social actor (CSA) studies, has been confirmed by a number of recent empirical investigations. In a study conducted by Christopher Bartneck et al. (2007), for instance, human subjects interacted with a robot on a prescribed task and then, at the end of the session, were asked to switch off the machine and wipe its memory. The robot, which was in terms of its programming no more sophisticated than a basic chatterbot, responded to this request by begging for mercy and pleading with the human user not to shut it down. As a result of this, Bartneck's research team recorded considerable hesitation on the part of the human subjects to comply with the shutdown request (Bartneck et al., 2007, p. 55). Even though the robot was 'just a machine'—and not even very intelligent—the social situation in which it worked with and responded to human users made human beings consider the right of the machine to continued existence. These results have been confirmed in two recent studies, one reported in the *International Journal of Social Robotics* (Rosenthal-von der Pütten et al., 2013) where researchers found that human subjects respond emotionally to robots and express empathic concern for machines irrespective of knowledge concerning the properties or inner workings of the mechanism, and another that uses physiological evidence, documented by electroencephalography, of humans' ability to empathize with robot pain (Suzuki et al., 2015). Although these experiments were conducted using physically embodied robots, similar results have been obtained and reported in situations involving software bots (Salichs & Malfaz, 2006; Zubek & Khoo, 2002).

Epistemological Problems

Although taken as providing evidence of 'pain', these demonstrations run into an epistemological problem insofar as suffering or the experience of pain is something that is not directly observable. How, for example, can one know whether an animal or even another person actually suffers? How is it possible to access and evaluate the suffering that is experienced by another? 'Modern philosophy', Matthew Calarco (2008) writes, 'true to its Cartesian and scientific aspirations, is interested in the indubitable rather than the undeniable. Philosophers want proof that animals actually suffer, that animals are aware of their suffering, and they require an argument for why animal suffering should count on equal par with human suffering' (p. 119). But such indubitable and certain knowledge appears to be unattainable. As Paul Churchland (1999) famously asked: 'How does one determine whether something other than oneself—an alien creature, a sophisticated robot, a socially active computer, or even another human—is really a thinking, feeling, conscious being; rather than, for example, an unconscious automaton whose behavior arises from something other than genuine mental states?' (p. 67).

This is, of course, what philosophers call the other minds problem. Although this problem is not necessarily intractable, as Steve Torrance (2013) has persuasively argued, the fact of the matter is we cannot, as Donna Haraway (2008) describes it, 'climb into the heads of others to get the full story from the inside' (p. 226). And the supposed solutions to this 'other minds problem', from reworkings and modifications of the Turing Test (Sparrow, 2004) to functionalist approaches that endeavour to work around this problem altogether (Wallach & Allen, 2009, p. 58), only make things more complicated and confused. 'There is', as Daniel Dennett (1998) points out, 'no proving that something that seems to have an inner life does in fact have one—if by "proving" we understand, as we often do, the evincing of evidence that can be seen to establish by principles already agreed upon that something is the case' (p. 172). To put it another way, if another socially interactive entity, like a software bot, issues a statement like 'Please don't do that, it hurts', we might not have any credible way to discount or disprove it.

Terminological Problems

To make matters even more complicated, we may not even know what 'pain' and 'the experience of pain' is in the first place. This point is something that is taken up and demonstrated by Dennett's 'Why You Can't Make a Computer That Feels Pain' (1998). In this provocatively titled essay, originally published decades before the debut of even a rudimentary working prototype, Dennett imagines trying to disprove the standard argument for human (and animal) exceptionalism 'by actually writing a pain program, or designing a pain-feeling robot' (Dennett, 1998, p. 191). At the end of what turns out to be a rather protracted and detailed consideration of the problem, Dennett concludes that we cannot, in fact, make a computer that feels pain. But the reason for drawing this conclusion does not derive from what one might expect, nor does it offer any kind of support for the advocates of moral exceptionalism. According to Dennett, the reason you cannot make a computer that feels pain is not the result of some technological limitation with the mechanism or its programming. It is a product of the fact that we remain unable to decide what pain is in the first place. The best we are able to do, as Dennett (1998) illustrates, is account for the various 'causes and effects of pain', but 'pain itself does not appear' (p. 218). What is demonstrated, therefore, is not that some workable concept of pain cannot come to be instantiated in the mechanism of a computer or the programming of a bot, either now or in the foreseeable future, but that the very concept of pain that would be instantiated is already arbitrary, inconclusive, and indeterminate. 'There can', Dennett (1998) writes at the end of the essay, 'be no true theory of pain, and so no computer or robot could instantiate the true theory of pain, which it would have to do to feel real pain' (p. 228).

Moral Problems

Finally, all this talk about the possibility of engineering pain or suffering in a mechanism entails its own particular moral dilemma. 'If (ro)bots might one day be capable of experiencing pain and other affective states', Wendell Wallach and Colin Allen (2009) write, 'a question that arises is whether it will be moral to build such systems—not because of how they might harm humans, but because of the pain these artificial systems will themselves experience. In other words, can the building of a (ro)bot with a somatic architecture capable of feeling intense pain be morally justified and should it be prohibited?' (p. 209). If it were in fact possible to construct a machine that 'feels pain' (however defined and instantiated) in order to demonstrate the limits of moral patiency, then doing so might be ethically suspect insofar as in constructing such a mechanism we do not do everything in our power to minimize its suffering. Consequently, moral philosophers, programmers and robotics engineers find themselves in a curious and not entirely comfortable situation. One needs to be able to construct such a mechanism in order to demonstrate moral patiency and the possibility of machine moral standing; but doing so would be, on that account, already to engage in an act that could potentially be considered immoral. Or to put it another way, the demonstration of machine moral patiency might itself be something that is quite painful for others.

Admittedly these four problems do not add up to a convincing proof, once and for all, that socialbots, or even one particular example of a socialbot, can or even should have something like rights. But they do complicate the assignment of rights and challenge us to reconsider how we make decisions about who deserves to be considered a moral patient and what does not. Although we might not have a satisfactory and thoroughly convincing argument for including machines in the community of moral patients, we also lack reasons to continue to exclude them from such consideration *tout court*.

Conclusion: Between a Rock and a Hard Place

My friend and colleague Joanna Bryson has a clever way to illustrate the 'robot invasion' that is currently taking place in all aspects of contemporary life. She holds up her smart phone and says, channelling the words of Obi-Wan Kenobi from the first *Star Wars* film,[2] 'these are the droids you're looking for'. What she means by this is simple. The robot invasion that has been so vividly illustrated in decades of science fiction literature and cinema will not occur as we expect. It will not take the form of a marauding army of robots descending on the planet from another time and place. It will instead be more like the Fall of the Roman Empire as everyday objects and applications become increasingly intelligent, capable and socially interactive. The 'droids' are not coming, they are already here in the form of friendly digital assistants, capable chatterbots, and social robots of various forms and configurations. As these increasingly autonomous machines come to occupy influential positions in contemporary culture—positions where they are not just tools or instruments of human action but socially interactive subjects in their own right—we will need to ask ourselves important but rather difficult questions: At what point might a robot, an algorithm, or other autonomous system be held responsible for the decisions it makes or the actions it deploys? Likewise, at what point might we have to consider seriously extending rights to these socially aware and interactive devices?

In response to these questions, there now appears to be at least three options, none of which are entirely comfortable or satisfactory. On the one hand, we can respond as we typically have, treating these mechanisms as mere instruments or tools. Bryson makes a case for this approach in her provocatively titled essay 'Robots Should be Slaves': 'My thesis is that robots should be built, marketed and considered legally as slaves, not companion peers' (Bryson, 2010, p. 63). Although this might sound harsh, this argument is persuasive, precisely because it draws on and is underwritten by the instrumental theory of technology—a theory that has considerable history and success behind it and that functions as the assumed default position for any and all considerations of technology. This decision—and it is a decision, even if it is the default—has both advantages and disadvantages. On the positive side, it reaffirms human exceptionalism, making it absolutely clear that it is only the human being who possesses rights and responsibilities. Technologies, no matter how sophisticated, intelligent and influential, are and will continue to be mere tools of human action, nothing more. But this approach, for all its usefulness, has a not-so-pleasant downside. It wilfully and deliberately produces a new class of instrumental servants or slaves, what we might call 'slavery 2.0' (Gunkel, 2012, p. 86), and rationalizes this decision as morally appropriate and justified. In other words, applying the instrumental theory to these new kinds of mechanisms, although seemingly reasonable and useful, might have devastating consequences for us and others.

On the other hand, we can decide to entertain the possibility of responsibilities and rights for social robots just as we had previously done for other non-human entities, like animals (Singer, 1975). And there is both moral and legal precedent for this outcome. In fact, we already live in a world populated by artificial entities who are considered legal persons having rights and responsibilities recognized and protected by both national and international law—the limited liability corporation (French, 1979). Once again, this decision sounds reasonable and justified. It extends moral standing to these other socially interactive entities and recognizes, following the predictions of Norbert Wiener (1954, p. 16), that the social situation of the future will involve not just human-to-human interactions but relationships between humans and machines and machines and machines. But this decision also has significant costs. It requires that we rethink everything we thought we knew about ourselves, technology and ethics. It requires that we learn to think beyond human exceptionalism, technological instrumentalism and all the other *-isms* that have helped us make sense of our world and our place in it. In effect, it calls for a thorough reconceptualization of who or what should be considered a legitimate moral subject.

Finally, we can try to balance these two extreme positions by taking an intermediate hybrid approach, distributing agency and patiency across a network of interacting human and machine components.[3] This particular version of 'actor network theory' is precisely the solution advanced by Deborah Johnson in her essay, 'Computer Systems: Moral Entities but not Moral Agents': 'When computer systems behave there is a triad of intentionality at work, the intentionality of the computer system designer, the intentionality of the system, and the intentionality of the user' (Johnson, 2006, p. 202). This proposal also has its advantages and disadvantages. In particular, it appears to be attentive to the exigencies of life in the twenty-first century. None of us, in fact, make decisions or act in a vacuum; we are always and already tangled up in networks of interactive elements that complicate the assignment of responsibility and rights. And these networks have always included others—not only other human beings but institutions, organizations, and even machinic elements like the socialbots that increasingly organize and influence our actions online. This combined approach, however, still requires that one decide what aspects of agency and patiency belong to the machine and what should be attributed to the human being. In other words, this hybrid approach, although attempting to strike a balance between strict 'instrumentalism' and 'machine morality', will still need to decide between *who* counts as a moral subject and *what* can be considered a mere object (Derrida, 2005, p. 80). And these decisions are often flexible, allowing one part of the network to protect itself by deflecting responsibility to another. This occurred, for example, during the Nuremberg trials at the end of World War II, when low-level functionaries deflected responsibility up the chain of command by claiming that they 'were just following orders'. But the deflection can also move in the other direction, as was the case in the prisoner abuse scandal at the Abu Ghraib prison in Iraq. In this situation, individuals in the upper echelon of the network deflected responsibility by arguing that the documented abuse was not ordered by command but was the deliberate action of a 'few bad apples' in the enlisted ranks.

In the end, how we decide to respond to the opportunities and challenges of this *machine question* will have a profound effect on the way we conceptualize our place in the world, who we decide to include in the community of moral subjects, and what we exclude from such consideration and why. But no matter how it is decided, it is a decision—quite literally a cut that institutes difference and makes a difference. We are, therefore, responsible both for deciding who is a moral subject and, in the process, for determining the very configuration and proper limits of ethics now and for the foreseeable future.

Notes

1. There is some documented evidence of animals being put on trial in medieval Europe, but these occurrences are considered something of an anomaly in the history of moral thought.
2. 'First' in terms of the temporal sequence of released films. From the perspective of the chronology developed across the different films that comprise the franchise, this 'first film' is actually the fourth episode.
3. This form of 'distributed agency' and its application to socialbots is developed and investigated by Bollmer and Rodley (2016), Latzko-Toth (2016) and Muhle (2016).

References

Bartneck, C., van der Hoek, M., Mubin, O., & Mahmud, A. A. (2007). Daisy, daisy, give me your answer do!—Switching off a robot. In *Proceedings of the 2nd ACM/IEEE international conference on human-robot interaction* (pp. 217–222). Washington, DC.

Bates, J. (1994). The role of emotion in believable agents. *Communications of the ACM, 37*, 122–125.

Bentham, J. (2005). *An introduction to the principles of morals and legislation* (J. H. Burns & H. L. Hart, Eds.). Oxford: Oxford University Press.

Blumberg, B., Todd, P., & Maes, M. (1996). No bad dogs: Ethological lessons for learning. In *Proceedings of the 4th international conference on simulation of adaptive behavior* (SAB96) (pp. 295–304). Cambridge, MA: MIT Press.

Bollmer, G., & Rodley, C. (2016). Speculations on the sociality of socialbots. In R. W. Gehl & M. Bakardjieva (Eds.), *Socialbots and their friends: Digital media and the automation of sociality*. New York: Routledge.

Boshmaf, Y., Muslukhov, I., Beznosov, K., & Ripeanu, M. (2011). The socialbot network: When bots socialize for fame and money. In *Proceedings of the 27th annual computer security applications conference* (pp. 93–102). Orlando, FL, USA, 5–9 December. New York, NY: ACM Press. Retrieved from http://lersse-dl.ece.ubc.ca/record/264/files/264.pdf

Breazeal, C., & Brooks, R. (2004). Robot emotion: A functional perspective. In J. M. Fellous & M. Arbib (Eds.), *Who needs emotions: The brain meets the robot* (pp. 271–310). Oxford: Oxford University Press.

Bryson, J. (2010). Robots should be slaves. In Yorick Wilks (Ed.), *Close engagements with artificial companions: Key social, psychological, ethical and design issues* (pp. 63–74). Amsterdam: John Benjamins.

Calarco, M. (2008). *Zoographies: The question of the animal from Heidegger to Derrida*. New York: Columbia University Press.

Churchland, P. M. (1999). *Matter and consciousness* (rev. ed.). Cambridge, MA: MIT Press.

Coeckelbergh, M. (2012). *Growing moral relations: Critique of moral status ascription*. New York: Palgrave Macmillan.

Dennett, D. C. (1998). *Brainstorms: Philosophical essays on mind and psychology*. Cambridge, MA: MIT Press.

Derrida, J. (2005). *Paper machine* (R. Bowlby, Trans.). Stanford, CA: Stanford University Press. (Original work published 2001).

Edwards, C., Edwards, A., Spence, P. R., & Shelton, A. K. (2013). Is that a bot running the social media feed? Testing the differences in perceptions of communication quality for a human agent and a bot agent on Twitter. *Computers in Human Behavior, 33*, 372–376.

Feenberg, A. (1991). *Critical theory of technology*. Oxford: Oxford University Press.

Floridi, L. (1999). Information ethics: On the philosophical foundation of computer ethics. *Ethics and Information Technology, 1*(1), 37–56.

Floridi, L., & Sanders, J. W. (2004). On the morality of artificial agents. *Minds and Machines, 14*, 349–379.

French, P. (1979). The corporation as a moral person. *American Philosophical Quarterly, 16*(3), 207–215.

Gehl, R. W. (2013). The computerized socialbot Turing test: New technologies of noo-power. Social Science Research Network (SSRN). Retrieved from http://ssrn.com/abstract=2280240

Goertzel, B. (2002). Thoughts on AI morality. *Dynamical Psychology: An International, Interdisciplinary Journal of Complex Mental Processes*. Retrieved from http://www.goertzel.org/dynapsyc/2002/AIMorality.htm

Google DeepMind. (2016). AlphaGo. Retrieved from https://deepmind.com/alpha-go.html

Gunkel, D. J. (2012). *The machine question: Critical perspectives on AI, robots and ethics*. Cambridge, MA: MIT Press.

Hajdin, M. (1994). *The boundaries of moral discourse*. Chicago: Loyola University Press.

Hall, J. S. (2001). Ethics for machines. *KurzweilAI.net*. Retrieved from http://www.kurzweilai.net/ethics-for-machines

Haraway, D. J. (2008). *When species meet*. Minneapolis, MN: University of Minnesota Press.

Heidegger, M. (1977). *The question concerning technology, and other essays* (W. Lovitt, Trans.). New York: Harper & Row. (Original work published 1954).

Johnson, D. G. (1985). *Computer ethics*. Upper Saddle River, NJ: Prentice Hall.

Johnson, D. G. (2006). Computer systems: Moral entities but not moral agents. *Ethics and Information Technology, 8*, 195–204.

Jones, S. (2014). People, things, memory and human-machine communication. *International Journal of Media & Cultural Politics, 10*(3), 245–258.

Jones, S. (2015). How I learned to stop worrying and love the bots. *Social Media and Society, 1*(1), 1–2.

Kokoro, Ltd. (2009). http://www.kokoro-dreams.co.jp/

Latzko-Toth, G. (2016). The socialisation of early Internet bots: IRC and the emerging ecology of human-robot interactions online. In R. W. Gehl & M. Bakardjieva (Eds.), *Socialbots and their friends: Digital media and the automation of sociality*. New York: Routledge.

Lyotard, J. F. (1984). *The postmodern condition: A report on knowledge* (G. Bennington & B. Massumi, Trans.). Minneapolis, MN: University of Minnesota Press. (Original work published 1979).

Matthias, A. (2004). The responsibility gap: Ascribing responsibility for the actions of learning automata. *Ethics and Information Technology, 6,* 175–183.

Metz, C. (2016). Google's AI wins a pivotal second game in match with go grandmaster. *Wired.* Retrieved from http://www.wired.com/2016/03/googles-ai-wins-pivotal-game-two-match-go-grandmaster/

Microsoft. (2016a). Meet Tay—Microsoft A.I. chatbot with zero chill. Retrieved from https://www.tay.ai/

Microsoft. (2016b). Learning from Tay's introduction. Retrieved from https://blogs.microsoft.com/blog/2016/03/25/learning-tays-introduction/

Misener, D. (2011). Rise of the socialbots: They could be influencing you online. *CBC News.* Retrieved from http://www.cbc.ca/news/technology/story/2011/03/29/f-vp-misener-socialbot-armies-election.html

Mowbray, M. (2002). Ethics for bots. Paper presented at the *14th international conference on system research, informatics, and cybernetics,* Baden-Baden, Germany, July 29–August 3. Retrieved from http://www.hpl.hp.com/techreports/2002/HPL-2002–48R1.pdf

Muhle, F. (2016). Embodied conversational agents as social actors? In R. W. Gehl & M. Bakardjieva (Eds.), *Socialbots and their friends: Digital media and the automation of sociality.* New York: Routledge.

Reeves, B., & Nass, C. (1996). *The media equation: How people treat computers, television, and new media like real people and places.* Cambridge: Cambridge University Press.

Regan, T. (1983). *The case for animal rights.* Berkeley, CA: University of California Press.

Risely, James. (24 March 2016). Microsoft's millennial chatbot Tay.ai pulled offline after internet teaches her racism. *GeekWire.* Retrieved from http://www.geekwire.com/2016/even-robot-teens-impressionable-microsofts-tay-ai-pulled-internet-teaches-racism/

Rosenthal-von der Pütten, A. M., Krämer, N. C., Hoffmann, L., Sobieraj, S., & Eimler, S. C. (2013). An experimental study on emotional reactions towards a robot. *International Journal of Social Robotics, 5*(1), 17–34.

Salichs, M. A., & Malfaz, M. (2006). Using emotions on autonomous agents: The role of happiness, sadness and fear. In *Proceedings of ASIB integrative approaches to machine consciousness* (pp. 157–164), April 4–5. Retrieved from http://users.sussex.ac.uk/~robertc/Papers/IntegrativeApproachesToMachineConsciousnessAISB06

Shannon, C., & Weaver, W. (1963). *The mathematical theory of communication.* Urbana, IL: University of Illinois Press.

Singer, P. (1975). *Animal liberation: A new ethics for our treatment of animals.* New York: New York Review of Books.

Siponen, M. (2004). A pragmatic evaluation of the theory of information ethics. *Ethics and Information Technology, 6,* 279–290.

Sparrow, R. (2004). The Turing triage test. *Ethics and Information Technology, 6*(4), 203–213.

Suzuki, Y., Galli, L., Ikeda, A., Itakura, S., & Kitazaki, M. (2015). Measuring empathy for human and robot hand pain using electroencephalography. *Scientific Reports, 5,* Article No. 15924. Retrieved from http://www.nature.com/articles/srep15924

Torrance, S. (2013). Artificial consciousness and artificial ethics: Between realism and social relationism. *Philosophy & Technology, 27*(1), 9–29.

Wallach, W., & Allen, C. (2009). *Moral machines: Teaching robots right from wrong.* Oxford: Oxford University Press.

Weil, P. (2016). The blurring Test. In R. W. Gehl & M. Bakardjieva (Eds.), *Socialbots and their friends: Digital media and the automation of sociality.* New York: Routledge.

Wiener, N. (1954). *The human use of human beings.* New York: Da Capo.

Zubek, R., & Khoo, A. (2002). Making the human care: On building engaging bots. *AAAI technical report SS-02–01.* Retrieved from http://www.aaai.org/Papers/Symposia/Spring/2002/SS-02–01/SS02–01–020.pdf

INDEX

Note: Boldface indicates a figure on the corresponding page.

9 781138 639393